WE ANSWERED WITH LOVE

WE ANSWERED WITH LOVE

PACIFIST SERVICE IN WORLD WAR I

The Letters of Leslie Hotson and Mary Peabody

Carla,
With love,
Nancy Haines

NANCY LEARNED HAINES

PG
BOOKS

Hopkinton, Massachusetts
Pleasant Green Books
2016

WE ANSWERED WITH LOVE
PACIFIST SERVICE IN WORLD WAR I

The Letters of Leslie Hotson and Mary Peabody

Book and cover design and composition
by Robin Brooks www.TheBeautyofBooks.com

The letters in this book have been used with permission from collateral descendants of Leslie and Mary Hotson.

ISBN: 978-0-9979848-0-4
Library of Congress Control Number: 2016954040

To my husband

who saw the story in these letters:

this book would not exist

without your enthusiastic support.

Table of Contents

Preface

IN THE SPRING OF 1918, a young Harvard sophomore, John Leslie Hotson, felt compelled to take a leave of absence from his studies. The Armed Forces had an urgent need for officers to lead the troops in the Great War. At the request of the government, American universities, including Harvard, made military training mandatory. Leslie was a committed pacifist and his education had to take second place to his principles. At the same time, he felt the call to be of service and to relieve some of the suffering caused by the war. His dear friend Mary May Peabody, a socialist and political activist, was a student at Radcliffe. Through her volunteer work with an organization working for peace, she connected Leslie with a group of Quakers doing relief and reconstruction work in France.

Leslie Hotson was approved to join the Friends Reconstruction Unit (FRU) in France. When he left Cambridge to embark on his journey of service, Mary encouraged the correspondence that eventually bound them together. Their stories are told in more than a hundred letters they exchanged during the year he was with the FRU. The letters are quite personal, but also offer a first-hand commentary on the issues of the day as experienced by pacifists striving to make their marks on the world. They share news of the great events happening around them. They tell about their daily activities, their dreams and hopes for the future, their deep faith, and their love of poetry, drama, and literature. They explore their ideals of living lives of service and eventually begin to discuss whether marriage would fit into their visions for the future.

Leslie and Mary wrote more than one hundred and thirty letters during the sixteen months of Leslie's leave of absence from Harvard; I was not able to use all of them in their entirety. Many of the letters were long and rambling, so I condensed some—mostly to reduce the amount of navel-gazing to which they, as young adults, were sometimes prone and to eliminate some of Mary's breezy, but largely irrelevant, gossip about her classmates. In editing their correspondence, I left their language and tone as close to the original as possible. I have not indicated these changes, in order to preserve the flow of the narrative. Ellipses in the letters were used by Mary and Leslie. Only minor corrections were made to spelling, tenses, and usage—fixing errors Leslie and Mary surely would not have made had they had a chance to revise these writings. I put the French and German phrases in italics and used brackets in the text for translations of French phrases and definitions of English words that are no longer commonly in use. Translations of long passages are incorporated into the text and noted in the endnotes.

A Friends Reconstruction Unit in front of
one of the newly built modular houses

Introduction: The American Friends Service Committee

IN APRIL 1917, THREE WEEKS AFTER America's entry into the Great War being waged in Europe, Quaker representatives from all branches of the Religious Society of Friends gathered in Philadelphia. Many older Friends felt that the pressures on their youth were overwhelming and that if Friends did not provide an alternative, these young men might be tempted to join the military. Their epistle from this meeting stated that "We are united in expressing our love for our country and our desire to serve her loyally. We offer our services to the Government of the United States in any constructive work in which we can conscientiously serve humanity."[1] From this meeting, they formed the American Friends Service Committee (AFSC). Vincent Nicholson, executive secretary, began receiving applications for reconstruction work in France. This project was named the Friends Reconstruction Unit (FRU).

In July, American Quakers held a Friends National Peace Conference in Winona Lake, Indiana. The attendees issued a message from the Society of Friends that "the alternative to war is not inactivity and cowardice. It is the irresistible and constructive power of good-will." They assumed that

Quaker men would be exempt from the draft, but presumed that Friends should not accept exemption from military service while doing nothing to express their positive faith and devotion.[2]

Logo adopted by the AFSC and worn on the uniforms of FRU workers.

Several years earlier, British Friends had begun to work in France. They issued a call to those "whose conscience forbade them to take up arms" to serve in other ways in the crisis. "Our duty is clear—to be courageous in the cause of love and in the hate of hate."[3] The English and Irish Friends identified three areas of service and established the Friends Ambulance Committee, the War Victims Relief Committee, and the Emergency Committee for Helping Aliens. They later added the Friends Service Committee for Suffering Conscientious Objectors. A few American Friends contributed funds to these efforts, and Philadelphia Friends sent four men to work with the Ambulance Unit as an experiment in cooperation.[4]

A group of prominent Quakers, including Rufus Jones and James Babbitt, recognized the desire for more service opportunities for American pacifists. The Quakers needed the cooperation of the military since they controlled the draft and the access to France, but they had difficulty in obtaining permits from the American War Office to work with British Friends.

President Woodrow Wilson and Secretary of War Newton Baker were somewhat sympathetic.[5] Wilson gave the Red Cross control of all American relief activities in France and appointed Grayson Murphy as Chief of the American Red Cross in France. Murphy was a graduate of the William Penn

Charter School[6] and had attended Haverford College. He suggested to Rufus Jones, a Haverford professor, that Friends form an organization for relief work in France in cooperation with the Civilian Service of the American Red Cross.[7] Lewis Gannett,[8] a conscientious objector (CO) from Harvard University, told the story that the first connection between the Red Cross and the Quakers had occurred quite by accident: Jones entered the committee room of the War Council at the Red Cross offices rather than a waiting room, "and thus established the relationship before the error was discovered."[9]

Murphy invited two prominent Friends, Morris Leeds and J. Henry Scattergood,[10] to travel to France to work on plans for the project. They agreed to form the Anglo-American Mission of the Society of Friends (Mission Anglo-Américaine de la Société des Amis) and were given permission to work with the English Friends doing relief and reconstruction work in France. This alliance gave the American Friends on-the-job training from sympathetic and experienced workers, enabling the Americans to become productive quickly.[11]

The American Friends offered the Red Cross a good reputation, a successful program, immediate publicity, and trained men to do the heavy work of building houses, repairing machinery, and helping on farms. A few young women were also sent to work in the hospitals and schools. At the same time, the association with the Red Cross was essential to obtaining necessary permits to gain access to the war zone, where the needs of the population were the greatest, and for providing transportation of building materials and equipment from America as well as within France. The Red Cross provided the funds for a modular housing factory, hospitals, farm equipment, cars, and trucks. The Quaker representative in Paris attended Red Cross staff meetings, and the head of the American Red Cross in France attended executive meetings of the Friends Mission.[12] The British Friends continued their previous association with the French Red Cross.

While working together, Friends recognized that the Red Cross had a different purpose in France. The Red Cross work was "an expression of the American people . . . and its work [was] in part an expression of their militant determination." There was also an element of national propaganda in maintaining morale and in increasing the agricultural production of France to save shipping space for men and armaments. Most of the FRU workers, on the other hand, saw their work as a positive expression of their faith and their pacifism. Their work in France arose from their desire to save what they could from the devastation brought on by the war. The Red Cross preferred the large scale, sweeping relief efforts, while the FRU relied on serving individual families and establishing connections.[13]

The first group of men, called the Haverford Unit, began their training on July 17, 1917. These members were not granted exemptions from the draft by the War Department; to be allowed to leave the country, a man of draft age had to sign a promise to return if he was called up for duty."[14]

Working in conjunction with the English Friends and the American Red Cross, the Quakers established their headquarters in Sermaize-les-Bains, France.[15] They set up their offices in the casino rooms of La Source, a luxury hotel about a mile from town. The hotel rooms were crowded with refugees; sanitation was poor and food and supplies short. Sermaize was "a dreadfully devastated town,"[16] which had been destroyed in the 1914 Battle of the Marne, but was under the control of the Allies by 1917. Many of the villages in the Marne region were reduced to rubble. Farm machinery was broken and farm horses were taken for military purposes. All young and able-bodied men had been drafted into the military. American Friends brought hope, as well as tools, labor, clothes, food, and medical supplies and services. As Henry Scattergood said, "We are here because we feel we must do something, not expecting an easier life than the millions of men who are following their light in other ways, and we are ready to do the hardest and lowliest kind of work. It is not that our blood is any less red or our patriotism less real . . . . "[17]

The Friends organized their work under four sections: medical, relief work, reconstruction, and agriculture. The American workers merged with the English workers, forming a small *équipe* or team for each devastated village.[18] By December 1917, 138 Americans were working at 27 locations including the two Quaker–run factories manufacturing modular buildings, ~~which~~ which could be quickly assembled to provide a community center or houses for homeless French families. Only a few FRU workers were placed in each village so that they could establish friendly relationships with the French people and so that their presence would not strain the limited resources of the village.

Most AFSC field workers proudly wore uniforms of dark gray cloth, similar to the uniforms worn by the British Friends. On their caps they wore the Quaker badge, the red and black eight-pointed star originally used by British Friends during their relief work in the Franco–Prussian War. This emblem was adopted by American Friends on November 13, 1917.[19] Since the agreement with the French government

Villagers in the Verdun region

forbade both religious proselytizing and speaking out against the war, the Quaker uniforms camouflaged their pacifism, but at the same time differentiated them from both the military and the Red Cross.

In early 1918, the AFSC formed the American Friends Unit No. 2, which had a more direct connection with the Red Cross, and members wore the symbol of the Red Cross on their uniform sleeves below the AFSC star. The director of the Red Cross Department of Civil Affairs, Homer Folks, had requested three hundred more workers to fill some of the needs in France. Because of passport and other difficulties, the second unit never numbered more than one hundred workers. The first members

of this unit arrived in France in March, and they were sent to projects all over France. Leslie Hotson was a member of Unit No. 2 and his letters tell one person's story of the work of Friends in France. Mary Peabody's letters complete the story by describing the work of pacifists and socialists at home in Cambridge, Massachusetts.

Three young men in the FRU uniform

Harvard students marching in Harvard Stadium, 1917

1

Answering the Call

LESLIE HOTSON LOOKED ACROSS THE SMALL TABLE at his companion.
He and Mary Peabody had been walking for hours along the banks of the
Charles River. This cozy cafe in Harvard Square was an inviting place to
warm up. Over hot cocoa, he continued to talk. He needed to unburden
himself, and she was an eager listener. He was a student at Harvard University, and she attended Harvard's sister college, Radcliffe. Their friendship
had begun through their shared interests in music and drama, poetry and
philosophy, and they found a mutual yearning to be of service for the
greater good.

John Leslie Hotson had grown up in Brooklyn, New York, the third
of four children. His parents were Canadian immigrants, and his father
worked as a law stenographer. At Harvard, Leslie majored in English and
worked as a private tutor in mathematics and French to supplement the
scholarships he had received. Leslie was outgoing, enthusiastic, and ener-
getic, with an infectious sense of humor. He found time to enjoy college
life while earning above-average grades. He sang bass in the glee club, acted
in plays put on by the drama club, and ran on the cross-country team.[1]

Mary May Peabody was an idealistic and determined woman. Her parents were divorced, and her mother supported their family with her earnings and with some family resources. They took in boarders, and Mary and her younger sister Helen lived at home to help with the work of maintaining the household. Mary earned extra money tutoring French grammar and conversation. She was outgoing and generous with her time. She could be counted on to get the work done, whether organizing a Class Day event, starting a French club, or planning a party. She was popular with students and teachers and had loyal friends, both female and male. She balanced her musical and literary interests with social justice activities and campaigned tirelessly for suffrage, socialism, and the rights of workers. She proudly considered herself a radical.[2]

America had entered the war being waged in Europe in 1917. For many Americans, this was a time of high ideals and fervent pacifism. All over the country, young men—poor and rich, illiterate and educated—were signing up to join the fight for freedom. Congress passed a law establishing compulsory military training for all college men over the age of twenty years and nine months. The law established the Student Army Training Corps (SATC) at all colleges and universities to develop the large cadre of officers needed for the war. By 1918, many of Leslie's classmates had already enlisted or were serving in Harvard's SATC. Leslie, however, refused to enroll in, or seek exemption from, the required military courses; he was not willing to participate in any preparations for war. Although he was only twenty years old and would not be subject to the draft until later that year, he felt called to action, "to be of service to people who are suffering, and to be of service in a practical way."[3]

Leslie's strong faith guided his determination. The Hotsons were members of the Church of the New Jerusalem or, simply, the New Church. Emmanuel Swedenborg, the church's founder, taught that truth is love in action and the essence of God is found in the desire to do service and live a useful life. Although some Swedenborgians were conscientious objectors, church teachings did not offer a theological basis for pacifism. Swedenborg had stated that "wars that have for an end the protection of one's country are not opposed to charity."[4] His church community could not offer Leslie options to support his personal rejection of military service.

Mary was determined to help Leslie find a way to serve. She had been volunteering at the offices of the League for Democratic Control (LDC), a Boston-area organization working for peace.[5] Her mother, Anna May Peabody, served on the Civil Liberties Committee, a group of dedicated staff and volunteers who aided men opposed to war on conscientious grounds, helping them prepare their cases before the proper tribunals. Mary eagerly told members of the League about her friend. Surely they could find a way for him to be of service without joining the military.

A few weeks after Mary and Leslie's discussion in the coffee shop, Anna Hallowell Davis offered to speak with Leslie. She served at the League with Mary's mother and represented the American Friends Service Committee (AFSC), a new Quaker organization calling for volunteers to help refugees in France. Horace Davis, Anna's son, had resigned from Harvard the previous fall to join the FRU working in France. The young pacifists at Harvard and Radcliffe relied heavily on Anna Davis's guidance and nurturing, and she hosted many gatherings of students at her home. Frances Witherspoon, a New York peace activist, called Anna Davis "the mother of conscientious objectors." In a letter to Frances Witherspoon, Anna wrote about the COs: "In our time, our men will prove to be the heroes and prophets of a better day."[6] Anna agreed to recommend Leslie for the FRU.

Leslie was quickly accepted. On April 17, 1918, he informed Harvard that he had enrolled in the American Friends' Reconstruction Unit and was awaiting instructions. He was now on a leave of absence from the university. He had given up his scholarship, and he wondered whether he would ever be able to return. His dreams of studying English literature and making his mark as a writer now seemed painfully elusive. Leslie was scheduled to sail for France on May 2. There was much to do, and he returned home to Brooklyn to prepare.

Leslie dearly missed Mary Peabody. Moreover, he was away from the intellectual stimulation of the Harvard community. He wanted to get his service adventure under way and, at the same time, wondered if he was up to the challenge. And he began to court Mary in his letters.

April 15, 1918, Leslie in Brooklyn to Mary on spring break in Chichester, New Hampshire

Dearest Mary,

I hope that you are having as beautiful spring weather in New Hampshire as we are in Brooklyn. Today the skies were mild and nature was gay.

I revisited my school this afternoon and greeted some of my old friends. So far I have noticed no change for the worse in their attitude towards me. Maybe I am not as bad as I look, Mary. A certain Miss Hazen (whose opinion I value) said that I looked happier and had lost a certain cynicalness of expression. I did not tell her who the cause of my happiness was. Dr. San Giovanni, with whom I talked in French, was quite surprised. He said, "*Vous savez que vous avez fait des pas gigantèsques avec votre français.*" [You know you have made some giant steps with your French.] I didn't tell him who had patiently and sweetly labored to help me learn. No, I didn't tell them. I came back home and looked again at you in your little brown frame. Do you know, the more my mother and father see you, the more they like you? If they didn't, I'd disinherit them.

Oh, I have some news! I am trying to persuade my brother Ronald to come up to Cambridge with me and stay a week. I want him to see Harvard. I think if he once sees it, he'll want to come to college, and <u>he can do it</u>, if he only wants to. What he needs is encouragement, because he thinks he's too old. He isn't, at all, you know. But you'll encourage him, too, won't you, Mary? Mother says that I can influence him, if anybody can, but she doesn't know you yet. I think I can get him to visit Harvard anyhow, and that's a big step. We'll fix him when we once have him in Cambridge, won't we? He is going to apply for the Quaker Unit, too. Think of it, we may go over together. I shouldn't ask anything better.

Those little verses that I sent you[7]—when I think them over, they seem so poor and inadequate! Why can't I say what I feel? If I could really <u>say</u> it, it would be calm, lovely, and deeply felt poetry. Oh, for a magic pen! I wonder if you ever feel or fancy that I am near you. If you don't, I must be near you unawares, loving but not loved.

We must read some of Swedenborg's <u>Conjugial Love</u>[8] together. It will search our hearts and minds with a surer and more enlightening touch, I am certain, than any other single thing we could read or talk about.

We can't misunderstand each other. It's impossible. We are so mutual in our sympathy, and so alike in our ideals, that we know each other. Still, we must see more of each other, talk with our deepest hearts, and dream golden dreams.

Till then! Are there hills, Mary? And dost thou lift up thine eyes to them?

Ever,

Your Leslie

May 16, 1918, Leslie in Brooklyn to Mary after a delay in his sailing date allowed him a visit with her in Cambridge

Dearest Mary—

O the wonder of the joy of my love for you! I may not express it, or give it voice. It is like being alone to view the rosy dawn—no one but yourself understands and feels its exquisite loveliness—and you are powerless to paint it in words. When I left you I was blind—blinded by the soft radiance of it. I was happy, yet torn—and I walked like a man who has won, lost, and won again.

All your words and glances are treasured in my heart as the dearest refuge I have. Yet on the train, while I was wondering and remembering, a curious feeling took possession of me. I suddenly felt a void in my spirit—my deep love seemed to have fled from me. I looked again at your picture, but all was a mist of wonder—like the morning haze that hangs over the most beautiful trees and meadows. I tried to understand it—and felt at last that you must really have had my heart with you. Mary, my darling, I am at your feet for ever—I cannot change my heart—and it is yours to raise me, or hold me by the hand and gaze without me into the distance.

In the morning my spray of lilac was not withered. Its perfume is the sweetest in the world and reminds me vividly of you and your love for it.[9]

I am writing this on the top of Lookout Mountain, the highest hill in Prospect Park. Down in the valley the green veils of the trees are at their most perfect youth, freshness, and variety. On the way here I passed, in the park, the little Moravian cemetery. In one way I like it better than ours by the Charles—its stones are very modest and small, and show only a little way above the ground. But that little burying ground does not overlook a winding river, and it has not one millionth the sweet memories that the other one keeps locked in its green bosom.

I have been reading Keats from the sweet book you gave me and the sonnet called "Remember." I try to say a little of what I feel in my own poor verses—but I am sad when I think what golden glory should shine in verses written for my Mary . . . .

I am sorry that I had not the time to call Harry Dana[10] from the South Station. I really had more things to *emballer* [to wrap up] than I had imagined possible. I have received some instructions from the Unit, but do not know just yet whether my passport has been granted.

Your face is before me as it was in the moonlight then—and it will be forever.

Leslie

May 17, 1918, Leslie in Brooklyn to Mary in Cambridge

Dearest Mary,

Your lovely little note came this morning to make my heart glad. It is dear of you to think of a steamer letter for me, and I promise, promise, promise not to open it until the shore has faded.

Somehow the fullness of my former life here in high school seems gone. It is a shell. There still is a sort of friendship. I go there (I went today) with the desire of pouring out my affection upon those whom I thought my dearest friends, and am received with a pseudo-welcome; I can see it in their eyes. Either it is because I have known real friendship at Cambridge and am spoiled for anything weaker, or that the people here are incapable of it. At any rate, I am looked upon with suspicion when they learn that I am a member of the Friends Unit. I find that some people here think that the Friends are pro-German, and that their work in some way is interested. I begin to realize what you heroic girls at Radcliffe have had to cope with and undergo, though I think that the intolerance here is more blind and unreasoned. The principal of the high school does not understand the possibility of sincere conscientious religious pacifism. One of the teachers, a Miss MacDowell, a religious pacifist, is at present standing trial for her convictions.[11]

You can really have no complete idea of what your presence and influence mean to me. Dearest, <u>you</u> hold me up in every trial and struggle. It is because of your love, purity, tenderness, and strength that I feel like the man who overcomes. And yet, the closer I come to you, the more I am aware that "underneath are the everlasting arms"—holding and embracing us all.

Mary, would you mind if I called you "thee"?[12] For me, you know, there is something sacred about the word, and I feel like using it for thee and only thee. It is the sacredness of my love for thee that makes me wish to have a word that is sweet and intimate. Tell me, dearest, if it is good or strange to thy feelings.

Oh that glorious sunset! Let us be symbolists and believe that the sunset was our deep, rich love and the moon and stars were the steadfast hope and faith, which we hold to through the days and months till the time to come!

I have a delightful occupation. It is a secret. It is one of the least practical, and yet one of the most enjoyable things I have ever done—in fact, there is nothing in Brooklyn that I would rather do. 'Tis like this: I sit still, with the <u>Oxford Book</u>[13] in my hands; between its leaves is the most beautiful face in the world. I read thy favorite poems, and after each splendid or strangely fair thought I look at thee—and thee seems to understand! Thy features seem to be made to sympathize with the loveliest emotions of which the immortal poets were capable. It would be curious to another, but it is beautifully natural to me—*car nous nous entendons, et nous comprenons la poèsie!* [because we understand each other deeply, and we appreciate poetry.]

My only prayer last night was that my picture might speak the truth and that I might someday, somehow be worthy to take thee by the hand. I must not protest my love too much, but live it—forever!

Thy,
Leslie

May 19, 1918, Mary in Cambridge to Leslie in Brooklyn

Dear Les,

I am sitting out on our little piazza upstairs that is all closed in with trees, and it is such a beautiful warm sunny day. I have just read over again your lovely poem. Leslie, it is beautiful—if you can write like that you must keep it up, you have the real thing. The first two lines especially are lovely, as is all the rest. You never can say that you can't express yourself again for I see the sweetness and sincerity of every word. When I think of your love for me I feel as though I had the keeping of a great treasure whose value is beyond my understanding yet. I only know that it is large and beautiful and when I take it out and look at it, I go away gently and happy. Sometime I will write you a poem and tell you just what I mean.

You mustn't think about me too much, Les. You will probably be in Brooklyn quite a while. Read some good books and go on walks with your brother. Be active and you will be happy. I felt so badly when I read your letter about the feeling in New York, because of <u>course</u> it is hard not to be understood by those you care most for—but you know you are doing right and that a great work lies ahead of you. Don't let the lapses in between cool your zeal. I don't need to say any of this, of course, because you see the light so brightly yourself. I just know it helps when friends say the same things you feel yourself. You didn't give me the information I asked for about your boat or the sailing day, but perhaps you haven't even a vague idea. I suppose a steamer letter would keep even if you didn't sail right away.

When you say in your letter that one of the teachers in your school is standing trial for her convictions do you mean figuratively or literally? How can people be so intolerant and call themselves Christian! I am sending you the clipping from the Radcliffe News as a report of the mass meeting.[14] I have had a talk since with the girl who says we don't "feel" and I think she knows now that we do. She was dear about listening to me and we parted the best of friends—better than ever before because we had each put the sincerity of the other to the test and admired her for it.

We had a wonderful meeting at Dr. Davis's house yesterday afternoon. His little room was full. We had a general discussion of our situation (during which Mrs. Davis read some letters from the COs at Devens[15] which were wonderful, so firm yet sweet) and finally decided that we favored a merging of the League with the Young Democracy.[16] The paper will be called Young Democracy hereafter and the planks are so constructive and splendid that we hope to greatly enlarge the membership with radical war people, labor groups of young people, etc. It was thrilling, Leslie—everything was on such a high plane. And do you know—you were there! Yes, tho' you didn't know it. Mrs. Davis brought over your picture and put it on the bookcase and from there you witnessed the meeting. Wasn't that a sweet thing for Mrs. Davis to do? Everyone noticed it and said "Oh yes, he has gone to do reconstruction work . . . he is such a fine fellow." They all love you, Leslie.

There are so many things to tell you (gossipy things I mean) that I don't know where to begin. On Friday the Jewett Players came out to college to tea and to see the Idler production of "Pomander Walk." They were so natural and dear. I got quite well acquainted with some of them in the course of the afternoon and Miss Road invited me to visit![17] Isn't that exciting? Mr. Gordon and the other men liked the college singing very much. They all seemed much

interested in what we are doing. Miss Road told me that they welcome a little change from rehearsing all day long—she just wished
she could come again sometime, and Mr. Gordon said he was coming to Radcliffe so that he could wear a "mortar board."

Radcliffe students socializing with the "Radio boys" at a dance

Last night I made the nicest friend—his name is Cosmo Ligorio—an Italian Radio boy [student at Naval Radio School]. There
was a dance at the boatclub to which we were invited for the sailors.
I didn't go till almost ten because I had been out to dinner with
Francis and roaming around Cambridge (I tell you all my foolish-
nesses to amuse you and because you know the value they have in
my scale of things.) I wore my little pink dress and some white flow-
ery stuff that looked very pretty with the pink. We danced out on
the piazza behind the club and down on the float under the moon
and stars—it was great fun. This Cosmo Ligorio began by talking
French and I never dreamed he was Italian till I happened to mention

Dante, and he said he had been brought up on it. Such a frank, wholesome fellow—thrilled to pieces to talk literature and beautiful things. He said when he left me at the house that he had never had such a happy evening in his life. Isn't it fun to make people happy because of the things that have been given you? I may never see that boy again, I probably won't, but we both got a lot out of a few hours.

I am really working awfully hard now, getting up early every morning to review Dante and reading a play a day. They are so dull to read alone! I haven't heard anything definite about a job yet, but I hope to get the one in Peterboro! [New Hampshire]

It is nearly time for me to start to church now. I must leave the rest for another time. Be sure and let me know anything definite you learn about your leaving.

Yes indeed, Leslie, you may call me "thee." It is a very beautiful custom; you have the true Quaker spirit of love for all, and it makes me especially happy to have you think me worthy of their name.

Thy true friend,
Mary

May 22, 1918, Mary in Cambridge to Leslie in Brooklyn

Dear Leslie,

It came over me with a dreadful empty feeling last night that you must have gone, sailed without my wishes for Bon Voyage. Oh dear I have been nearly killing myself to get my work done so that I could write you a real poem for the steamer letter—and now you have gone and won't get this letter till weeks from now somewhere in France.

The last days I have just waited for mail times to get news from you, always hoping to hear something definite so that I could cling to that last straw, but now I know I won't hear for a very long time—When I get desperate I am going to write to Ronald and ask him when you sailed. You <u>will</u> write me soon, won't you?

Nothing has any fun in it any more, somehow, oh Leslie, I can't keep the tears from coming into my eyes when I think how dear and splendid you are! It is just a week from last night that you left Cambridge, but it seems years—time is such a comparative thing after all—and I miss you so terribly. It is terrible your going away so suddenly and so quietly (for you must have gone or I would have heard from you). They must have hurried things up the last minute and of course you were not allowed to tell where you sailed. Never mind— I shall hope to hear from you before very, very long. I hope that you got quite a long letter from me written on Sunday the 19th before you sailed; if you didn't it will probably be forwarded all right. I am sending this to Brooklyn with a note to Ronald asking for any information he may have.

Don't forget, Les, (but I know you won't) those you have left behind. We want you to be strong but to take care of yourself too. Your work is going to be thrilling and you will put all your heart into it. Good luck! Good luck! or rather *Bon courage! Mon ami, tu sera le conquereur et tu as toujours avec toi les souheits de ceux qui t'aiment. Le plus belle chose qu'on m'a jamais dit c'est à que tu a dit dans ta lettre—qu'on me connaissent tu as plus que jamais ta foi en Dieu. C'est cette foi là qui te guidera par les chemins difficiles vers notre lumière de l'idéale. Ta fidèle amie,* [Good luck! My friend, you will be the conqueror and you will always have with you the wishes of those who love you. The most beautiful thing anyone ever said to me is what you said in your letter—it makes me realize that you always have more faith than ever in God. It is this faith that will guide you past difficult things towards your light of the ideal. Your faithful friend,]

Mary

I haven't been able to write a special poem yet for you so I am sending this little one just for fun. It might just as well be about the last night you were here tho' I wrote it quite a while ago. I always manage to get in a star somewhere!

Cover Me Over With Shadows

Cover me over with shadows
I am weary of light and the day,
Let the wings of the night enfold me
And noiselessly bear me away.

I am lifted on darkening pinions
Till the numberless shadows seem
Intermingled within the ocean
Of one unending dream.

On the edge of the world they are calling,
But the echoes scatter afar
And are lost in the infinite silence
That veils the last white star.

Ronald Hotson, Leslie's brother

2

Ronald's Story

LESLIE CONTINUED TO AWAIT INSTRUCTIONS about sailing to France. He was able to visit Mary in Cambridge a few times, but for the most part he wandered around Brooklyn. For Mary, spring was the time for parties and dances, term papers, final exams, Class Day activities, elections for class officers, and her growing involvement in the socialist and radical clubs.

However, their letters that spring were overshadowed by their concern for Ronald and news of his stance as a conscientious objector. Leslie greatly admired his older brother Ronald, one of a very small number of pacifists who refused all alternative service. These men were known as "absolutists," COs who had been drafted and were officially soldiers but would not cooperate with the military in any way. Ronald sincerely believed that participating in war was so abhorrent that he was willing to suffer rather than compromise his moral principles. He saw no option but to resist any actions that would further the ability of the military to wage war.

Ronald's actions violated the Selective Service Act of May 18, 1917, which required all men from 21 to 30 years of age to register for military service.[1] Members of denominations, such as Quakers and Mennonites, could sometimes receive an exemption or were offered alternative service, but others had to prove their sincerity before often-hostile exemption boards. Obtaining an exemption would not be easy for the Hotson brothers; they were Swedenborgians, not members of a historic peace church.[2]

In the spring of 1918, Ronald was 23 years old and working for the Typewriter Speed Key Company as a linotype mechanic and machine shop foreman. On May 20, he was drafted and summoned to appear before the Exemption Board. Ronald made his appeal for exemption on the basis of the strong pacifism engendered by his mother and his Christian belief against the use of violence. The board refused to grant Ronald official status as a conscientious objector, and he was ordered to report for military duty.

The next day he was sent to Fort Slocum at the western end of Long Island Sound, one of the busiest Army recruiting stations in the country.[3] Young men were arriving at this base by the thousands, all eager to get to the front. They were full of patriotic fervor, anxious to do battle, and more than ready to turn their angry energy onto a CO, seeing him as a coward and a traitor who might even be pro-German. Here, Ronald began his stand as an absolutist objector and refused to cooperate with the military. He was imprisoned awaiting court martial.

The enlisted men bullied and abused him, trying to break his spirit or to get him to fight back. The officers condoned, and even participated in, persecuting him. They were concerned that his presence on base was detrimental to good order and to troop morale, and feared that his actions could induce others to defy the draft law. Further, the soldiers hoped to show that he was insincere in his stance, strengthening the case against him when he came up for court martial.

Ronald, a slight, bespectacled young man, made a ready target. A military uniform was forced on him by four soldiers after his own clothes were ripped off. He was strong from his work in the machine shop and could have defended himself. Instead, he simply suffered the cruelties without striking back or fighting off his attackers, further inflaming the bullies. Several times, he was beaten so badly he had to be taken to the hospital. On at least one occasion, he was moved to the guardhouse for his own safety. As he later reported to the Committee of 100 Friends of COs,

> "They (sergeant and 'help' consisting of privates ordered to the task) grabbed me; they seemed to be afraid to knock me outright, and contented themselves by obtaining the same result by various and sundry pressure. They could not drag me, and had to carry me bodily, struggling and squirming, across the camp to the Co. 4 Barracks. They dropped me several times, and one brute knocked my head from side to side until I could struggle no longer. My coat had been torn off, my collar and shirt torn open. They knocked me out. I came to on the veranda of the Co. 4 Barracks. After a bit, they took me to the hospital."[4]

Three days later, he was transferred to Cramp's Shipyards[5] in Philadelphia, another facility in which COs were treated brutally and often starved. Again he refused to put on a military uniform. Word got to the Hotson family in Brooklyn. Leslie was frantic. His brother needed immediate help. Leslie called Anna Davis, who had been advising Ronald about his own application to the FRU and who knew firsthand of Ronald's sincerity. She urged the Hotsons to reach out to the New York Bureau of Legal Advice, a left-wing pacifist organization. Its founder, Frances Witherspoon, was making a name for herself in defending other absolutist COs. She had the contacts and access to the courts to try to intercede on Ronald's behalf.

Anna Davis and Frances Witherspoon had the same advice—Leslie should not attempt to visit Ronald. He too would be seen as a "yellow-bellied pacifist," a traitor to the country for refusing to enlist. His presence might further antagonize the military command at the shipyard. Ronald's mother Lillie, a tiny, fiercely determined woman, went to visit him instead. Lillie Hotson had intentionally raised her boys as pacifists and encouraged them to apply for conscientious objector status. She deeply admired Ronald for taking an absolutist stand. But this was her son; she could not stand to see him suffer needlessly.

Lillie met with the authorities at the camp. They would not let her see Ronald unless he put on the uniform, nor could she send word to him. She was determined to get better treatment for her son. Anna Davis had given her the names of Friends in Philadelphia who were working on behalf of the Quaker COs. Lillie Hotson met with Samuel Bunting[6] on the staff of the American Friends Service Committee. Mr. Bunting was permitted to see Ronald and said later that Ronald "hadn't budged an inch" from his position. He was weak from being given very little to eat, and the beatings had left him bruised and in pain. But his spirit was strong and he was bearing up under the hardship.[7]

Quakers in Philadelphia intervened on Ronald's behalf, and he was moved to the immigration station in Gloucester City, New Jersey. Under the advice of Samuel Bunting, he agreed to put on the uniform while he was being transferred. He was not happy about this compromise, but realized it was necessary to avoid being lynched, "to ensure my safety from shipyard savages."[8]

The authorities at Gloucester City were not as cruel to COs. Captain Bell, who was in charge, may even have been sympathetic to their stand against participating in the war. Ronald was able to move about the grounds and could even take a few hours a day of liberty outside the station. He agreed to wear the uniform—but without insignia—when he went off base to avoid embarrassing the captain, writing "he in turn agrees that it shall in no wise prejudice my standing as a CO, and he is sincere and honest."[9] Captain Bell tried to persuade him to accept hospital service or to work in France at a hospital for life-long crippled soldiers, both considered by the Army to be acceptable non-combatant alternatives. But Ronald explained that he could "take no part whatever in an organization formed to prosecute war, nor [could he] in any way aid in supporting such organization nor obey orders, military or civil, tending to strengthen it."[10]

In June, Ronald was moved to Camp Dix, New Jersey, to await court martial with forty other absolutist COs. The group included several Mennonites, many Quakers, men from other denominations taking their stand on religious grounds, and a few socialist and secular conscientious objectors. He no longer had the freedom that Captain Bell had given him at Gloucester City, but at least the COs were segregated in a clean barracks, mostly for their protection from the angry soldiers.

In the fall, he was given the opportunity to go to France with the Friends Unit, but he chose not go at that time. On September 4, he wrote to Harold Evans, one of the founders of the AFSC and a member of the Board: "I've been of two minds about it. On the one hand, I approve of the good being done, and desire to help if I can. On the other hand—well, being at last out of the immediate proximity of the military, I feel as one reprieved from Hades. I loathe and detest the whole outfit so heartily that I bristle like a dog at the mere sight of a uniform—quite involuntary, and irrespective of its occupant. I conceive that in the reconstruction work I would probably come more or less into contact with the various military systems, French and American, with their slave psychology and dehumanizing discipline of their soldiers. I'm sick of them, now, at all events. It may be the reaction to past experiences."

After the war ended, he finally went to France with the FRU, joining Leslie in Paris.

Panaromic view of Camp Dix Cantonment in 1918

May 22, 1918, Leslie in Brooklyn to Mary in Cambridge

Dearest Mary,

Forgive me for not answering thy lovely letter more promptly. I certainly should have if I could; but the fever from the inoculations began to bother me on Sunday and hasn't left me yet. I couldn't be very active to be happy, but that letter cheered me mightily.

Women certainly must have intuitions. How did thee know that I should probably be in Brooklyn for quite a while? Up until yesterday morning I had reckoned to be sailing today as that was the date the Committee had told me, and the one I was instructed to put on my application for passport. Well, I had heard nothing by Monday morning, so I wired to ask if I was to sail this week. Yesterday, I received the answer—"Passport received. Prepare to sail about June 5." I was quite anxious before I heard, but now I am thankful, because it is much better to be sick at home than at sea.

Mary, a thing has happened with unexpected suddenness. Ronald has been called into the Army and sent to Camp Slocum. He is an absolutist CO, of course. They gave him exactly one day's notice. We understand from Miss Witherspoon that the conditions are worse for COs at Camp Slocum than at Camp Upton,[11] where we had hoped he would be sent. He has a splendid spirit, and I shall be proud of him and more proud every day. I will send thee his address when we get it. I know he would love to hear from Helen and thee. There are no girls he knows whose principles are so lofty as yours.

I was not discouraged at the feeling here—merely disappointed. About that religious pacifist teacher—her trial was before the Board of Education, and the penalty was dismissal, with the understanding that she is not to be employed by any other public high school in the city.

I have written to Mrs. Davis, thanking her for sending me that priceless book, The Record of a Quaker Conscience[12]—I gave it to Ronald—he will need it more than I. Let us hope that the officials will not take it from him. I thanked her, too, for bringing me to the meeting on Saturday. She knew how I should have loved to be there in person. I am so glad that they had such a fine meeting.

How I envy thee that afternoon with the Jewett Players! It must have been delightful. I do hope that thee has not seen the last of Cosmo Ligorio. It must have been charming for you both— to dance in the moonlight by the river and to talk about things you both love in literature. It is altogether too bad that you can't have him to thy house! I can imagine how beautiful thee must have been that evening—no wonder the lad vowed he had never spent a happier time.

While I am "laid up," I have been thinking and dreaming— mostly the latter—of learning Italian. I love it so, thee knows. My future is quite unclear as yet. The life of a scholar, teacher, and writer attracts me strongly, and yet I feel that I ought to get working for the common people. Maybe something will show me my best path when the time comes. How I should love to spend a year with thee in Florence!

Thy,
Leslie

May 23, 1918, Leslie in Brooklyn to Mary in Cambridge

Dearest,

Oh, I am so sorry and troubled to have kept thee in suspense! Things all added in to make it pretty bad. Thee knows that I had been instructed by the Committee to be ready to sail May 22, and I had been hanging on every mail—and nothing, no word until Tuesday, a day after I had telegraphed. Till then I had been pretty well torn in mind with the fact of possibly having to get ready in almost no time and the news on Monday of Ronald's call. Maybe that helped to lay me out flat.

The letter I wrote thee yesterday—thee musn't judge the writing too severely. That was the first time I have ever had to stop to rest physically in the middle of a letter. How foolish of me to pick up a fever at this late date! Darling Mary, I'll promise to never, never do it again. (I'll have an occasion to keep the promise, too, because I got my last inoculation yesterday.) I feel on the high road to *bien-être* [well-being] now.

Dear Mary, thee mustn't work so hard—though I love thee dearly for wanting to make me happy with a poem. I love thy [poem] "Cover me over with shadows"—that key-thought is beautiful to picture, the deep longing of the weary to be gathered in the soft and cool and dark, and thy poem does much more. The last stanza is especially sweet—hearing, in perfect rest, the distant voices, and losing them gradually and effortlessly into the Nowhere beyond the world's edge. I had a dream something like that when I was in bed.

Ronald's real trials have not yet begun, I suppose. We have not received an exact address from him yet, and but one letter, in which he said that he had arrived at Fort Slocum (near New Rochelle) and was expecting possibly to be sent away soon to some more permanent station—Slocum being more like a clearing camp.

Thy lovely words of strengthening courage and faith have heartened me tremendously. I felt even physically stronger when I read them.

Your,
Leslie

May 27, 1918, Leslie at Grand Central Station, New York, to Mary in Cambridge

Dearest—

I have just read again your letter that came this morning, and the steady, sweet, peaceful tone of it is like a soothing hand on a troubled forehead. Yes, Mary dear, I am entirely well again, and to prove it I have written thee a little sonnet, my first and quite probably my last, if it doesn't please the princess who holds my heart with golden bands.

News about Ronald! About 10 o'clock Saturday evening a telegram was phoned to our house from him: "Come at once." We took it to mean Mother, and she went by the 12:45 a.m. train, and did not come back until this afternoon.

When she got to the camp in Philadelphia, after waiting a long while, some officers came out to reason with her about Ronald. It appeared that he had taken off the uniform, which they had forced on him. She was calm, and told them that she was of the same mind Ronald was. They told her she could not see him unless he put on the uniform and, later, that she could not send in word to him.

She went downtown, and was sweetly received by the Friends. She attended one of their meetings, and was introduced to Mr. Bunting (to whom Ronald and I had applied for the Unit.) She says he is a splendid man. Him she told about Ronald, and that he had taken off the uniform. Mr. Bunting took an extra suit of clothes for Ronald and went. He was permitted to see Ronald, who had a blanket around him. Mr. Bunting said later that Ronald was well and "hadn't budged an inch" (from his CO position.) He had the marks of several blows on his face, but he had not struck back. They had been giving him very little to eat. It appears that he had meant me to come, but Mother and Mr. Bunting are glad that she went after all, because their refusal to let her communicate with him makes his case stronger. Mr. Bunting is going to look after him and has already telegraphed to Dr. Keppel[13] at Washington. I'm mighty proud of Ronald, I can tell you. And my mother gets so much strength and comfort from her faith!

Bunting says that after holding up passports for a long time, the government has just sent him a big bunch; and since there are certain women needed at once in France, I'll have to wait until June 12 at least! *Sapristi!* [Heavens!] I'm getting quite a vacation. But I know I didn't leave college early under false pretenses, so I am conscience-light on that point.

I have started <u>A Nobleman's Nest</u> by Turgenieff [Turgenev], and find it very interesting. Bliss Perry's[14] admiration for Turgenieff as a literary artist is deep, and I want to appreciate him too.

Accept my hearty congratulations for the lucky Radcliffe Cercle.[15] It has chosen a remarkably fine president for the next year. To think that I shall be away when all thy pleasures and triumphs of college are at their height. The thought is not happy, so I don't dwell on it.

Bonne chance. Je prie pour tes examens. Pauvres petites! Ils en out besoin, car tu vas les tuer, cruelle! À plus tard, [Good luck. I pray for your exams. Poor little ones! There will be no more need of them, because you will kill them, you cruel woman! Until later,]

Leslie

May 29, 1918, Leslie in Brooklyn to Mary in Cambridge

Dearest Mary,

Here is the first letter from Ronald since Saturday since they began to starve him.[16] His fortitude and faith are admirable, and show so beautifully the strength of Christian love. I wrote him the night before last, and hope the letter reached him. I will write again today, and if this treatment of him persists, I am going down soon to visit him. Will you please send this letter of Ronald's to Mrs. Davis, when you have read it? I think that she would be interested, even though she has not met him. Mary, he will be weak from lack of food, probably, so don't expect very much from him in the way of answering letters. He will love to hear from Helen and you—and I will send you copies of his letters home.

Mary dear, I am looking out of the window and hoping for a letter from thee. Don't study too much; thee won't have to, as I am going to pray for thee in the examinations.

Ever,
Thy Leslie

May 30, 1918, Mary in Cambridge to Leslie in New York

Dear Les,

It is beautiful! That is all I can say when I read your sonnet over and over. I like it the best of anything you have written, it sounds so mature—I mean the thought seems to have dictated the words and the words just came musically. I don't know how much you worked on it, but it sounds like something you had thought out and then written very spontaneously. I love every word of it, *mon poète* [my poet], and will never forgive you if it is your last sonnet. Have you begun to study Italian that you can quote so well? Anyway, I always knew that you had the "gift of tongues" (I don't mean the kind we heard about in morning prayers once! but the linguistic and poetic kind). Leslie, I think your little poem is a gem; its brightness is lightening up these gloomy days of finals.

I am so glad you are all well again, but poor Ronald—isn't it perfectly outrageous that he should be treated so. How you must feel not knowing what will be done with him next, and yet you must be so proud of him. He is a true soldier of the Cross. I am going to write to him right away, Leslie—I wonder if they would let him have a book if I sent him one. We have that lovely story called <u>A Soldier of Life</u>,[17] which I thought would help pass the weary hours and also give him strength. I am so glad that the Quakers are going to keep an eye on him. I think they treat the COs better if they have <u>friends</u> at hand. I am going to tell Mrs. Davis about Ronald and perhaps she will write to him too.

You are having a fine lesson in patience, aren't you—waiting to sail. I am glad tho' that you are having a little time to read—you may not have any for two years after you leave. I read <u>A Nobleman's Nest</u> this winter and thought it was perfectly splendid, so strong yet so sympathetic. You ought to read <u>Virgin Soil</u> by Turgenieff too: it is about the Spirit that ran thru' Russia before the Revolution, and it shows two types of men—the simple, practical yet kindly man who throws in his strength for justice and the poetic visionary who goes too far—that is, he is too temperamental to stand the strain. Read it and see what I can't explain.

It is funny I can't seem to say what I want to now-a-days. I guess it is because I am really awfully tired. I saw the strangest things last night. All kinds of people out of books and prisons visited me and I couldn't go to sleep. It was very silly. I had to go thru' a process of argumentation with myself each time to prove that there was really nobody there—and finally they would go away.

The other day Mrs. Hallowell[18] gave her lecture on "The Friends in France" to Mother's little Lend-a-Hand Club. The children sold the tickets for 25¢ each, and they had a fine crowd. They made $40 to send to the Quakers. The lecture made me perfectly crazy to get over there to France and help—and Mrs. H. encouraged me; she said she hadn't heard of any rigid age limit—so perhaps I will go next summer! Oh if I only could! I practically have my position for this summer. Tutoring and being companion to a little girl of 10 years—what her teachers call "a difficult child." I will have $100 a month, which I feel is a triumph—if I succeed in understanding and helping her.

It is so cold and rainy here tonight that we are all sitting around the open fire—Patsy is frantic because she thinks she smells a mouse in the corner, her tail goes round and round with excitement. A while ago Helen and I were singing Shubert's "Serenade" and Schumann's "Ich Grolle Nicht" and some of the Swiss songs we are so fond of. What a blessing music is, I don't know what I'd do without a little now and then—do you get a chance to sing now-a-days? Do tell me what you do all day—you seem so far away and detached, somehow, Leslie. Let's <u>converse</u> more thru' our letters. Yet when I do that I ramble on for pages without saying anything in particular, which isn't very interesting but sometimes little common things seem to give the atmosphere of reality, don't you think so.

Au revoir mon ami. Peut-être nous nous serrons la prochaine fois à Paris—Marie. [Good-bye, my friend. Perhaps the next time we will be together will be in Paris—]

Mary

May 31, 1918, Leslie in Brooklyn to Mary in Cambridge

Dearest Mary,

How I love to read words from thee! Thy letter was sweet, and I felt the atmosphere of over-strain in it that gave an air of gentleness—my heart goes out to thee—really, my Mary must not work so hard. *Soigne toi, ma vie!* [Take care of yourself, my life!]

I am so glad that the sonnet pleased thee. Thee is gifted with second sight! That is just how I wrote it—got a complete idea first, and the words flowed to express it. No, I found the quotation by chance; and it suggested the analogy for me and my dream of thee. The Oxford Book gave me an exalted mood, but little suggestion.

Through the efforts of the Friends, Ronald has been allowed some liberty, after five days without food. He has been ordered from Washington, transferred to c/o Lieut. Vawter, Immigration Station, Gloucester, N.J. He has had to put on the uniform to get out of the Shipyards without being lynched, but he has accepted no service, taken no oath, and has a signed statement from his officer that his status has not changed. So he really made them give in, and he has not budged an inch. He is just over the river from Philadelphia, and has five hours free time, I understand, every other day. Yes, Mary, please send him the book—he needs every help he can get. He is having strong temptation—they are treating him with kindness, and even some of his friends urge him to accept the Army's offer to work in a hospital in France for disabled and insane soldiers. He cannot take it, because it would mean taking an oath to support the arms of the United States, and he feels he must carry a clean record against the idea of military, organized force.

Samuel Bunting was in New York yesterday at the New York Annual Meeting of Friends. I went over and saw him, and he told me things about the Unit, about Quakerism, and best of all, about Ronald. (He was one of the two Friends that visited Ronald and really got the relief from Washington.) I am more enthusiastic than ever over the prospect of being given the opportunity of working with such fine men as they. I stayed for part of the meeting; it was quite a revelation to me. Samuel admires Ronald's firmness and strength. The Friends are so kind, so strong, so sympathetic, so capable, and so wise!

The memory of our times together this spring is growing with me. As I read The Oxford Book, I think of the time we gathered the flowers and read poetry on that green hillside. I shall never forget thy presence and the music of thy voice, reading the words of beauty. It suddenly came over me today—what a precious treasure Mary has in her voice—the range, clarity, and sweetness of it!

May I go on? I love to write to thee, and since I have seemed far away and detached (O Mary! I have been close to you almost every minute!) and since thee might like to read a letter to ease thy mind of Music 4 and French 9 finals, I shall take a little minute more. I have been reading quite a little, studying French, helping Mother somewhat in the house, and trying to write. The day certainly passes without my time hanging upon my hands. My typewriter has arrived from Cambridge, and I have written the lines on it.

What does thee suppose! A card from Boris Stern[19]—*en route pour le front!* [on the way to the front!] He sends his regards to thee, and wants to hear from his Cambridge friends. I am going to write to him soon. He wants to hear about the Socialist Club, about which I know nothing, except that our study circle had a fine meeting that

last time I was there. Has Trixie—excuse me, has Miss Jones[20] written to him? She could cheer him up considerably, I think. He is a
fine lad—sympathetic and affectionate—and having no faith in another life, is giving everything he has to protect Russia and democracy, as he sees it.

Wasn't that a remarkable letter of Ronald's! We received another today, and the note of deliverance and thanksgiving for
strength was touching. He says "before, I felt and thought and believed, now I <u>know</u>." He has been through a very deep valley, and has
been brought forth in safety and faith by an Arm which makes the
weak stronger than the mighty.

*Encore une fois, ma chère, si tu m'aimes un peu, soigne-toi bien, et
ne travaille pas trop. Tu réussiras dans tes examens sans la moindre
doute. Au plaisir, mon étoile—je ne puis pas être rez-de-chaussée quand
je vois ta figure dans la fenêtre de mon âme.* [Again, my dear, if you
love me a little, take good care of yourself, and don't work too hard.
You will succeed in your exams without the slightest doubt. I will
see you again, my star—I cannot stay on the ground when I see your
figure in the window of my soul.]

Ton,
Leslie

Quand partes-tu pour ta situation? [When are you leaving for your
job?]

May 31, 1918, Mary in Cambridge to Leslie in Brooklyn

Dear Les,

    Mon ami, isn't it terrible the suffering that Ronald is having! Yet in the same breath I say how splendidly beautiful is his strength and faith. That letter is extraordinary—when people read it years from now, they will find it hard to believe, and they will admire as they did the Christian martyrs the strength and gentleness of such a man. I cried, Leslie, I couldn't help it, when I read Ronald's letter. Poor boy, he must feel so alone; and yet his wonderful spirit keeps up his heart. I wonder if they can be keeping his mail from him. I wrote to him, being careful what I said because I didn't want to get him into trouble. By now he must be in the hospital. Oh Leslie how do you bear it—you are so brave. I felt so weak and useless in the world when I read Ronald's letter. I just pray that if ever I should be put to the test I would have the strength he has.

    Last night over the telephone Mrs. Davis told me that Ronald had a very good chance of going in the Quaker Unit if the Gov't would let him off. In fact she seemed almost sure that he would go if he could get off. Do you think there is any hope? (With the Gov't I mean.) Why won't the Gov't let him do it as alternative service, everyone knows the splendid work of the Quakers, and yet what their principles are all the time. I am going to send the letter to Mrs. Davis right away. Are your plans for sailing still about the twelfth? Dr. Dana told me to tell you that he might turn up on the same boat. He really wants awfully to go, but he doesn't think he could get a passport.

    I won't study too hard, Les, tho' I am afraid it would take more than prayers to save my exams. I am sending you a little wild rose that I picked down by the river. I hope it will still smell a little sweet when it gets to you; it was so fragrant when I picked it.

Addio amico mio [Good-bye, my friend (Italian)]
Mary

June 1, 1918, Leslie in Brooklyn to Mary in Cambridge

Dearest Mary,

Ronald's sufferings are over for the present! Due to the urgent report of the Friends to Washington of his case, he was transferred on Wednesday last, to an alien internment station at Gloucester City, a few miles down the Delaware from Philadelphia, in New Jersey. Maybe I told thee this? I can't remember. He had to be carried out of Cramp's Shipyards; and the last two days of his five of starvation, he had to have a guard of two dozen heavily armed soldiers, because the Shipyard crowd was so threatening—menacing him with everything from ordinary hanging to peculiar tortures of burning, roasting, etc. to which the facilities of a great shipyard are adapted. O my dear, Ronald had a gay time—one that he will not soon forget! But now he is getting excellent treatment, excellent food, a cool solitary cell to sleep in, and <u>five</u> <u>hours</u> <u>free</u> <u>time</u> every other <u>day</u>!

I went down to Philadelphia yesterday to see him, and met him at the Arch Street Friends Center.[21] Oh, it did my heart good to see him again, safe! I ate him up with my eyes. Mary, he has stood up wonderfully, a little thinner, but strong, and <u>happy</u>. He has a more determined, lofty spirit about him than before—his ideals are evident. There is a look in his eye—a look which never was there before—a look which I have rarely seen. He says life is sweeter to him, humanity means more, and the Lord is very present.

I came as a surprise. I guess he was pleased to see someone who loves him. I had him all afternoon to myself! (It really wasn't piggy, Mary, because I had no one to divide him with.) We went together back to his station, which is really a beautiful place—trees and ground around it, and one side facing the Delaware. There are no restrictions on his mail anymore; but his mail that was sent to Cramps is being held (somewhat spitefully, I'm afraid) by the captain there; who is a rather two-faced individual. Ronald is under a Lieutenant now, who is putting him on good behavior, giving him more liberty than any CO ever got before, I think, and watching him very closely. Ronald is tactful, polite, and on his guard. He is wearing the uniform, without any insignia, as a favor to the captain (another, a Captain Bell, a man of honor and kindness. Ronald says the superior of Lieut. Vawter) and will take it off the minute anyone tries to make him serve, or obey a military order of any kind. He told me oh so many things about his treatment, and the character of the regulars and of the drafted men. And of brutalities, too. He has been through a heavy trial, and he says that the only thing that held him up to the last was his faith in the divine Love.

Mary dear, thee must not cry like that for him. He is richer now by far than I am. I am not sorry for him now; I wonder at him, and admire and love him. And as for thy being useless—ah, thee does not know: the memory of the three strong and sweet ones at thy home—the knowledge of their steadfastness and faith in the ideal of human love, sustained him, Mary, more than anyone knows . . .

They must be holding thy letter at the Shipyards; but he will get it soon, I trust. Write him anything that will bear the inspection of the lieutenant (though the last letters he got were unopened, 'tis best to be safe).

I suppose thee has seen the ruling, just out, about COs? Mrs. Davis must have shown thee a copy of it. I went over it with Ronald. He believes now that they will send him, sooner or later, to some camp to be interrogated by these worthy gentlemen. He is glad now that he went through the terrible time, because he says that practically everybody, including the reptile captain at Cramp's, is convinced of his sincerity. Imagine him standing every conceivable abuse, and keeping courteous and patient and firm through it all! It is wonderful. I fear he has much more strength than I should. He even convinced the brutalized men . . . But about that ruling, Ronald is not sure yet what he will do. He may refuse both agricultural and Quaker unit service, as being a mere means of slipping out for himself. He almost feels that to do what the military wants him as a CO to do is to spot the record of objection to war service that he is trying to make. He needs time and reflection to decide. I don't suppose that he will be immediately ordered away from the strange but very congenial and pleasant place where he now is, but one cannot tell. Oh, what a power there is now about him! To have "bucked the machine" and <u>won</u> with God's help! He didn't give up—he didn't betray his faith. Even if they had killed him he would have been the victor!

Mary, a brother like that is a <u>brother</u>: a man whom I can love and revere through everything and forever. And just think—when he heard that we had sent thee his letter, he was sorry, because he was afraid that, led away by his pain and weakness, he might have complained unduly! Why, there wasn't a word or thought that wasn't faithful,

fearless, and calm . . . I think that he feels, at least, that he is not intending to ask favors from the military authorities—and that to ask
them if he may be allowed to go with the Quakers is admitting a military control which he will not recognize. His mind, though, is not
made up. But the beautiful thing is that I feel that he is far above
them in power—no more subservience to Moloch[22]—they cannot
do anything to his real self—and he is wondering what <u>he</u> will let
<u>them</u> do! Oh, how free it makes you feel! Forgive me for going on in
this unbounded fashion—I hope thee doesn't mind—and I am full
of strong feelings.

I have heard nothing further about my proposed trip to
France—I hope that it will not be delayed any longer than the
twelfth, *ma chère,* because I want to get somewhere where I can undergo and be of service. Ronald's triumph has made me wild to be
tried. Oh, I hope Dr. Davis can come! That would be truly delightful. Yet I can't help feeling that there is much in his doubt that perhaps he ought to stand by the radicals here. Somehow I think that
that is what I should do—but of course I know little—ridiculously
little about the state of things.

*Courage, ma bien-aimée, ayons toujours la foi, l'espoir, et notre
étoile. Oh, quel bonheur si vous pourriez venir en France! L'avenir est
une nuée impenetrable, mais pas sombre au cynique—nous avons la foi
et l'amour: les clefs qui courent tout.* [Courage, my beloved, always keep
the faith, the hope, and our star. Oh, what happiness if you are able
to come to France! The future is an impenetrable cloud, but not
somber or cynical—we have the faith and the love: the keys that
open everything.]

Love,
Leslie

June 3, 1918, Mary in Cambridge to Leslie in Brooklyn

Dear Comrade,

When I came home from the Music 4 examination I curled up in the Phillips Brooks corner and read your letter and the poem. When I finished I felt as if I had been talking with you, that you had really been there. It was such a nice letter, Leslie, and made me forget about my old exams. Music 4 went pretty well. During it Prof. Spaulding came up to me on tiptoe and whispered in my ear "Now be careful, Miss Peabody, and don't let your emotional nature run away with you." Wasn't that funny! I assured him that I would do my best. Then just after he had gone, a big military band started up in the common right beside the college and played for two steady hours while the Radios drilled. I noted the fact at the end of the exam for Prof. S.'s benefit. It was perfectly terrible to keep your mind on the questions. I would just get an answer formulated in my mind between marches when "Dixie" or something else would start up. Another thing that disturbed me was that one of my friends was being married at the church on the corner, and I saw her go in and out and drive away with her husband (one of the Chem. Professors—Forbes—do you know him?)

Oh I am so glad about Ronald—that he has no immediate suffering. I don't understand just what he is doing now. I heard that they are going to send the COs out west to farm—do you suppose there is any truth in it?

Molière is calling me. I must get at French 9. *Au revoir, mon ami,* when you pray for my other exams please don't send a band and a wedding!

It is your poem that will make me pass them—*N'ayez pas peur!*
[Fear not!]

Ton,
Marie

June 5, 1918, Leslie in Brooklyn to Mary in Cambridge

Dearest Mary,[23]

How is Zoology 2 coming? Know that I am praying for you this
morning during your exam. It will go better that way, I imagine, according to the Catholic Church, than to try to pray afterwards or
ahead of time. Oh, pardon me for my irreverence, I pray you. These
words are a little too ill-considered.

How happy I am that you will have time to rest before the last
two exams! Be wise, and don't study for them. You know enough to
pass both of them, and to earn two As, without more study. Rest and
reflection, in my opinion, are the best ways to prepare. And my opinion isn't one to throw lightly aside—because, you know, I am one of
the instructors employed by The Kind Widow (so says Mr. Allard.)
Yes, indeed! Smile, my beautiful one, and the sun will shine again for
me. I'm saying some foolish things—are you willing to accept them?

Mary, would thee be pleased if my mother should call at thy
house next Sunday morning, and ask thee to take her to church[24]?
Tis a surprise for thee—she has decided that she must come and
see thy mother, Helen, and thee, Mrs. Davis, some New Church
friends, Cambridge, the closing of Evelyn's[25] school, etc. Oh I hope
Mrs. Davis hasn't told thee and spoiled the surprise! I've been

thinking about it for nearly two weeks now. (Sh! I'm largely responsible for it. She was doubtful about taking such a trip, but I knew how she would love everything and everybody I know there.)

Bonne nuit, mon coeur, sois la Marie forte et douce que j'aime plus chaque jour. Je dis "Courage" mais tu as plus de courage que je n'aurai jamais. Pour toi, le meilleu, [Good night, my heart, be the strong and sweet Mary I love every day. I say, "Courage," but you have more courage than I ever will have. For you, the best,]

Leslie

June 7, 1918, Leslie in Brooklyn to Mary in Cambridge

Thursday Night

Dearest Mary,

Thy last letter was splendid. I did send the first part of it to Ronald, today. Yes, Mary, I agree with thy way of looking upon the thing. My last letter but one just boiled over with my joy and thankfulness in having a brother who was a hero by Christ's help, and who with it had conquered his own natural part and won the victory against brute force—and the consequent joy of freedom was almost too much for me. But really when I was talking with Ronald at Philadelphia, I ached to persuade him to come with the Unit; but I felt strongly that he needed time to reflect and pray for guidance. So I said nothing; but since then I think he is inclining to accept the Unit work, and I felt justified in sending him thy letter and adding a word from me. We can hope, and hope strongly. Mary, it was sweet of thee to write such a fine letter. It will mean much to him.

Yes, poor little Evelyn was very worried about Ronald; she is happier now that he came out of it all. Mother intends to stay for the closing party of her school (at Waltham, you remember) which will be either Tuesday or Wednesday night.

I have heard no more about my sailing; I do hope it will be soon! They are having a busy time over there with the new throngs of refugees, and I long to help. Surely I will let thee know the moment I hear anything at all.

I have started Tolstoi's <u>War and Peace</u>! You remember that I read <u>Anna Karenina</u> last fall. My admiration for the great Russian grows daily. One big thing I see just now is his marvelous power to transcribe not only what he sees people do, but their play of expression, and above all, their thoughts. Maybe it is he who makes me feel so inarticulate. I see things that Tolstoi could paint indelibly in a minute—and I grope vainly for any words to describe them. I feel absolutely dumb; it's the strangest feeling! Maybe after a while I'll write some verses about the great leaders (i.e. Shakespeare, Dante, Milton, Tolstoi, etc.) and the speechless throng—some of whom learn from them, and more of whom learn from the Bible, and still more from the dictates of an inner voice, strong against all temptation. Learn some things from the first—but to love and love God and man forever from the last two.

Ai-je le droit de dire, "nous nous entendons?" Dis-le-moi que je sois content. À tout jamais, [Do I have the right to say, "We understand each other deeply?" Say it is so to me so that I will be happy. Forever,]

Les

P. S. Ronald got thy first letter yesterday! It made him happy.

June 8, 1918, Leslie in Brooklyn to Mary in Cambridge

Friday Evening

Dearest Mary,[26]

My mother will be very happy to see your mother, Helen, and you! She will tell you some things about Ronald. How happy one is to have the best mother in the world. You have her, you say; and I affirm that I have her. We are both happy, because we have reason to be, and it's not an impossibility. It's not logical, you see, but nevertheless it's true. I hope that Mother doesn't disturb you Sunday morning, yes, morning. Shhh! The little trip for her is a birthday present. It's a wonderful present, in her opinion and in mine. Her presence will be as good for me as it will be for you.

The other day I read three essays from a book by Bliss Perry[27]: "The Amateur Spirit" (the title essay), "The Life of a College Professor," and "College Professors and the Public." Mary, thee would enjoy them so much! One gets so much of the spirit of the author in them—Perry is never anyone but his splendid self—thee would feel as if thee had met him and had an inspiring talk. He means more to many of the boys at Harvard than all the rest of the college. He is an earnest, scientific scholar—and yet he is not "hard-shelled"; he has still his modesty, sympathy, idealism, and humanity—the *amateur* or lover spirit! Those essays opened my eyes to much in the life of a professor, and I have more esteem than ever for such a calling. One thing I know, and that is that I must write and write, to learn the hard lesson of composition! My calling may come when I can write respectably!

Thy erring and loving,
Les

June 9, 1918, Mary in Cambridge to Leslie in Brooklyn

Dear Les,

I have just seen your mother onto the car to go and see Eve-lyn—we have had such a lovely visit together. I feel as tho' I know <u>you</u> a great deal better now. You all have that same beautiful spirit and your mother is just a darling!—that is all I can say. I would say saint, but that always sounds cold to me, and she is warm-hearted besides being so spiritually strong. We went to your little church to-gether, and it was such a lovely service. There were ever so many people who knew you who spoke to her afterwards.

You know, I was so disappointed. I got up early this morning and went to meet your mother at the train—I must have been a minute or two late because we missed each other. I waited for about half an hour thinking perhaps she was not dressed and gone—and then I came slowly out to Cambridge not knowing where to find her to bring her home to breakfast. I was reading a French play as I came down Hilliard Street, and just as I got into the house the bell rang and it was your mother. She said she had seen me go down the street reading and had thought to herself, "well, there is a tall girl"— and she had seen me in the station too. Wasn't that funny—if we had only known each other we never would have missed. We all had breakfast out on the balcony and then your mother and I made a little call on Dr. Dana—he came into the parlor with a great pile of books in his arms, which he hastily put down and greeted your mother in his frank, enthusiastic way. He was so glad to see her and asked all about Ronald and you. The Craigie House[28] is beautiful now with the garden coming along.

Oh a piece of news—an aunt of mine left me $1,000 the other day. I won't have to worry about my expenses for the Unit if I go, will I? And now mother won't have to take so many roomers—hurrah! Oh Les, I am so tired of studying—I wish you were going to be here for Class Day. My cousin has invited us to spreads and then there is dancing and fun in the evening. Please just fly up here in an invisible cloak and join in the fun! When the lessons and gaiety are all over, there will be a big drop—and then how I shall miss you and your frequent letters if you have gone. The ocean is so wide, so wide. Never mind, you won't forget me and I won't forget you, and perhaps someday when you are over there you will find a little note mysteriously delivered at your quarters saying *"Je suis ici—vien me voir,"* [I am here—come see me.] Won't it be exciting if it really happens. I shall live thru next year of college hoping for it.

Les, you have a beautiful mother; she is just like mine. How we should treasure them. *Ces jours-ci, si je ne reçois pas de tes nouvelles, je te croirais parti. Dis à Ronald de me laisser savoir n'est-ce pas-il saura un des premiers quand tu pars.* [These days, if I don't receive your news, I'll believe that you have left. Tell Ronald to let me know. He will be one of the first to know when you leave.]

Addio,
Mary

Tuesday Afternoon, June 11

Dear Leslie,

Another exam out of the way! Zoo went pretty well this afternoon tho' I finished in an hour and a half. Something must have been the matter, but it seemed awfully short.

Your letter about Ronald came this morning and I have been thinking very hard about it. Of course he must do what he thinks best, but I do hope he will decide to go with the Quakers. I have just been talking with Mrs. Davis over the telephone, and she says there is every reason for him to get into the Unit. She says she wants terribly to see Ronald, his letter impressed her so very much. She says that the Quakers feel they must do something to help the suffering even if they don't believe in war. Do you think, Leslie, that Ronald's plea could be any stronger than it has been? Haven't the authorities seen him at death's door for his principles? They have given in, and the new rulings show that they recognize that a man's conscience cannot be forced. They are doing their best in a very difficult situation. Dr. Dana says the men on that board are perfectly splendid men. He was very enthusiastic about the triumph for us that the rulings showed. Wouldn't it be great if you and Ronald could go over together—you could do such splendid work each with the other there for encouragement. I think he ought to go for your sake!

There is nothing, not even eating a meal, that people do now-a-days which isn't in some indirect way helping the government—and people can't be too extreme—I think a case is stronger when not carried too far. Of course, I believe when it comes to the point of swearing allegiance to the government at war when you do not believe in war is not right, but I do think that when that government gives in to your position and allows you to do something which you wanted to do before, you ought to do it. At least I don't see that you are gaining anything by being locked up and forgotten when you might be doing a splendid work under the banner of love of the Quakers. If you think it is safe to send this part of my letter to Ronald, tell him to tear it up when he has read it please! I hope it doesn't sound hard and unsympathetic, but I can't bear to think of his going back to prison.

Ton,
Mary

June 10, 1918, Leslie in Brooklyn to Mary in Cambridge

Dearest Mary,

Look at me—the happiest boy in Brooklyn; two letters from *ma très-belle* [my very beautiful] came today! Mary dear, I had no right to expect a letter so immediately in answer to mine. It does me good to be patient: I'm becoming too exacting and selfish, I'm afraid. I'm the one to be forgiven.

How glad I am that Mother was able to meet you dear people in Cambridge! She must have spent a perfect day yesterday, at thy home, at church, and at Evelyn's school. And how she must have enjoyed thy companionship to church! Did Mr. Worcester[29] preach? He is that gentle, loving, lofty soul I used to speak of. I hope Mother may see you again before she leaves Boston—it would be such a pleasure for her. I know it would, Mary, *vois-tu* [you see], because

I'm her son! But thy exams come tomorrow and Thursday, don't they? Oh dear, dear, thee must study, I suppose, as thy letter said. *Bonne chance! Je prierai pour toi, sans faute.* [Good luck ! I will pray for you, without fail.]

I got a fine letter from Ronald today. He says that Mr. Bunting will let me know as soon as he can when to sail, but this is the tenth and no notice. I doubt that I shall sail on the twelfth; *mais espérons!* [but let us hope!] Yes, Mary, if they put me off again, Mrs. Davis wants me to come up and help the League and I've promised to go. Oh, if thee goes away before I get there (if I should come), I'll tie the James's grave-stone[30] around my neck and jump into *la rivière carolingienne!*[31] [He probably meant the Charles River between Boston and Cambridge.]

Ronald also says in his letter, "The sunset was a thing to remember with delight. I stayed out on the pier until nearly nine, reading the book that Mary sent me. It is one of the most absorbing I have ever read—this <u>Soldier of Life</u>. My renewed 'eagerness of spirit' may make it more vivid, perhaps. I love to read by the water, lift my eyes from the print to rest them on the river not still, yet never hurried waves, and hear the small voices of the waters talking with the stones of the pier, laughing at them, whispering refreshing little bits of nonsense to them, and giving them a little slap now and then, just for playfulness." He says further that he was so engrossed in the book that he sat up most of the night with it. I'm grateful too, Mary, to thee for sending him that book. It must mean a great deal to him.

Bien, ma chère, la cuisine m'appelle. Tu rirais: comme je suis gauche! Mais je dis à Clarence—"Patience, mon enfant, tu mangeras tôt ou tard! Oh, la belle vie! Cuisinieusement, [Well, my dear one, cooking calls. You will laugh: how gauche I am! But I said to

Clarence[32]—"Patience, my child, you will eat sooner or later!" Oh, the beautiful life. In the spirit of cooking,]

Les

June 12, 1918, Leslie in Brooklyn to Mary in Cambridge

Dearest Mary,

Thy sweet, sympathetic letter of Saturday was mis-sent by the post office. I did not get it until after the Sunday one.

I received a letter from Ronald today, saying that he was over to the Friends' Institute yesterday and that they told him positively that I wasn't to sail this week, and probably not within two weeks. *Voilà la guerre! Un mois perdu de ta douce compagne—aber "ich grolle nicht"! Tu sais bien ce que tu es pour moi, et je ne dois pas te le dire trop de fois.* [Such is war! One month lost of your sweet companionship—but "I bear no grudge." You know well what you mean to me, and I don't need to tell you too many times.]

Did thee see my mother again? Isn't it a shame that her visit had to come just when the old exams have your time all locked up and put away? She was hoping to be able to have a longer visit, but I think she enjoyed to the full every minute. I am to meet her and Evelyn at South Station at nine-thirty tomorrow morning. Thy last exam comes to-morrow, *n'est-ce pas?* How glad I am that they are all over and done.

What a beautifully mysterious thing that steamer letter of thine is! It's tantalizing and alluring. And the dainty seal on the back— "*Gare à qui le touche avant huit heures du soir, premier jour du voyage!*"

["A warning to anyone who touches it before eight o'clock on the first night of the voyage."]

Poor Ronald is just a little lonesome there (Camp Dix, New Jersey); he has been warned not to talk with the interned prisoners, and he has none of his former friends in Philadelphia. I must write to him more. He is a splendid brother. I'm so glad thee has seen him.

Je prie quelques heures auprès de toi, et le pouvoir de dire tout ce que est dans mon coeur. À demain, ma chère! [I pray for some time beside you, and for the ability to say all that is in my heart. See you tomorrow, my dear!]

Les

June 20, 1918, Mary in Ashburnham,[33] *to Leslie in Brooklyn*

Oh Les,

You don't know how I felt this morning when I got a letter from Mother saying that you were going before I should see you again. I have walked two miles to the Post Office and found your letter, which I was just hoping for. All I can say here, writing at the inky old public desk, is that I am bitterly disappointed and have a strange lost feeling that won't go away. *Mon ami, j'ai peur que tu me fuis— mais enfin nous ne pouvions que dire au revoir encore une fois, et, comme ça, nous fait tout les deux beaucoup de peine. Peut-être c'est mieux ainsi.* [My friend, I'm afraid that you are running from me—but at the end we will only be able to say good-bye again, and, just like that, we will both cause each other great pain. Perhaps it's better like this.]

If for some reason you don't get the letter I wrote to New York you will know that I am thinking of you and wishing you all courage and all happiness in your great adventure.

Ta fidèle camarade [Thy faithful comrade],
Mary

Oh Les—you will write to me won't you—I shall be so eager for your letters. I suppose when you sail I won't be able to write till I know your address—but you must know that of headquarters in Paris—you must tell me that. Please please tell me when you are safe on the other side. I wish my steamer letter were a thousand times what it is—it is so poor. Oh I must stop—I could go on forever. *Au revoir, au revoir, mon bon, bon ami.* [Goodbye, goodbye, my dear, dear friend.]

June 26, 1918, Leslie in Cambridge to Mary in Cambridge after having unexpected time to visit with her

Dearest Mary,

I hope thee will get a good rest tonight; the excitement of the music, the short sleep, the packing, and the ride in the train must have tired thee. I reproached myself last night for not bringing thee back to Cambridge earlier.

I was rather *bouleversé* [shaken up] this morning, to get a letter from Mother saying that she had a telegram from the Friends to me "Would you prefer sailing this week or next? Reply immediately."

She replied "Next week." Since I must visit at home, visit Ronald at Dix, and get my things at Philadelphia, I must leave Cambridge (or rather, Boston) Thursday morning on the ten a.m. So I shall not meet thee at 6:15 on Friday. We shall not go together to the concert that evening, and Mrs. Davis will not have both thee and me to dinner on Saturday. It's rather hard for me, but when I think how much easier this circumstance will make thy mother's mind and thee, I think it is better so. I imagine thee looked forward to our parting with a feeling of uneasiness, not due to the fact of our separating, but an apprehension that I might take too much from thy words or tone. That apprehension is gone, now that I am slipping off like this, and I am glad for thy sake. But I wish I might take thy hand and look into thine eyes only once more!

I had a fine talk with Harold Rotzel.[34] He's a splendid Christian; he told me how he came to his decision to do his utmost to follow Christ. When I hear him talk, and see the light in his eye when he says that he will live with bare necessities all his life, I know that he is living on love—the "meat ye know not of." But he says a difficulty arises, because if he sacrifices pulpits for conscience's sake, the hardships necessarily fall back upon his wife and child. He had not decided upon this mode of life when he married, but she is true and does not complain. He says, "Of course, if you can get somebody to enter marriage with you with such an understanding beforehand, it is easier." That delightful spirit of freedom and labor for mankind was on me all day. I have not heard my call yet, but I feel that somehow it is near. It is that golden dream of beauty that keeps my weak spirit from mournful despair when I think on the possibility of never marrying in this world. Be joyful, Mary, and of good heart while in Ashburnham. True Christianity is the only real thing—the rest is man's erroneous logic.

Ton camarade à toujours, [Your comrade forever,]
Les

July 1, 1918, Leslie in Trenton, New Jersey, to Mary in Canada

48th Company, 12th Battalion, 153rd Depot Brigade Camp Dix, N.J

Dearest Mary,

An imposing superscription, *n'est-ce pas?* I have been here since noon on Saturday, with fifty COs, visiting Ronald. Over Saturday night, I slept at a lodging in Wrightstown, just outside of camp; but last night, with several of the men having gone home on pass, I stayed all night in the barracks—strictly against the rules. It was great. The two days I have spent with these men, living their life, has given me understanding of their faith and inspiration from their devotion. Ronald did not overpraise them in his last letters—they have a quiet nobility and yet a true humility that are unique in my experience of men. I have spent more time getting acquainted with them than I have in going about camp. You should see them read their Bibles and talk of the beauties of the Christian religion. And all the time, outside, the drafted men are being herded and cursed like sheep into the ranks. I can see by experience that Ronald is right in saying that militarization acts to deaden all initiative, constructive work, natural loves, and spiritual life.

The COs here say that Dix is the best camp in the country for such as they. There is no doubt that the captain treats them with consideration if not kindness. But it isn't more than a week since James, a splendid chap (a friend of Lewis Gannett), now in the guard house, was being stuck with bayonets for refusing to work. And one of the fellows here was beaten unconscious and starved four days in this same camp. I have met the two fellows who won't accept the farm furlough, and are to be sent to Fort Leavenworth. Donnell[35], one of them, would like to go with the Unit, but won't be allowed to.

The finest thing, almost, that was ever said to me was last night: Anderson, a Bible student who slept on the cot next me, said confidentially, "Even if the officers did come up, they'd never know that you weren't one of us."

I received thy letter this morning—Mother sent it on from Brooklyn. I was so glad that thy visit to Ashburnham was not the trial that thee had expected. And if thy father, seeing a picture of me, thought that there might be <u>one</u> exception to the mass of insincere and cowardly COs, what <u>would</u> he say if he saw what I see here—these devoted men among whom I feel awed and humbled? So much of the contempt and harsh criticism of people is due to lack of knowledge!

Ronald telephoned early this morning for me to Sam'l Bunting. The latter informed him that I am to sail neither Wednesday nor Saturday, but Friday! <u>So</u>, my dear, I <u>did</u> run away unnecessarily, when I might have stayed to bid thee good-bye . . . I have just asked to be taken out and shot for disappointment, but they refuse to waste ammunition on me; I'll have to go on living, *après tout* [after all]. I am going down to Philadelphia tonight to spend tomorrow getting my things. I expect to be back in Brooklyn through Wednesday and Thursday.

Ronald wants me to say that he thinks that one of his letters to you must have been lost on the way; and that he wants to write to thee and Helen very soon. He is looking very well; Mother says that on her visit here, a week ago, she had never seen him in such good health.

I am glad to have two days at home just before I sail: I may be able to write some small verses. It will be much less than a month, I am sure—the delay before you hear that the boat has reached Bordeaux. The Friends will certainly hear, and they will release the postcards I leave with them. I'm afraid it will be more than a month, though, before thee gets a letter. It will be a good one, I hope! *Oui, la confrèrie, la camaraderie de l'humanité; c'est mon idéale, en verité. Éternellement,* [Yes, the brotherhood, the comraderie of humanity; that is my ideal, in truth. Eternally,]

Leslie

July 4, 1918, Leslie in Brooklyn to Mary in Canada

Dearest Mary,

I am at home again, having brought my equipment here yesterday. By the time I got it home here, it had grown in size and weight about three times! I got my passport and had it visaed at the French Consulate. I tried some of the French that thee taught me, and it worked like a charm.

This is probably the last thee will hear from me for some time. How I shall miss thy letters! I value them more and more each day; but of late I have had a good feeling that thee is thinking of me . . . and that feeling drives away my clouds of uncertainty and doubt miraculously. I feel calmer in mind and heart than I have for a long time.

My address, according to the last instructions, is to be Friends Unit No. 2, American Red Cross, #4 Place de la Concorde, Paris. I am leaving some addressed postcards here; mother will mail them when she hears that the boat arrived. So you all <u>should</u> hear from me in about eleven or twelve days! That isn't so long as I had feared.

Six of the eight prospective companions that I have met so far are farmers from Iowa (pronounce: <u>Eye</u>'-o-way). The seventh is an instructor of Bible, English, and German at Exeter Academy, named Libby[36]—a splendid man, and very affable. I suppose that there will be more in the party, but as yet, I have not met them.

My dear, true comrade, *au revoir pour peu de temps.* [good-bye for a short time.]

Leslie

Le « Rochambeau » paquebot destiné au transport des passagers de 2 et 3e classes du Havre à New-York. Longueur 163 m, largeur 19 m, 40, profondeur 13 m, 20, tirant d'eau 8 m, 18, déplacement 12.500 tonnes. Ce paquebot est construit en acier, a 4 ponts couplés, il est muni de 2 machines alternatives et de 2 à turbines actionnant ensemble 4 hélices. La puissance de ses machines est de 11.000 chevaux, la vitesse de 19 nœuds. Le bateau peut recevoir 1 884 passagers et 400 hommes d'équipage, ce qui fait un total de 2.284 âmes. Il est muni des appareils de télégraphie sans fil à longues distances qui lui permettent de rester pendant toute la traversée en communication avec l'Europe ou l'Amérique.

50 LE HAVRE. — Le « Rochambeau », de la Cie Générale Transatlantique — LL.

S.S. Rochambeau, *the ship on which Leslie sailed to France*

3

Aboard the Rochambeau

ON JULY 8, LESLIE BOARDED THE FRENCH LINER S.S. *Rochambeau*[1] to sail to France. America had few large passenger liners suitable for trans-Atlantic transport. During the war, more than half of all American troops were carried on British or British-controlled vessels, with others on French and Italian ships.[2] Leslie traveled with a small group of men from the Friends Unit, as it was not possible to get a large number of berths on any one ship. As part of the Red Cross, he and the other AFSC workers traveled as officers in first class.

Leslie had a lively time on board. The soldiers staged boxing and wrestling matches, and there were concerts, a celebration of the French holiday Bastille Day, and a Liberty Loan fundraiser. He read poetry, discussed literature, practiced his French, and talked with Polish soldiers, Chinese laborers, French citizens, French light brigade troops or *chasseurs*, and American soldiers.

Despite the light-hearted reports in Leslie's letters of shipboard life, travel in July of 1918 was dangerous. The ship was armed for defense because of the threat of attack when traveling between New York and France.

U-boats, the German "underwater-boats" or submarines, were being used to enforce a naval blockade against enemy shipping. The primary targets of the U-boat campaigns were the merchant convoys bringing supplies from the United States to Great Britain. The German submarine offensive in the Western Atlantic accelerated in early 1918. Germany had developed large cruiser U-boats suitable for extended operations; six operated off the coast of America during this period. Britain and the United States had instituted a convoy system for ships sailing out of Canadian and American ports, including New York. Convoys of mixed troopships and cargo ships sailing directly from New York to French ports on the Bay of Biscay were escorted by armored cruisers or battleships. The safe arrival of the freighters and transports, with supplies and men, helped bring about the defeat of the U-boats and of Germany.[3]

Owen Stephens, a FRU member who had traveled on the *Rochambeau* in September 1917, described life on the ship: "When we turned in, we found the steel cap of our porthole clamped down to keep any light from showing outside. That night we went to bed discussing just what kind of a hole we thought a torpedo would make in the side of the ship, in what direction she would explode, how large an opening she would tear and how deep. None of us were afraid it would happen; we found it an interesting topic and to some extent appropriate . . . The ship is now taking a zigzag course, changing her direction through 30 degrees and back every couple of miles. Both guns are ready for action and two men are by the one forward all the time. Two lookouts stand in the bow, two in the crow's nest, and four on the bridge, with binoculars, all continually scanning the surface of the sea."[4]

As soon as they were under way, Leslie found a quiet place to open and savor the little steamer letter he had carried for more than a month. He knew he would read and reread this letter—it would be his only communication from Mary until he landed in France. That did not stop him from writing letters to her that he planned to mail from Paris.

The *Rochambeau* arrived safely at its destination. And shortly after he arrived, he finally received a packet of letters from his sweetheart.

Mary, meanwhile, was spending the summer with a family at one of the campgrounds on the shore of Lake Magog in Assiniboine Provincial Park, Quebec, Canada, near Mount Orford. She wrote a long letter about her daily life while she waited to hear from Leslie.

June 10, 1918, The Steamer Letter (given by Mary to Leslie with the note that "This steamer letter is not to be opened until the evening of your first day out.")

Dear Les,

This is a picture of fairy land with the fairy castle off in the distance. Do you recognize it? When you read this you will be out on the wide empty sea, but when you look at these pictures a magic spell will waft you back to Cambridge to the banks of the dear old Charles. This grass is the wand, picked by the bank. Here we are, isn't it lovely with the wind in the grasses and the setting sun on the clouds. Shall we sing a little while? Let's begin with "Sweet and Low" (you must really sing it to keep up the spell) and now Shubert's "Serenade" and "Sweet Afton" [a poem by Robert Burns set to music by Spilman]. But we musn't stop without singing Lace's "Old Sweet Song"—that is my favorite.

Just a Song at Twilight

When the lights are low— — —

Yes, Les, I can hear you singing it. Isn't it a dear old song.

Now look off over the sea—nothing in sight—and yet if you look hard enough you can imagine something white coming over the waves—you see the magic brought me down the Charles and right out to sea. Let's go down to the very bow of the boat and watch it cut into the water. It is a wonderful sensation isn't it, to feel the wind in your face and look way off to sea. You feel so small and helpless and yet so safe rocked in the cradle of the deep.

How I wish I were really there with you, going to help the sufferers overseas. What adventures you will have.

It seems so funny to be sitting here at my desk with Forbes Robertson[5] and you looking at me from among my books—and yet when you get (read) this you will be sitting on the deck of a big steamer way out at sea, and thinking of your family and friends back on the distant land. Yes, we are thinking about you, Les, and wishing

you the very best of good luck and courage in your work. Don't forget, will you, that the things which soon seem every day to you are
new and full of interest for us—and tell us the little touches that
give local color, so that we can just picture you in our mind's eye. I
shall try to write you as interesting letters as I know how, telling you
all the doings and thinkings back here in old America.

Les, I hope we won't seem very far away. When you or I read
our Oxford Book it will be like stepping onto the flying carpet that
carries you wherever you wish. I have just taken mine from the row
in front of me and it opened to Shelley's "West Wind"—Have you
got your copy there? It is down in your cabin? Well, why don't you
get it and we will read some together. Begin with the best—the
"West Wind"—how I love it, it is so full of pictures beautifully colored and powerful. Yes, the last six lines are what you are going to
do someday, Les, I prophecy!

Now let's read Keats's "Ode to a Nightingale" because it goes
on an imaginary journey like the beginning of this letter. As you
read the last lines you wonder what is vision, and what is reality

after all. But we know, don't we—the real things are beyond sense in the glorious land of the ideal—this little blue book is just a store-house of symbols, magic wands to conjure up the infinite beauties of eternity—Read Wordsworth's "Ode to Immortality." It is a glo-rious thing. See on p. 611 that rare place beginning "Our birth is but a sleep and a forgetting"—Les, "trailing clouds of glory do we come"—no wonder we have visions of glory to achieve—and we are led by the philosophies of a little child. It is too wonderful, we cannot understand the whole vision—it would be too bright and dazzle us, and so as Dante was led by Beatrice to Revelation—we find the revelation of the ultimate truths in all the beauty of the world. How glorious it is to be alive. You know, my *"joie de vivre"* never diminishes. Something may come between me and it now and then like clouds before the sun—but those clouds always blow quickly by, and the light is brighter than ever. Isn't that the way it is with you? You feel the fullness of life as I do, I know—you feel strong and happy—"for the young men shall see visions"[6] is the hope of the world.

It must be growing dark now because my letter is long and I asked you to read it at twilight.

Bonne nuit, mon ami, que la mer te port sain et sauf sur l'autre côté—Bon Voyage tout le temps que tu es parte. La Camarade te suit en esprit—Pense que quand tu es heureux qu'elle réjouit avec toi; et quand tu est malheureux elle te plaint de tout son cœur. Mais tu ne va pas être jamais triste! La vie est glorieuse et il y a le monde a conquérir dans l'esprit de l'amour divin. [Good night, my friend, as the ocean transports you safe and sound to the other side—May you have good travels for all the time that you are away. This Comrade follows you in spirit—Think that when you are happy that she rejoices with you, and when you are unhappy she objects with all her heart. But you must not ever be unhappy! Life is glorious and there is a world to win in the spirit of divine love.]

Good-bye, Leslie—take care of yourself. I think of you more often than you know—all the best things in life are wished for you by your comrade.

Mary

July 8, 1918, Leslie on board the Rochambeau *to Mary in Magog, Canada*

Dearest Mary,

I have just read thy letter for the sixth time. I shall read it many times over, for the meadows of memory and hope that it opens to me are rich in wild flowers. I wonder if thee ever comes to gather flowers there. The first page of the magic note calls me to take the wings of the wind and fly to fairyland. I am again with thee in the land of beauty, gazing upon the distant castle with its white walls rising in a Druid half-ring. I sing "Sweet and Low" and a fine-spun, exquisite thrill strikes through me, for I hear thy voice in an overtone too fine for other ears . . . But the spell breaks. Back again in the flesh-locked natural body, I say to myself that I am on a great ship, which takes me farther from thee every moment. But the spirit putting at naught the confines of matter sings to me that instead of going away, I am really approaching thee . . . .

I have been wanting to write to thee and say what I mean to say, but I have felt as thee did at the public desk in Ashburnham: the ship is very full, and it is difficult to find a place, in this good weather, where one can be alone. I started this just now down in the salon, but two of the YMCA men were going so lugubriously down the long, long trail and coming so wretchedly to the end of a perfect day that I have escaped and hunted out a hole here in the shadow of the life-rafts on the top deck, where no one is perpetrating anything, and the home fires are not ordered so raucously to be kept burning.

Francis Sayre,[7] the son-in-law of the President, is in this bunch of Y.M.s [members of the YMCA] going to France. He's a great lad—very manly and democratic. I liked him the moment that I set eyes on him. I may have a chance to talk with him at length, as Mr. Libby (of the Fellowship, and leader of our party) did this morning. He (F.S.) and his wife are anxious to learn—they really want to know about socialism. Madame Blouet (a friend of our dear Louis Allard) is giving him a French lesson every day at two o'clock. He knows quite a very little and is making excellent efforts to learn more. Madame gave me a delightful hour and a half yesterday. I am learning, I hope. Her French is a great deal, in fact remarkably like M. Allard's; that makes it easy and pleasant for me.

They staged boxing and wrestling bouts on the foredeck yesterday between the Polish soldiers and the American doughboys. Neither side was markedly superior to the other. But national partisanship was strongly manifested, although no hard feeling resulted, so far as I could see.

Friday, July 12

Yesterday there was a concert, gotten up by the passengers in the salon. The reason for my name appearing on the program is that I rather brazenly put it there. Here is the way of it: At dinner on Wednesday, the chairman of the committee, a French banker who speaks staccato French and atrocious English, got up and asked (in French thank goodness) for somebody to sing the "Marseillaise" at the concert. There was no responding forest of hands,

COMPAGNIE GÉNÉRALE TRANSATLANTIQUE

Cover of program for concert, given on board by the passengers, July 11, 1918

apparently; so after waiting about an hour after the meal, I took my courage between two rather cold hands, and offered, if no one

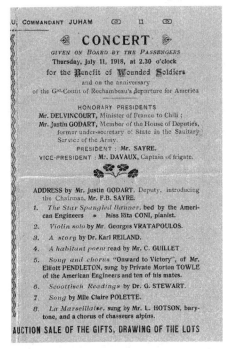

Reverse side of program for concert

else could be found, to do it. Golly, I was taken up! He called my bluff, as Shakespeare says, and I was in for it. Well, I got coached up by the wife of the French minister to Chili (a rather supercilious creature, who fondles an insect with a black nose; she calls it a "lap dog") and by Mme. Blouet. They differed in their separate interpretations, but I got quite a little help from it. We had the concert, and it did not go badly: 5,876 fr. 75 cent. was the receipts.

The *Chasseurs Alpins*[8] (the Blue Devils, you know, who have been touring the U.S. and Canada, boosting the third Liberty Loan) came in on the chorus of the "Marseillaise." They were so well received that they had to sing two encores—"La Madelon" and "Le Poilu." Some of the bidding for the donated things of which the auction was composed was spirited. A certain American financier was great fun. Whenever anything was put up, he would lift his head absently and remark loudly, "Two dollars!" The repetition was comic. But often he ran things way up, because he liked them or because some Frenchman was bidding against him. One sketch of a Marne trench by a certain artist on board sold for $25.

Today I went out on the after deck at twilight and struck up a conversation with one of the *chasseurs* to whom I had not already spoken, and asked him if he had sung in the concert. He told me that he had—"Madelon," "Poilu," and "La Marseillaise." "But 'La Marseillaise,' *les couplets* were sung by an American, I think; you see, he did not sing it well." He wasn't paying a great deal of attention to me because he was trying to catch an American girl's eye. What he said was almost unconscious and right from the heart. I agreed with him that the American knew very little of French, and so could not be expected to perform well.

Saturday, July 13

There are eleven Chinese boys on board, sailing for France to interpret between laborers from China and the English there. Lao Hok Tsun, is a boy of 19—he looks about 15. He has learned to speak good English in two years. He is delightful—sharp as [a] steel trap, and has a rollicking sense of fun. Everybody likes him and tries to get acquainted with him. He wants to learn French—and I believe he has picked up more in a shorter time than anyone on board. In return for a lesson I gave him, he wrote a lot of Chinese, and told me about it. My last name sounds like his two given names: Hok Tsun (you don't pronounce the K.) He wrote my name for me—its sound is a little different from his, but it would take a close ear to detect the difference. The first one, Ho, means "thirst." The other, "new"; I like it. It means to me "new thirst for knowledge."

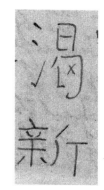

One of the *chasseurs*, Gratien Yorard, taught me "La Madelon" today. I'm going to pick up all the songs I can while I'm in France. You know how I love them.

Sunday, July 14

Dearest Mary,

Last night I did what I have done several times when the weather is warm, and the cabin is close—I slept on the deck. I awoke just as the day was breaking through the clouds in the east, over the shining lace-tipped waves. We are sailing right into the dawn. I went down and hurriedly dressed, not to miss the glory, and am back here on deck, watching the purples, roses, and pinks of the dawn. Who could look upon the wealth of beauty and not believe in God's loving bounty to his children? The ship is rolling more than it was yesterday, and gives a feeling of freedom of motion that it had not before . . . . Now there hangs a soft cloud in the east—surely the roseate breath rising from a boundless garden of royal flowers beyond the horizon has reached the sky and imbued the clouds.

One would suppose that material separation would tend to make my thoughts and memories of thee dim. Three days ago, without reflecting about it, I felt thee nearer than ever; and since then the feeling has become a conviction. Never did thee seem such a true comrade and loving friend as now. This conviction of nearness and strong support proves to me after I have cut the cords of place-association and left home behind, that in spite of all and through all, thee is with me. Thee can have no idea of what that means to me, when I remember to realize with ever-new joy that it is thee who is my comrade. You

know me very well, Mary; put thyself in my place and think about it
... There, have I not a right to be grateful and happy?

I have been trying for days to write some verses, and they refuse
stubbornly to be written. I hope to have them done before I must
mail this letter.

Later ...

Today, you know, is the great French holiday. A few minutes ago
the starboard gun on the afterdeck was fired to salute the French flag,
which is flying at the stern. Just now I have been forward to take a picture of the four hundred Polish soldiers at Mass on the forward steer-
age deck. I took them when they were kneeling.

I have been wondering what thee is doing at thy lovely Quebec
lake, and am vainly wishing that I might share its beauty with thee.
Does thee get to see many sunrises? If I were thee, I should cultivate
them more; that is because to me they seem the opening and not
the closing of the most beautiful things, that they inspire me to
more efforts. No, I am wrong; thee has reason to love the sunsets
best for thee has so much strength that thee needs no encouragement—merely the closing gentleness of the day to bring rest and
peace for more work. Mary, thee has a strong will—but it is a good
will, good will towards all. And thee has the qualities a Christian
must have—implacability to evil, and gentleness toward people. I
think I might approach the necessary implacability to evil, but it
will be very hard for me to be gentle toward people. Thee has the
secret; no, it is not a secret, but a goal, and thee has reached it. Thy
comradeship has been and will always be a helping hand for me to
learn kindness.

There was a review of the *chasseurs* and some selected American soldiers on the promenade deck today. They are a reckless crew, all right, the *chasseurs*, but you should have seen them, or rather heard them ground arms and sing "La Marseillaise"! I tried to get some pictures of them, but I am afraid the light was not very good.

Later—I am writing the rest of this letter, watching the sun set over the stern of the ship. The setting promises to be superb. There is a line of yellowish-white clouds down on the western horizon. I have never seen clouds of the same nature before. They are like yellow smoke; and a haze seems to separate the nearer from the farther ones. The sun is enriching the crests with silver and gold, and the rays of light coming over and under the line of cloud makes the haze or mist in the clouds even more remarkable.

There is a girl on board who speaks such perfect French and such faultless United States that I am at a loss to give her a nationality. I was very interested to see her talking with two friends of hers—one a blond American sergeant of Engineers, and the other the nattiest and handsomest Blue Devil—a sergeant of *chasseurs*. Both boys were rather young and blue-eyed. The *chasseur* had the highest decorations of war. She would talk first with one, and then with the other. When she said something to the Frenchman, it was with a play of expression and a few slight gestures, which she immediately modified and reduced when she changed to the English! Neither of the boys could understand what the other said. She is one of the first I have seen who can talk like thee: with music, with grace, and with *relief d'expression* [multi-faceted expressions]. But she and the others lack either heart, mind, or spirit—maybe all— while thee has them all in abundance; and also thee has something else which is undying, and which is not common.

Oh, Mary—how I wish thee could see what I see now! The salute to the flag from the bow cannon, the lowering of the colors against the golden west, and the picturesque knot of *Chasseurs Alpins* buglers, rakish in their black tams and splendid with their bright bugles. There they go—a beautiful call; two bugles answering two, a fugue—(or is it a canon? Let's call it the latter; more warlike, you know) and an ending in chords. Now the sun is so low that the clouds in front of it are the lightest violet—but over the top of the line of violet I see peaks of cloud still deeply rose. Now the clouds directly before the sun have lifted, and I see what I remember to have seen before only in Doré's pictures in the Inferno:[9] red darts radiating outward and downward to the horizon—it is perfect! Now the clouds are still lower, and the blood of the sun is showing only in holes burned through the veiling mists. The moon coming into her own gains her cool brightness and floats crescent over the violet cloud and the steel-grey sea.

Night is coming on, *ma mie*, with its romantic, cryptic shadows; it will bring velvet blackness and oblivion of light—but the glorious dawn is not many hours off.

I see here some of the mysterious power of the military, and the beauty of the bugle salute to the French flag; but militarism is what plunges us into the black perdition of war—the night before God's dawn, which we pray is not far.

Tu as longtemps connu celle que j'ai aimée et que j'aimerai à jamais. Prie-t elle d'être Marie, la Marie que j'aime, toujours et moi, je serai content. Ah, mais je suis content maintenant—et ça veut dire qu'elle est encore Marie. Bonne nuit, ma camarade! [You have known well for a long time the one I love and will love forever. Please be that Mary, the Mary I love always—and I will be content. Ah, but

I am content now—and that means she is still Mary. Good night, my comrade!]

    Ton,

    Leslie

July 17, 1918, Mary in Magog, Quebec, Canada, to Leslie aboard the Rochambeau *(sent to Paris)*

Dear Les,

    Now for a good old talk! As I write this you must be either in or very near *la belle France* and I am looking every day for your postal. I think I shall wait and send this when I get that so that you will know I have heard. I won't tell how many times I have thought of you on your traverse because you know it and also it would take too long. I don't know where to begin to tell you all I want to. At eight o'clock of your first evening out I was sitting on the hill watching the sunset over the mountains and lake and I read the "Ode to Immortality" just as I thought you were reading it. Isn't it a glorious thing. It just thrilled me through and through. Then pretending that you were there, I said, "And now let's sing"—and what do you suppose, a hermit thrush burst into song right nearby. Wasn't that lovely! You chose a beautiful messenger.

    It must have seemed a long time on the boat when you were eager to get to work. I remember that I did much reading and gazing out to sea. I hope you had interesting companions to make the time fly. Goodness, but I shall be glad to get your first letter; it seems centuries since I have heard from you. Your last letter written on July 5th was a surprise because I hadn't expected to hear from you again. I am glad you liked my last letter. I am going to try to make all my letters interesting and tell you all the news I can think of. I am going to be here until about September 10, I think. It is doing me worlds of good to be out of doors all the time in this glorious place. I am getting well rested and sun burned.

The days are very much alike so if I tell you about one you can get an idea of what it is like all the time. I wake up about 6:30 with the sun shining in my tent and look up into the big maple trees that are just alive with birds. The little log cabin and the other tents are as quiet as can be when I go barefoot thru the wet grass to make the fire and start breakfast. Patsy, who sleeps in a box in my tent, accompanies me and sniffs around after chipmunks and digs holes for my approbation. I have great fun juggling the things around on the little stove for there are eight of us and we eat a great deal and a great variety. We have breakfast at a long table on the cabin porch overlooking the lake, which early in the morning is always veiled in mist. With a concert of birds around us and the sun shining thru the leaves, we eat porridge covered with rich cream and ground up maple sugar!

After breakfast there are all kinds of things to do, and my stint is to get the dinner into the fireless cooker[10] and then go for the mail if there is time. The funny French-Canadian mail driver expects to see me sitting on the fence waiting for him and calls out a cheery *"Bon jour, Mamselle—une lettre pour vous."* ["Good day, Miss—letter for you."] He asked me one day if I was twelve years old! I don't wonder he thought so when I had my hair in braids and wore bloomers and a sailor blouse. I laughed and said, *"Oh je ne dis pas mon âge.*" ["Oh, I don't tell how old I am."] and the next day I appeared in a long dress, shoes and stockings, and my hair up—I wish you could have seen that man's face, it was a study in astonishment and incredulity. "*Oh Mam'selle,*" he said, "*Vous êtes vielle de dix ans pendant la nuit.*" ["You have become ten years older during the night."] I asked him which way he liked me best and he said in English as he whipped up his horse, "I like you at twelve years"— Henceforth I shall be that age when I go for the mail.

Theodora and I have our French lesson every morning from 10 to 11, and I really think she is learning something. Her mind is slow but very sure, and she is becoming accustomed to hearing the French and even talks a little. We all go in swimming in the morning, and the lake is perfectly glorious. My uncle made a fine raft from which we dive, and we race and play ball in the water. The feeling of abandon that one has in swimming can't be equaled. The lake is so huge I always feel like laughing heartily at my own self-confidence. Don't worry, Les, I shan't do anything crazy. My aunt worries terribly if people are reckless, so for her sake I won't give way to my fits of foolish daring. I shall miss the thrills though.

I have had to take care of myself lately somewhat because I have been having some of my horrid old hay fever asthma. There is a large field of timothy near here, which is my particular enemy and I guess that is the cause of it. I have a great time at night trying not to wake people up when I burn my little sparkly pastilles.[11] Then I sit up in bed and watch the weird shapes that keep changing in the trees around the tent. Finally I go off to sleep again. It won't last much longer because pretty soon they are going to cut the timothy and with it will go my asthma. It is funny I should have it again this year when I had none last year. But I didn't have enough inoculations this time, I know. I found out that asthma has nothing to do with your lungs. It is more in the bronchial tubes—so that is why my large lung capacity doesn't help me out any.

I am perfectly absorbed in <u>La Guerre et La Paix</u> [*War and Peace*]. It is powerfully written. I have only gotten as far as Pierre's conversion and I find it hard to make out how deep his feelings really go. I think Andre is more interesting, of course, and his sister is a beautiful character. What a striking place that was where he came home as if from the dead the day his little son was born. Did you finish the book—I wondered if you took it with you on the boat?

I must go and help get supper now. I will go on with this later.

July 18th. It is now sunset of the next day and we have had a most strenuous afternoon with a Red Cross sewing meeting at camp. Sixteen women from all around came at dawn in their best apparel and proceeded to say nothing. I got all the young people together, and we soon broke the ice and were off in peals of laughter. I think both you and I have a faculty for making people feel at home and jolly when we want to. All you have to do is find common ground and you are at home at once, *n'est-ce, pas?* Tomorrow we are going to climb Owl's Head, one of the highest mountains around, about 3,300 ft. I have a plan with a young camper down the lake to swim across the lake and back again someday, about two miles—if I can manage it without my aunt's worrying—of course, we shall have a boat alongside.

I hear from Helen every once in a while—she says Mrs. Davis is perfectly angelic to her but that the office is a "screaming nightmare." She has never tackled "business" before and it quite takes her by storm. She is learning the typewriter pretty well and says she isn't ashamed to do it when the postman comes in any more. A letter from her the other day said that the postman had paid her a great compliment—he said, "Well, I have seen lots of stenographers, but I never saw one work the way you do when the boss is out!"

Sunday July 21. I am off by myself on a beautiful point by the lake—the water is lapping softly against the rocks down below and just a minute ago a real bald-headed eagle came and rested on the pine tree not three yards away from me. They are such glorious birds. I am glad we have them for our country's emblem. That is, they are beautiful when they soar and dip over the lake; I don't know what bad qualities of greed or fierceness they possess!

We climbed the mountain as planned, and on the way a storm came up making the trees shine and the ground smell sweet. When the sun came out the woods were brilliant with gems. We got soaking wet and then dried off (it is such fun to welcome any weather) and the storm cleared away so that the view from the top was glorious. Lakes scattered everywhere like a map, and mountains fading away into misty blues in the distance. I wished you could have been there (a wish I find myself often making, by the way). When we came home from the climb, every one went to bed early—but the moon was so brilliant, I couldn't bring myself to go. I climbed a great maple tree near my tent and saw the country far and wide flooded in the moonlight—I shall never forget it. As so often happens to me when I am impressed by something very beautiful, bits of the Psalms and other places in the Bible come to me. I seem to be so much more familiar with that great book since English 35. I am so glad I could hear it.

After this sight I was less inclined than ever to go to bed and so I went in swimming. (Don't worry, I didn't go out beyond my depth.) It was glorious! Glorious!—I am going to try to write a poem about how the moon shone through the trees on the shore as I swam along in the black water and heard a cow bell tinkle lazily in the distance and some voices singing far away. Oh, Les, Life is very beautiful—I so often feel that I don't deserve such happiness as I get from nature and then I know that just because of the joy it gives me, so much more must I give to others now and always. I think we young people are very apt to dream for the future and forget the present—don't you think so—so I am trying to live my dream every day. That is what you are doing, too, I know, and on so much bigger a scale than I am. May joy and faith and courage be yours every single day.

This morning, it being Sunday, we had such a lovely little service in the cabin to which the neighbors came. The sermon was on looking westward to foretell the weather and so looking ahead to the ideal and eternity. Somehow everything seemed to be black to me for a while and I had a good cry after church was over. Don't think me weak, Les. It was just the horror of this awful war that came over me and the thought of all the splendid lives that had gone beyond the Western gate, which somehow because we are human seems irreconcilably sad. Soon however I became calm again and was much better for my cry, for now I seem to have thrown off a weight and can look freely upward at the clouds. I shan't give up being an idealist because of the bumps I get—will you?

I have been reading some Dante lately, those beautiful cantos in "Purgatorio" where Beatrice first appears to Dante. There is a young Italian artist at a camp on the lake who says he is coming to read some time. His name is Antonio Fraioli and he is very interesting.

He made a sketch of me the other day but I can't say it looks much like me. I think he is a better musician than artist. There are very few campers on the lake this year and almost no motor boats—so that it is much wilder, and the eagles have come back to nest on the shores. The war seems to cause a return to wildness and barbarism in more ways than one, doesn't it!

Soigne-toi et ayes confiance dans tes idéales, ainsi tu seras fort pour le travail, que chaque fois que tu le fais de ton mieux, même plus haut vers la lumière—Je me dis cela aussi tous les jours. [Take care of yourself and have confidence in your ideals, so that you will be strong for the work, that each time you do your best, you will be that much closer to the light—I say this also to myself every day.]

Ton camarade,
Marie

FRU members enjoying their free time at the Students' Hostel in Paris

4

Summer Sojourn

LESLIE FINALLY ARRIVED IN PARIS on July 17, 1918. He was eager to get started on his reconstruction work. He was in France, but still faced bureaucratic hurdles before he could begin the work for which he joined. The French authorities were reluctant to allow civilians to enter the battle zone, although by the autumn of 1917 they had given free access to Quaker relief workers. Nevertheless, he needed to wait for U. S. Army Intelligence to issue the special papers, the *carnets rouges* [red notebooks], which entitled civilian relief personnel to stay and move about in a military zone.[1] This took time and required that the AFSC office negotiate with the Red Cross and the U.S. Army for permission to travel into the areas most damaged by the fighting.

Leslie was part of the Haverford Training Unit No. 2. Due to an increased need for field workers in France, the American Red Cross had contacted the AFSC in March 1918. This second group was made up of COs who had been accepted, trained, equipped, and transported by the AFSC. They had agreed in advance to accept Red Cross supervision from the time they stepped foot in France until they could be moved to their field assignments. The Red Cross bore their expenses after their arrival in return for permission to use their services on a voluntary basis in some non-combatant military work: serving in station-canteens, meeting and feeding refugees, unloading hospital trains, assisting with wounded and shell-shocked soldiers, and relieving Army personnel from civilian chores.[2]

While in Paris, Leslie stayed at the Unit No. 2 headquarters at the Students' Hostel in the Latin Quarter. The building had originally been a monastery, called the Monastery of the Guardian Angel, and some of the fountains and relics, as well as the chapel with its vaulted roof, still remained. In 1906, it was renovated by an American woman connected with the Y.W.C.A. and renamed the Students' Hostel, serving as a dormitory for British and American women attending art school. By the time Leslie arrived, the entire dormitory had been given over to members of the Friends Unit. They could receive medical treatment in the dispensary, use the hostel bathhouse, and enjoy writing letters home in the charming tea garden. They also were given access to excursions, classes, library privileges, and admission to lectures on art and literature—a wonderful gift for a young Harvard literature and theater major.[3]

To fill his time, Leslie volunteered to help the Red Cross. But the young men did not only work while in Paris. The city was not under siege and was still a vibrant place of culture and entertainment. Leslie was in his element. He went frequently to the theater, visited the museums, traveled in the countryside south of Paris, and practiced his French with some of the French citizens who worked with the Red Cross.

He also began regularly attending a Quaker meeting for worship, a practice that he followed during his entire time with the Unit. The meeting was held in the common room of the hostel. By the time Leslie left France, he identified himself as a Quaker, although he never formally joined the Society of Friends.

Mary was still working in Quebec. Her days were filled with camp chores, swimming in the cold, clear lake, and tutoring a young girl.

July 21, 1918, Leslie in Paris to Mary in Magog, Canada

Dearest Mary,

There are so many things that I have seen and done about which I should love to talk with thee for hours and yet I have to confine my thoughts to a letter! Bother time and space, anyhow!

Our voyage ended perfectly. Toward the last there was timidity and anxiety shown by the Congressmen and some of the Y. M.s whom we had to have on the boat with us. There was unparalleled rejoicing when, on the evening of the day before we sighted land, a French chaser [escort ship] met us, dashing up at about thirty knots, and zig-zagging prettily behind us close until we entered the mouth of the Gironde.[4]

The first sign of land that we saw was a dirigible, yellowish gray . . . then the Phare de La Gironde. It was about six o'clock in the evening; we held for the *embouchure* [mouth of the river]. As the land grew larger and nearer, we saw the most beautiful red-roofed houses and cottages on the left bank. Two aeroplanes sailed high over us toward the land. Then we were made aware of the sunset. Mary, it seemed to come to me like a silent rebuke for what I had said in my last letter about dawn being more beautiful than the setting of the sun. All about me I heard people saying that they had never seen so beautiful a sight in the world. While I was gazing, I felt an excited tap on my shoulder. It was Madame Blouet—"*Voyez-*

vous?" ["Do you see?"] pointing proudly to the glory. "*Même le ciel vous dit 'soyez le bienvenu!'* " ["Even the sky is saying 'Welcome!' to you!"] Everyone on board shared in the feast of beauty, even if, like the heroic Congressmen, they only got a crumb. People went without their natural supper to fill their soul with good things.

In front of the sun was a hill of cloud, floating in the blue of the west. The sun could not send his rays straight to us, but he shot them

up into the sky. The fan-shaped light rays leaping like spears into the rich blue touched the top of the cloud-hill with snow; while the bottom, nearer the sun, showed a border of rich gold—and the red downward rays (of which I spoke in my last letter) were more beautiful than those first ones—not relatively, but completely.

And when the sun came out from beneath the cloud, the path of wonder stretched down over the glittering waves even to the ship. And then, Mary, does thee know what we saw? The golden-gray airship, coming in from the sea, sailed slowly and peacefully into the sun! When I saw that, I felt that the cup of my joy was full and that thee was there to drink it with me. Thee surely was on the boat then, because without thee I could never have tasted that sweetest draught.

We came up the Gironde by moonlight and docked at Bordeaux at one in the morning. There was very little sleep for anyone that night. In the morning, we landed, rattled through Bordeaux, and caught the 11:08 for Paris. The Red Cross had three special cars—and we were all very comfortable. Wednesday the 17th was a very hot day; we got out and drank water at every big stop. It was great sport to hunt for the water-pipe, and fill our bottles, and climb on the train just as it started. But the beauty of the country held me. I think I stood more than half the way, out in the corridor, with my head and shoulders out the window. The vineyards, crops of grain, and the trees and hedges were in their greatest glory. I never saw a lovelier countryside; it looked more like a fairyland made by an artist than a habitation of man. The Lord seemed to wish to heap us with bounties, for towards evening the sunset colors over the land made a beauty that was different, but hardly less superb than that over the sea.

When we arrived in Paris, we were met at the station and taken in a horse-drawn omnibus to our house, through the dark, deserted streets of the beautiful city. We are living at the headquarters of the French Unit No. 2, at the Students' Hostel, 93 Boulevard St. Michel. It is in the student quarters, by the Luxembourg Gardens, and not far from the Sorbonne—a beautiful location—Horace Davis says it is better than any occupied by the Red Cross in Paris. The beautiful building, which was loaned to us rent-free by some American women, was an Art School Dormitory for young English and American students—some of their pictures are on the walls of the rooms.

When thee told me to take thy love to "dear old Paris," I did not appreciate what that meant; now I do think it is the most beautiful city I have ever seen. It probably is the most lovely metropolis in the world. We have been so busy that I have seen only a few of its wonders . . . Notre Dame, Place de la Concorde, Gardens of the Tuileries, and a few others. I have still to see thousands of things, as thee knows.

Horace Davis met me at the station. He was the only familiar face in the crowd. How glad I was to see him! Day before yesterday he took me for a walk, through the Luxembourg Gardens, into the oldest part of Paris. We went through a marvelous *ruelle* [alley] and came to a court that must have been exactly like it was in the [French] Revolution—maybe before. Then we went out on the Pont des Arts and talked as we looked down towards l'Île de la Cité and Notre Dame . . . .

Friends Unit No. 2 has been busy at the construction of about forty bungalows for consumptives [patients with tuberculosis] out at Malabry, seven miles S.W. of Paris. The estate of Malabry is on a height of land and is by the Versailles road. The chateau is being fitted up as a hospital. Our new bunch got up at five a. m. yesterday and went out to work for a day. It is a beautiful spot, and the forty boys there are doing great work. Some of the boys who are here in Paris are working on shifts in the *gares* [train stations], unloading wounded from the trains. I'm hoping to get a chance at it tomorrow. We are doing this only to relieve suffering in a great emergency, and are doing it entirely voluntarily, being under the direction of the Civil Affairs Bureau of the Red Cross. Tonight I am hoping to go to the Théâtre Français and hear "Horace" and "Les Fourberies de Scapin."[5] I am going to see if I can't get some work here where I shall be with French people or with children. That is where I feel I can be of the greatest service I am capable of. One of my greatest difficulties will be to make my spirit stronger than my body.

It is late Sunday afternoon. I have finished the verses called "The Thought of Thee" and have attempted a few others. Just think, Mary—it will be at least September 1 before I get thy answer to my first letter. That is no short time; it is part of the test, I suppose. But after that, God willing, there will be no interval so appalling; and in the meantime, I shall read that steamer letter.

It is true, Mary—my knowing thee has strengthened my faith in the Lord. Thy presence seems to make clear and interpret what it meant in the words of the Bible. When I know thee is near me, I always have more strength; it is wonderful, but true. Sing our favorite songs again, and I'll be there to sing them too. *Dieu te garde toujours.* [God protect you always.]

Ton,
Les

July 26, 1918, Leslie in Paris to Mary in Magog, Canada

Dearest Mary,

It is early morning. A gentle rain falls from a quiet but troubled sky. The carillon of a church is ringing the turn of the quarter hour, and the little sparrows are twittering in the little shaded garden behind the house. We have just got back from Gare de la Chapelle, where we have worked for the past week. No wounded came in last night, so we slept in stretches until six this morning.

Mary, has this been a beautiful summer for thee—has thee been given the opportunity to dream dreams and see visions? Oh, if I might have shared them with thee! Mary, I wish I could write thee this time more about the interesting places, people, and happenings here; yet I cannot.[6] I feel that I am standing at the threshold of the world, making ready to enter it. The outer impressions I receive just now help, but do not decide the preparation. It seems to me as though somehow, unconsciously almost, I were deciding the terms on which I am to meet the world—and that decision is brought about by my faith, and by my thoughts of thee. Every thought except that of religion seems to fade into emptiness beside thee. Yet when I think of thee in relation to things, they take on a new richness and beauty by thy presence.

But, Mary dearest, thee remembers what we said—I will always live by it. My decision does not decide thee . . . thee is as free as ever. And thee mustn't decide out of pity for me: because nothing can be a tragedy while God is in heaven. I am learning to be strong enough to wait . . . until the next world, if necessary. Thee can never be lost to me, no matter what comes.

My heart goes out to the wounded boys whom we are handling at the Chapelle station. The more I do of it, the more I feel that it is a privilege to be allowed to try to help them. And the more different kinds of men I meet, the more good I see in them. They may, some of them, be misguided: but who of us isn't? And as a rule they are so young and unhardened, so dazed by the business. There have been several whom I shall never forget, though I saw them only for a few minutes. One slight lad, who had two fingers cut off and a bad wound in his leg from a piece of shrapnel, was suffering keenly when we took him from his berth onto the stretcher. I did my best to make him comfortable and talked to him. His voice was very weak, but so appealing that I was drawn to him. The next day when we were loading a hospital train at Vanguard Station to go south, I heard somebody say "Hello, Billy," and there was the same boy. The tone of his voice and the look on his face made those two words almost the loveliest I have ever heard . . . .

The housekeepers in our hostel here on the Boulevard St. Michel are all either refugees or *rapatries* [repatriated citizens who had been caught behind German lines or captured and returned because they were too old or too young to be of use]. How close it brings the suffering to have them tell, simply, as is their way, what they have seen and been through!

I am still alive, Mary, though the taxicabs of Paris have done their worst and are still doing their best to put me out. The pace they hit on these crooked little streets is "<u>scan</u>-alus," as Laksuh, your Southern friend, would say.

Soigne-toi bien, ma mie. Tu ne sais pas à quel point tu m'es chère. Songe à nos beaux jours à Cambridge, et chante. J'aime à croire que tu chantes presque toujours, car mon cœur chante tout le temps les chansons que nous aimons les mieux. Que Dieu te garde—[Take good care of yourself, my dear friend. You don't know how dear you are to me. Dream of our wonderful times in Cambridge, and sing. I love to believe that you are always singing, as my heart sings all the time the songs that we love the best. I pray that God protects you—]

Les

July 31, 1918, Leslie in Paris to Mary in Magog, Canada, stamped "Passed by DASE Censor A. E. F."

Dearest Mary,

A delightful, shaded garden lies behind our house, and I am looking into it between sentences. The afternoon is still, and nature has lifted a gauze of impalpable delicacy between us and the sun. As I look at the varied shades of green on God's trees, the memory of the back-wash of war that I have seen rises before me like a mud-digged thing of disgust. And yet it was only two o'clock this morning that I saw it last—the pain, the dirt, the foul air, the wrecks of God-given bodies—and what is worse, the complacent regarding of death agony given and received . . . it is a miasma. The more I see of it, the less formidable and awe-inspiring does War appear. As a real force it is nothing. Those who tremble before it, to be sure, try to catch hold of its Juggernaut car, and pull along with it, taking Fury and Murder as their masters, and struggle, sweating and anxious, to save themselves or theirs from physical death. But those who stand fearless to be slain in body, by this man-made Fiend, do not surrender their love and faith: by which two, men live.

How humble and like a child one feels before the mystery of the life after death! Those who know not of it and seek the answers to all their questions on this earth, become great men on knowledge, in their own eyes. What we would do is to gain, through the natural beauty of Nature, a conception of the spiritual beauty of Heaven's nature: to reach, through our frail human nature and understanding of the Christ-like spirituality. Think of the joy of that struggle— which is the real struggle upward over sin. It is along that way that you and no other can help me, and I feel the never-ending inner urging forward . . . .

We are still helping to do the work with the wounded who come into the *gares*—to get them out of the trains into ambulances.

My French is improving, like cheese, with time—imperceptibly. I am getting on the trail of the gurgled <u>r</u>; by the time I come home I may be able to utter it!

Au revoir, ma chère chère amie—Que Dieu to garde pour tes amis! [Good-bye, my dear, dear friend—I pray that God will protect you for your friends!]

Les

August 1, 1918, Mary in Magog, Canada, to Leslie in Paris

Dear Les,

I am all alone in camp this afternoon with Patsy—the others having gone to a country fair in the village. I wish you could see the view from where I am sitting now—the lake is so very blue and the mountains so green and strong. I wonder what kind of place you are living in, whether you are at Paris or nearer the front and what you are doing. In fact I have hundreds of "wonders" which I just hope a letter from you will before very long do away with in part.

The very day after I wrote to you last I got a special delivery from your mother saying that you had arrived safely in France—the cable had come from Mr. Bunting. I can tell you I was glad to get her letter and I wrote and told her so.

I had the funniest dream the other night—I dreamt that I was on a steamer bound for Europe to do reconstruction work and all my friends were on board. They appeared to be doing each one what was his peculiar work or rather talent. Joe was there writing poetry—sitting out on the bow looking off to sea dreamily. Helen was painting, Francis acting out French poetry, and Robert Messmes was coiling ropes and looking after the ship. I couldn't describe all the others; it would take too long, but it was awfully funny and so real. The best part however was that all of us were talking about something splendid that you had done in construction work (it evidently was your example that had spurred us all to cross the Atlantic). I don't remember what it was, but it was something quite wonderful!

Seriously, as soon as I get through college I am going to take a course in nursing and one in dietetics, household economy, and gardening. I want to be able to really do something when I go over to help construct. Mrs. Davis says that the women they send must be trained; because they have so many to choose from, they want to take the ablest.

Au revoir, Les, pour cette fois—joie et courage! [Good-bye, Les, for now—joy and courage!]

Ta camarade,
Mary

August 5, 1918, Leslie in Paris to Mary at Camp Magog [passed by SASE Censors A. E. F.]

Dearest Mary,

I wonder if thee is disappointed that I do not write more inter-estingly and in detail about what I am doing. Part of the reason is that my work so far has been with wounded American soldiers, and what I see and hear hurts me so that I try to forget it. And then, when I settle my mind to let it recoup its health with thoughts of love and beauty, I like to write to thee in that spirit. Maybe it is only a phase and will pass; but when I get my work (if ever I do) with the *refugés* and *rapatries*, it is possible that what I say will be more interesting—possibly not . . . .

I am exchanging English for French with a *professeur de lycée* [high school teacher], one Lebettre. He lives at Melun, about forty-five kilometres from Paris, being a refugee with his family from Lille. The man is a linguist, having learned Russian, Polish, German, and English. He knows English though only as I know French—needing practice in speaking and hearing it. He is going to talk to me about Tolstoi, Turgenieff, and others. Education for little Leslie, *pas*? He invited me to come down to Melun, and I'm going to go before long.

The majority of the boys here are from the West and Quakers, as clean, honest, frank, transparent, and likable a set as one could find anywhere. I have found one, though, who is a kindred spirit to me. His name is James Stanislawsky. His father is of Polish lineage, and his mother was born in County Cork; they are Hicksite Friends,[7] and live in Oakland, California. He likes poetry, is inter-ested in the Irish School, writes a little himself, and knows what the IWW[8] really is. I wish he could come to Harvard and get into the

Workshop. He'd be a good member, because of his originality, imagination, sensitive touch, and energy.

I went up to the University Union the other day. It occupies a
beautiful building right beside the Thèâtre Français. I signed up in
the Harvard Bureau, and met one of my classmates, who is an
under-secretary there. Young Widener,[9] who used to sit behind me
year before last in Louis Allard's French 6 section, blew in. He was
wearing the most expensive and <u>chic</u> first lieutenant's uniform I have
ever seen on a mortal, and his identification tag was solid gold. And
would thee believe it, he recognized me! He simpered as of old and
remarked how long ago that French 6 class seemed. Then with studied nonchalance, he referred to Quentin Roosevelt's[10] sudden death.
Quentin used to sit beside him and whisper and giggle while Louis
was trying to give us his lecture, making the latter very excited.

De plus en plus ton, [More and more yours,]
Leslie

*August 5, 1918, Leslie in Paris to Mary in Cambridge, forwarded to Magog,
Canada*

Dearest Mary,

I am happy today! There are several reasons why I should not
be so: it is a dull, drizzling day. The sky, uncertain whether to frown
and cry, or only to frown, has compromised on a rain followed by
a fine mist. Bertha, [a large caliber howitzer cannon used by the
Germans] after a protracted silence, has begun again, dropping a

few plums in at fifteen-minute intervals, and Madame Brocailles' nerves are almost ragged out by the associations that the sound calls up—but somehow or other I am happy and I want to let thee know it. Thee can say to thyself when thee gets this letter, "on August the fifth, Leslie Hotson, being still a boy in years and in heart, was very happy—though Hell ran amuck through the world, for love was stronger than hate, God still opened heaven to man through created nature and his Word and had granted to Leslie to find his ideal of woman."

August 9

Yesterday I went to the *Marriage de Figaro* at the Odeon. Day before yesterday I had bought a text of the play for thirty centimes ($00.054) and had read it through before the performance. So, thee sees, I enjoyed it doubly. The acting was finished and spirited ... and again I thought of thee ... The thought, so dear and welcome, was brought by the voices of the players. The best actresses, in the variation and range of their tones, try to express the highest and most characteristically feminine. Their nuances of tone, running the gamut of high emotion, recalled thy voice and brought thee near, so that I was in thy company at the play.

Last night I learned that Horace Davis had returned from his vacation tour with Bill Southworth[11] in the Alps; I climbed the stairs at the Britannique,[12] and found him sunburnt about the nose, and glad to see me. He reported a great trip; that he, Horace Davis, had never seen a man so improvident, so hit or miss as Bill, nor one who got through somehow, anyhow, so amazingly and with such charm; that their itinerary called for more than was humanly possible; that rather than be inhuman, they left out a mountain; and that they were nearly very sick from heat and fatigue at one time, and at another were lost in a snowstorm.

Horace has decided to stay in France for perhaps a year, perhaps until the end of the war. Anyhow, I'm glad. He's a treasure for me—not only in that he has been here almost a twelvemonth, knows everything and everybody, and gives me dope about people and affairs that I could get nowhere else—but in that I can talk with him—with one I love, admire, and trust, about the past, perfect, present progressive, and future. I met Lewis Gannett there last night, too. Did thee know him? I saw him for only a short time and liked him at once.

Bon, ma mie, joues de la vie et de la chance de pouvoir travailler pour le bien. L'été s'en va, et je n'ai pas encore reçu mot de l'autre côté de la mer—mais je lis les pensées de mon coeur, qui sont tous à vous, et j'attends content. Nous avons pourquoi savoir gré au bon Dieu purement parce que nous sommes. Et moi, j'en ai d'avantage puisque j'aime—et ce mot renferme toute la beauté qui existe—toi . . . Amour à jamais—au revoir pour le moment. [Well, my dear friend, use life and the chance to be able to work for the good. Summer is on its way, and I haven't yet received word from the other side of the ocean—but I read the thoughts of my heart, which are all of you, and I stay content. We have much to be grateful for purely from our good God because we exist. And I, I have an advantage because I love—this word contains all the beauty that exists—you . . . Love forever—good-bye for the moment.]

Les

August 8, 1918, Mary in Magog, Quebec, to Leslie in Paris

Mon cher ami, comme j'étais heureuse de recevoir hier deux lettres de toi. [My dear friend, how happy I was yesterday to receive two letters from you.]

Yes, Les, I went up to get the mail yesterday never dreaming of the surprise in store for me—it took me nearly all morning to read your splendid letters and when I got through I felt as though I were over there seeing it all. Your descriptions are so vivid and you know just what to tell to make it interesting. I have written you two letters to Place de la Concorde. I hope they will be forwarded. One I wrote when I was worried at not hearing of your landing and the other after I heard you had arrived.

It is great you are so comfortably situated in Paris—dear old Paris—I knew how you would love it. I hope you will get out to Versailles sometime, it is like a place of dreams. You certainly must have been glad to see Horace Davis and have an old friend show you around your new home. Gracious, your telling about it makes me positively homesick for the other side. I hope it won't be long before I am over there too.

Everything is much the same here except that now I am running the camp alone, my aunt and uncle having gone down to Boston to see my cousin [Frederick Eliot][13] before he sails. We were expecting Mother to come up the other day, but Helen has strained her eyes working at the League, poor little girl, and Mother didn't want to leave her. Helen feels terribly at having to give up before she expected to but the doctor says she must not use her eyes for a week. As soon as she is out of his care she is going to Ashburnham for a visit and then coming up here where I shall take care of her and make her get strong and well.

....

How I wish this could get to you in time to wish you a happy birthday and your twenty-first too. You are certainly not wasting a minute in claiming your independence. You are independent of everything but your conscience and that, as the servant of the Invisible, is your master. Happy is every man who can say that <u>of himself</u>.

I wish you, Les, all the best things of this life but gained by enough struggle so that their value is really appreciated. I wish you the joy of seeing happiness in people's faces, knowing that you have helped to put it there (that means many friends), and I wish you the great peaceful joy that comes from faith in the invincible and infinite.

Au revoir, mon camarade. Pour le moment nous avons le même âge. (Mon anniversaire n'est que le 29 Sept.) J'espère que tu es en bonne santé, soigne toi bien! [Good-bye, my comrade. For the moment we are the same age. (My birthday isn't until the 29th of September.) I hope you are healthy, take good care of yourself!]

Ton camarade,
Mary

August 12, 1918, Leslie in Paris to Mary in Magog, Canada

Dearest Mary,

It has come! After I had settled down to a sufficiently apathetic attitude of waiting (for I had no right to expect any letters before the answer to my first, i.e. circa August 27), today I am roused to happiness by the first word from overseas, which is from thee. My eagerness in reading it was pathetic. I read so intently that when I came to a place as for example where thee told about swimming by moonlight, my heart stopped and my brain went on reading mechanically; I entirely missed the next phrases—read them but not understood—while reassuring myself of thy safety. I did not realize this until the second time through, when the phrases just following things that touched life and death were new to me, though they had been staring me in the face all the time. I think that thee is more a comrade of me just now than ever before: I have been slipping a little, letting my high thoughts go, dropping to a lower level. Thy letter holds out a strong hand to me, and with thy help I am getting back. Thee is very near now, holding up my hands, helping me to keep them outstretched toward the holy mountain. What a beautiful thing is perfect confidence! It is what I have in thee and what thee cannot yet have in me, because I am not worthy of it.

Horace Davis, three boys from Unit 2, and I went out to Saint-Germain-en-Laye[14] yesterday. We sat up on the *impériale* [upper deck] and watched the suburban beauty glide by. Gifford,[15] whose home is near Whittier College on the Pacific coast, said that it was far prettier than California. We went through the museum of antiquities in the Chateau de St.-Germain. The present building is a restoration in greater part of the original castle of François I ... The relics of the Stone Age, Bronze Age, Iron Age, and old historic days of France collected there were fascinating. I learned that they had safety-pins in Gaul before 400 B.C.! We found Gallic helmets closely resembling the trench helmets of the modern *poilu*, [French infantryman; literally, "hairy one"] and horses' bits identical in shape with those now made. We saw the relics of the ancient men who dwelt in houses resting upon piles driven into lake-bottoms, so to escape the ferocious beasts and monsters of the forest. Imagine a party of them, chased by a pack of wolves, coming into the moon-light out of the woods, hardly taking time to turn and loose an arrow, darting along their wooden causeway, across the *pont-levis* [drawbridge] and lifting it behind them. The mere fact of these *la-custral* [lakeside] (so-called) dwellings drives the dramatic reality of the savage wilds into one with the force of a speeding flint-headed arrow. There were saber-toothed tigers, enormous bears, and fear-some mammoths.

From the edge of the Forest of St.-Germain we looked out over the gracious valley south toward Paris. Into the wooded spaces again, we walked several miles to the town of Maisons Laffitte. There was a remarkable effect in the trees as we walked. A combi-nation of sunlight, pale green leaves, and a thin haze turned the sur-roundings into fairyland. I saw then in Nature the phenomenon which art-theatres try to simulate by gauze drops, ingeniously lighted, between flats of scenery. When we walked, we felt our limbs moving; but like Alice running with the Red Queen in Through the Looking-Glass, we seemed to be standing still.

No, I didn't bring a copy of War and Peace on the boat. I must finish it properly though, and I'm anxious to as I have just grazed the last third or quarter of it. I have been buying some French books in little paper editions—eleven volumes the other day cost me a total of 36 cents. The type is *très lisible* [very legible] even if the paper is cheap.

I have not yet been assigned to any regular job. The work with the wounded at the station is desultory but *saisissant* [gripping]. Rumors run to the effect that I may be sent out with a Red Cross official as an interpreter. That will be excellent if this work is to be with the *rapatries*. And I shall be able to study the French people and imbibe their language. My guttural "r" is improving!

August 13

Mary, the day after tomorrow is *Jeundi le 15, jour de l'Assomption* [Thursday the 15th, the day of the Assumption.] Madame Brocaille (Marie) says that it is the *grande fête* for all, and especially for those who bear the Virgin's name.

On the following day, I will reach my milestone and go in one bound from infancy to the full estate of a man. *Gaudeamus igitur!* [So, let us rejoice!] No . . . it's no good, I can't think of myself as a man yet, and I certainly am not going to make myself older than I am.

Ce que tu dis au sujet de vivre nos rêves tous les jours—je sais que c'est là que je manqué. Mais tes lettres et la pensée de toi sont l'aides les plus puissantes pour moi. Cette guerre n'écrase pas mes idéales: Elle les prouve et les assure! Nos mains ont touchés. Encore au revoir, mais en souriant—[What you said about living our dreams every day—I know that is what I lack. But your letters and the thought of you are the most powerful aids for me. This war doesn't crush my ideals:

It proves and ensures them! Our hands have touched. Again good-bye, but smiling—]

Ton,
Les

August 16, 1918, Mary in Magog, Canada, to Leslie in Paris

Dear Leslie,

Today is your birthday and such a beautiful day it is too! The sun is warm and bright but soft white clouds go sailing by and the wind is in the treetops. I had a beautiful letter from you this morning that has made me serious but happy. I too feel the way you do, that events and sights of the day are not what I care most to write about to you—it is the thoughts that arise from them that we like to interchange, our spiritual interpretations of beauty. We seem each of us wonderfully to understand the other's ideas and feelings on these things—that is part of true friendship, a very beautiful part. Indeed I knew what a great door was going to open for you onto the world, in your new work. To every one of us some time comes something like a Great Awakening, and we see the values of things more truly than we have ever done before. Tell me of them when you write, Leslie, and leave me out—for I know how you feel, *amico mio*—I understand—you see I don't want to be selfish and take up too much of your thoughts. Let us write to each other as dearest friends.

I am now reading Jack London's socialistic novel The Iron Heel. It is intensely interesting, giving a very clear exposition of socialism. Tho' the book was published in 1908, it predicted a war between

Germany and the U.S.—but the author was confident that the socialist parties in all the countries would rise in a general strike and stop it. Oh, if the German socialists had only had the courage to stand firm. I think their brothers in the other countries would have done the same, don't you?

I wonder how the progress of the war affects you—we hear of great victories for the Allies, which must mean fearful suffering and death. Why, why don't we hear any talk about a Peace Conference at least tentatively? When I get a letter from you it is so real, and I put myself so soundly in your place that it is hard to realize that all of that happened three weeks ago—and then I begin to wonder what you are doing <u>now</u>.

Oh, Leslie, I had such a lovely letter from Evelyn the other day. She was greatly excited because they had heard from you. I am going to write to her right away. The day after I heard from Evelyn I had a long letter from Ronald—what a splendid fellow he is—you are all of the same metal! He has been suffering badly from inoculations. He says Clarence has been drafted and has decided to follow in his footsteps. Think of it. You didn't think Clarence would do that, did you? Ronald wrote so beautifully of his love for you—He said that your religion teaches that those who really love must be separated by space or time, and then he said, "My friends are lovingly near me whenever I think of them with love and the desire for their companionship. My family are constantly with me, as they love me and I love them dearly. Leslie is perhaps nearest of all just now—yet in time and space, he is months and leagues away." You know, Leslie, I think that both you and Ronald are going to be ministers some day, and there couldn't be more splendid ones—for you both live what you believe.

The lake last night was a fairyland. Les—about eight o'clock we started down the lake for a dance, and I wished that I could have gone on forever on that silver blue water, instead of going to the old dance. Everything was delicate pinks and blues and the mountains faded away into mysterious soft haze—oh, it was beautiful—I can't describe it—I can only say that it filled me with the strange sad happiness that I feel in the presence of great beauty—all the world seems a dream, a mysterious and beautiful dream from which I did not care to awake. Even the noise and crowd of the dance could not rouse me. Les, I have gone off dreaming again, and I don't care what discouragements I have, I am going to keep on loving the intangible and glorious things and try to help others to love them. What a wonderful chance you have—I was so touched by your story of the young wounded man who recognized you at the station—no one seeing your face could very well forget it—the light of the distant vision always shines through people's eyes.

We leave here about the 14th of Sept. for Boston—the summer has gone so fast I can't believe it.

Ton fidèle camarade,
Marie

August 18, 1918, Leslie in Paris to Mary in Magog, Canada

Dearest Mary,

Joys, like catastrophes, never come singly. The day after I had received thy treasured letter, I got one, or rather three from home! It was the first word Mother, Father, and Evelyn wrote to me, and remembered my birthday! And I heard that Ronald had been allowed to go home for two days. Think of it! Mother said she was never more overjoyed in her life.

My *jour de fête* [birthday] was quite surprising for me, because they had found it out, and brought on a cake with candles at supper. And what does thee suppose they wanted me to do . . . Blow out all the candles at one ruff . . . If I didn't succeed, those left burning would represent the number of years before my marriage. Didn't I pray for a lung capacity like thine though! I blew my whirlwindiest, but two candles refused to be abolished. Two . . . two . . . *C'est un peu trop d'espérer, n'est-ce pas—mais enfin, qui sait? Deux ou un peu plus, ou jamais—c'est entendu* . . . [It's a bit too much to hope, isn't it—but in the end, who knows? Two or a little more, or never—it's all right.]

Mary, I went to Versailles today for the first time; it rather overwhelmed me. One cannot envisage the splendor of the place before seeing it. I came out dazzled from the halls of the great king's fame, art, and glory, into the vaulted aisles of the forest; it was more than ever God's cathedral. The quiet tones and grace of the trees outshone the gold, marble, and glitter. Here was a thing to appeal to the sense of beauty just as the palace; but there was death, while here was life—the mysterious and priceless gift which flows from God. When the building crumbles the trees will grow green over it. One should go to the *Palais* naive, carefree, and forgetting—

ready to regale the eyes and the sense of the aesthetic with a royal repast—in order to appreciate it to the full. If one reflects upon the billion francs it cost; and whence that billion came, and how—with what pain, sweat, and blood—oh! one longs to fly from it to the calm corridors of the forest or to broad-bosomed hills—to a life free from marble, porphyry,[16] and gilt such as this: ground in agony from the faces of the poor.

Enough of it! The thoughts I had were bitter, but not so gnawing but that I could enjoy the loveliness of the art of man . . . .

August 19

The Paris Friends' Meeting is held here. I like the Friends' method of silent prayer. Last night no one spoke for a full fifteen minutes after the opening lesson from the Bible, and I for one got much more help from meditating upon my own evils in that time than I would have received from a baker's dozen of average sermons. We need more introspection and thought than we usually allow ourselves in this busy world; doesn't thee think so? Heaven knows we have enough temptations, and I need a little space to see them straight and know myself . . . It shows poor preparation and a slow mind, but I am not able to do otherwise.

I must lean constantly upon God and my belief in the next life. It is as if I were standing with thee on the foredeck of a great silent ship, sailing in the moon-track westward . . . as if Providence had let me aspire to thy comradeship . . . as if I were to be happy. A threatening cloud comes out of the south, and swift and black as a bat wing, with the roar of a startled lion, the storm bursts over the vessel . . . It cannot come nigh thee, but me it snatches off with a rush and heave down then up into the blackness and turmoil. One glimpse of the tall ship nobly driving the snarling waves before it, like an antlered stag, in a pack of recreant wolves, and I am all but crushed and dragged under by jostling, brutal waters. Then my faith cries out to God. He lifts me up, and I walk upon the waters. And sooner or later, I shall come again to the ship . . . while it is yet on the sea, if God wills. If not, when it is safely berthed in the last harbor . . . But as yet the storm is able to drag me from the ship. If my faith were greater, it would not have such power . . . .

Voici une petite feuille de lierre prise d'un vieux mur à Versailles, près du Jardin du Trianon. Elle n'a pas les associations de la gabuette de fée que tu, as mise dans ma lettre de bon voyage, mais elle t'apporte l'assurance de la foi que j'ai trouvée en mon cœur pour toi. Mais pour l'amour—pour porter mon amour à ton oreille, je n'ai plus au souhait une grive à t'envoyer. Mais écoute les souffles du vent sur la brune dans les cimes des arbres. C'est moi qui te dis tout bas 'J t'aime, je t'aime!' Mon cœur parle, Marie—prête l'oreille du sien . . . Si! Si! C'est la voix de l'amour de l'âme, de Leslie. [Here is a small leaf of ivy taken from an old wall at Versailles, close to the Trianon Gardens. It doesn't have the associations of the fairy's wand as you wrote in my bon voyage letter, but it assures me of the faith that I found in my heart for you. But for love—to carry my love for you to your ear, I have nothing more than the hope of a bird to bring it to you. But listen to the breath from the breeze at twilight at the top of the trees. It's I who is saying very softly, 'I love you, I love you!' My heart says, Mary— listen to it . . . Yes! Yes! It is the voice of love from the soul of Leslie.]

August 21, 1918, Leslie in Paris to Mary in Magog, Canada

Dearest Mary,

I have just received thy second letter. After reading it four times, I am at last able to lay it down for a while. It is so good to hear from thee—to see between the lines what strength and cheer thee has in the face of pain. The brightness of thy letter is like a cooling drink. I have been rather weary in spirit in the last day or two—and thy words, which I was hoping for, have roused me from the chains. We haven't yet got into correspondence with each other (I hope to get the answer from my first letter to thee in about a week. Don't letters written to be thrown like bread upon the water seem hard to write?) And at such a distance and time interval, intimacy has no easy task to maintain itself.

Mary, thy greatest concern is for work for humanity, isn't it—I can tell from the tone of thy beautiful letters. But I have been wandering about in my own heart, expecting to find a like overwhelming call—and it isn't there. Everywhere, turn as I might, I found thee—thee—Mary. Why should thee make me subordinate the whole mass of humanity to my love for thee? It seems wrong and yet it is not wrong. True love, forever young, harms no one but him whom it wounds instead of saves. It is because thee does not love any one above all that thee can hold still calmly and with single heart to the great purpose. Sometimes I wish I could cut the sweet bonds which bind me—and yet I may not; I would lose something irrevocable— my ideal of love and truth. God and fathers and mothers can love beings continually who do not love in return. I ask myself if I can.

This may all be a mood. But aren't moods real? What are they if not reflections drawn from the well of experience? Thy moods are bewitching. I would not have thee otherwise than with thy quick reception and appreciation of things that arrive whether awake or in dreams. All the courses of nursing, dietetics, home economics, and gardening in the world cannot make thee put thy *joie de vivre* on the shelf, can they? Say <u>no</u>![17]

Today there is a suffocating heat. Horace took me to the "Petit Bain Parisien"—a swimming pool in the Seine, close to the bridge at La Concorde. There we swam to refresh ourselves. I didn't have the mystery of the moon to lighten me—nothing but the plain, merciless day, a little camouflaged by some drapes. And the whisper of the treetops—where was it? Replaced by the chatter of the barely-dressed Frenchmen who were swimming there. The distant ringing sound—where did it come from? The noise of the bodies in the water . . . There was one chap, joyfully idiotic, who just jumped in with all his clothes on, and who splashed around in the water as if he were punching himself. Then he climbed to a high diving board, with a bucket in his left hand and a scrub brush in the other. Someone called to him, "The Goths! To the cellar!" And without hesitating he jumped underwater—to avoid the shelling, and to clean the floor of the fish.

Yesterday I helped to deliver two beds to a disaster-stricken family who live in the Gentilly area. I helped to interpret, and after a long while we finally got rid of them . . . the beds, I mean, not the family, who was charming. But the most beautiful thing came when we were back at the little van, "Henry Ford." A group of young children had formed—and when I greeted them, "Hello, my little ones!" all of them said, "Hello, American Sir! Hello!" and held out their hands to us. Touching and holding these thin, little hands—ah! How heavy my heart felt. I wanted to kiss them, but I didn't dare.

Tonight, I had dinner at the Britannique, which is in the Parisian team's area of the Mission, invited by Horace Davis. And then, after he put on his new uniform (he looks very dashing wearing it), we had

Refugee boys near Sermaize watching the FRU workers build a house

headed towards the house of the countess, a friend of Louis Allard. When we got there, we found ourselves, in of all places in the big world, very close to the back right leg of the Eiffel Tower. But she wasn't home—she had left Paris for the country. So, there we were looking around the left bank of the Seine by the light of the moon, heading towards "Les Invalides," [Hôtel National des Invalides] having deep discussions about life and death, about the hot weather, about feeling like members of high society for the night. The light of the moon was so clear that one could have believed that the panorama was a winter scene—covered with snow—it was good for our sense of beauty, and what is even better, to refresh us.

Clarence, I hear, has come around to a point where he will take the same stand that Ronald did. Good for him! (I think that he has been called.) Mother—thee can picture her happiness. I hope he won't be treated as Ronald was.

Courage et bonheur est mon souhait pour toi. Pour toujours, [Courage and happiness are my wishes for you. Forever,]

Les

August 30, 1918, Leslie in Paris to Mary in Magog, Canada

Dearest Mary,

Last night, at the invitation of Horace, I went down to the Britannique to call on Hilda Holme,[18] who is up from Le Glandier, Pompadour. There is the school for Belgian children, whose out of school life has been lightened by Friends. Henry Strater[19] (who has more personal charm than any other man in the Unit, according to Horace) is needed elsewhere, and they are short-handed . . . I went down, as I say, to talk with her about the place, but when I got there I bumped into a fudge-party with H. H. presiding at the chafing dish; so I went away happy but unhappy—full of fudge, but empty of information. The work with the Belgian children is about the most expressive of the Friends Mission; if it is at all feasible I should like to enter it . . . Time will tell, I suspect; it often does.

We had a Quaker wedding here the other day. A Mary Pancoast married a Dr. Jesse Packer,[20] to whom she had been engaged in America. It was a solemn occasion—and the first wedding, I believe, that I ever attended. The wedding takes place in Friends meeting— a cloud of witnesses. Silent prayer opens the worship; and it is only after a fitting time that the two rise, take each other by the hand, when the groom says "In the presence of God and the Friends assembled, I, So and So, take thee, Such and Such a One, as my wife. I promise to be unto thee a faithful and loving husband as long as we shall live" (or words very similar; I am not certain that I have quoted correctly). The bride responds in reciprocal fashion, and they resume their seats, united. The silent prayer of the Friends for their happiness and grace in the sight of God goes on. If any Friend feels the call to speak his heart aloud, he does so. Then the record of the marriage, couched in the quaint terms of the earlier Friends, is read, and the couple signs, followed by the overseers and the cloud of witnesses—*fini!* Horace was what corresponds to *garcon d'honneur* [best man]—he held the paper for them to sign. The room with its quiet furnishings and lofty ceiling was even more beautiful with vases of flowers on the table. The sun streamed in at the tall windows on the bowed heads of the praying Friends—one felt blessed and consecrated merely to be in the company.

Afterward we went out into the quiet garden back of the hostel for ice-cream and cake. Thee cannot realize what those homely words mean to us here, thousands of miles from American freezers and ovens. The food was delicious, too . . . but some of us had no time to meditate upon the wedding—we left immediately for the station to unload American wounded from a train into ambulances. We of the Unit were put in charge of squads of Y.M.C.A. men who hadn't been there before. We have the system of work well in our minds, and the Red Cross knows it . . . .

Je laisse tout l'avenir de mon amour entre tes mains. Si tu penses quelquefois à moi souviens-toi de mon amour pour tes yeux, ton cœur, et tes idéales. C'est à cause de toi que je me dis courage et patience toujours. Ah, si je suis heureux! Quel autre connait si bien que moi la portée de la voix de Dieu dans ton âme? Je dis ce que je sais . . . et je sais que je t'aime . . . . [I leave the entire future of my love in your hands. If you sometimes think of me, remember my love for your eyes, your heart, and your ideals. It is because of you that I talk to myself always about courage and patience. Oh, how happy I am! What other man knows as well as I do the way that has opened from the voice of God in your soul? I say that I know . . . and I know that I love you . . . .]

Leslie

August 27, 1918, Mary in Magog, Canada, to Leslie in Paris

Dear Les,

Yesterday came two letters from you, one written on July 31st and the other on August 5th—funny they should have come together, isn't it. I was surprised to see the American stamps on them and for one strange second I thought something must have happened and you had come back—then of course I saw your address in the corner and the next second I was reading them.

Hurrah for your progress in French—if you keep it up you will soon be rolling your liquid "r's" like Louis himself. I am getting on in Italian, having conversed quite a bit with Antonio. He is going back to New York in a day or two. We parted the best of <u>friends</u> though I don't know yet whether he quite understands what friendship is—he seems very young to me in some ways—tho' old in others. He says he is going to write and I shall be interested to see what his letters are like.

Since I wrote the first part of this letter I have been on a visit. One of my country playmates, a girl about my age who has lately married and set up a farm with her husband about 15 miles from here. I had a glimpse of real country life with its routine of chores and monotonous housework without any outlook. I plunged into the work with the rest and so was happy—but I can tell you that if I ever live on a farm I shall make other interests somehow—start a library or a local club for discussion, acting, walking, etc. It is great to run a farm and be in the beautiful country under the open sky— it is an ideal work if you don't let your mind go to seed—don't you think so? My whole visit made me feel as tho' I had stepped into another world and made me surer than ever that you can't do good for others unless you live as they live and share in their problems.

It is Sunday afternoon; camp is very quiet for everyone is resting or reading—a fine chance for my talk with you. I feel as though it were only yesterday that you went away, and when I talk about the things we both love, the ocean dries up and disappears. I can't but admit, however, that the talk is very one-sided with my imagination doing good work and that I would give a good deal to have a real talk for just a little while!

Sept. 7

It is quite a long time since I wrote the foregoing. The days go by full of work and thoughts. A week from today we leave this lovely place and go down to Cambridge—I shall hate in a way to leave all the beauty here, but for a week or more I have been restless to get back to college and the busy whirl. Mother had a letter from your mother the other day saying that your father is going to France in the fall and that she and Evelyn are coming to live in Cambridge. Isn't that fun—probably Evelyn is going to stay with us a week or two' until your mother gets the house shut up and finds a place in Cambridge. All this is no news to you of course—what changes each day brings with it! We are so glad that we shall get to know your mother and Evelyn better, but I feel sorry that they had to close your home.

Yes, do keep at your writing, Les—you have a gift for it, and what is more, your mind is full of things to say. I hope you will find someone to criticize and encourage you—even if you don't, keep at it. You are a good judge yourself and there is nothing like practice.

Au revoir, mon ami—courage. When distance seems long or tasks hard, let's both remember that the same sun and stars shine the world over and beauty and faith endure forever. You must be happy in your splendid work.

As ever your comrade,
Mary

September 3, 1918, Leslie in Paris to Mary in Magog, Canada

Dearest Mary,

My heart had been waiting for thy beautiful letter which came last night. Further, I had been hoping for some poetry. Maybe it was my wish that decided thee not to deprive me of the joy I take in thy verse . . . The deep love and admiration which shines through thy sonnet to Helen makes it, I think, the most beautiful thing of thine thus far. Yet only a few can feel its full loveliness—those who know what Helen is to thee: a perfect sister and comrade. "With light of sunrise still upon thine eyes" is priceless. Helen's eyes were made for the dawn.

But here is a little piece of real news. Zavitz,[21] who has been working down at Le Glandier, Pompadour, with Hilda Holme and several others among the Belgian children there, came to our hostel yesterday. He says that they are to start two new schools for the Belgian children, one hundred at each, in the Basses Pyrénées— one toot sweet [from the French *tout suite*, meaning immediately] and the other in a couple of months. They want one man and one woman worker for each place. The children's ages are from seven to fourteen, but the greater part are from ten to twelve. The men workers will be recruited, I think, from our Second Unit, but there is a shortage of women . . . Mary—one moment! Will thee please put on thy bonnet and come over with me to the mountain border of France near Spain, to teach a hundred children to play? Thee can get over all right—I don't think this twenty-five years of age limit [for women in the FRU] is hard and fast. That work appeals to me strongly; and with someone congenial, or (what is too much to hope for) with thee—what an opportunity! Well, no one has yet accepted me for the job, so don't start across until thee hears from me again. One teaches them games, outdoor and indoor sports— one takes them on hikes—one answers their questions—one has a chance to try to influence them for good—one works with minds still open to ideas—one gets far from the mud and dried blood. I have a feeling that such work would help educate me as well as the children—if I am not drafted.

Please tell thy mother that I read the Testament she gave me every night . . . The gospel words mean more to me each time I read them. How simple and yet how wonderful is truth! Ten thousand sophistries to justify the thing we abhor cannot overpower the smallest part of the Lord's Word.

Thee has heard about Clarence? On August 9, which was the last letter I got from home, he was at camp in Georgia. He too is standing for the truth as he sees it. How happy the news has made me! Let us hope that all of us may act according to our highest light always . . . .

I wish thee the happiest birthday ever—I shall be thinking of thee—and a glorious senior year (if thee decides not to run down to les Basses Pyrénées with me). Give my regards to Margaret, to Miss Beatrice Jones, A. B., and to Harry Dana, please.

If thee is still Mary, I am *encore* [again] Leslie . . . who thinks more of thee than he can tell.

Les

September 11, 1918, Mary in Magog, Canada, to Leslie in Paris

Dear Les,

I am happy today too—not in spite of the weather as in your case, but with the weather which is cold and fresh and golden. These last autumn days up here are glorious, just to show us how foolish we are to go down to the city.

Your jubilant letter was so refreshing—I took a two-mile swim on the *joie de vivre* it imparted and broke the record by swimming it in 73 minutes. Your letters 6 and 7 came together and the next day came 5—I had a regular feast of news.

I was just reading *Le Mariage de Figaro* the other day—Louis advised us to for Fr. 16. I am glad you saw it so well acted. Yes, I know the air *"Marlbrough s'en va-t-en guerre"*—the song must have been lovely. You are so lucky to see all these plays—it will help you a lot when you write yourself.

I am glad Horace has decided to stay, for your sake; it is great to have a friend who knows all the ropes. By the way, it looks as though Victor Heatherston might be over there before long—he has been so well treated at Devens, and they tell him that if he gets into the Unit, they will let him go—of course, things may change, but they seem to be going swimmingly now.

Both Bob Dunn and George Hallett have gone to camp—I don't know how they are faring. Brent Allinson[22] has gone to prison for his 15 years sentence to be in a tiny little cell with another man—it is too horrible to think of. They can't cage his poet's soul though—I just hope all the suffering hasn't taken away his songs.

What fun you had on your birthday—with all your letters and the cake. Now, Les, you mustn't be superstitious. Whoever you marry—it will be a good way off, I should think, because you must remember your own ambition and how much preparation it takes now-a-days for any life work. You must finish college, and perhaps go on for an A.M. or even Ph.D. Whether you teach, minister, or write, it takes years of training and men who try to do this and support a wife are undertaking more than is humanly possible. Of course the woman could go on studying and working, too—and I have known people who have been most happy doing this—also I am the last person in the world to say, "wait until you have a position in the world"—but what I mean is that no woman ought to hamper a man in the preparation for his career. There are so many, many problems, now that some women are going in for the same things as men, and both have careers—But the man can have two careers, while the woman only one, and the highest is the home. But she need never be shut in by the walls of her home—all the world is around her as before, only in a different way. The man and the woman work together there for the rest of the world. It is an ideal situation—I wish you were here by the fire, Les—we would talk of many things.

Sometimes I think that I ought to write you only cold, matter-of-fact letters, so that if you were mistaken, you would gradually forget the past and what you have said. You see, *mon ami*, I can't bear to think that you shouldn't be free to change your mind when you like. You are seeing and feeling so many new things and you too are "passionate," as the girls said of me—you are romantic and therefore more easily influenced than others—when you come to your matter-of-fact senses you may regret, and it is those regrets that I want to spare you. I know I have said all this before, and it will look cold and hard when written, but there are so many splendid women in the world that could fill your ideal much better than I—you too must keep on searching, Les—I mean it. This is the advice of a faithful comrade.

13 Hilliard St., Sept. 16th

Here we are back again in dear old Cambridge. I found your letter (no. 8) here when I arrived. It was rather blue, Les, and took away from the joy of coming home except that as I read I said to myself "by now he is as happy as a lark again." Please don't get "*entre chien et loup*" [between dog and wolf or, poetically, that uncertain threshold between hope and fear[23]] again! Whatever the future has in store, it doesn't do any good to see darkness now.

Who do you suppose is staying with us for a while—Evelyn! She went to the Latin School for the first time today. I took her down and introduced her to the principal, whom I know. She has made out her program with Radcliffe in view—and I just hope it won't be too hard. She is going to stay with us until your mother comes up from Brooklyn—I don't know and I don't think they are sure—when that will be. Evelyn is such a darling—it is a perfect pleasure to have her in the house.

Radcliffe students talking on campus

The atmosphere here in Cambridge is so strange this fall; the Radio School[24] is all quarantined for Spanish Influenza—a very catching and serious disease that has already taken the toll of many lives; they say they have it under control here but that it is now spreading to Devens and other places.

They say that Harvard is to be a regular military training school this winter, the boys having the pay of privates and only taking a couple of courses such as science and math, in addition to the military science and training. It all counts for a degree too—just think of it— I don't think this is compulsory for all, however.

Bonne chance et bon courage. Ton fidèle camarade, [Good luck and have courage. Your faithful comrade,]

Mary

September 13, 1918, Leslie in Bourges to Mary in Cambridge

Dearest Mary,

Out of town at last! But wait until I whisper the bad news in thy ear—we have heard recently from the children's school at Le Glandier, that they need only one man; and apparently that is not I, for the present, at least; but I'm still hoping that by the time thee comes over I shall be in line for a similar job. So, if thee has thy bonnet on, come along! We'll do or die.

I'm waiting for thee near Bourges, a large town which has grown from 42 to 110 in thousands since the beginning of the war. The Chateau de Montifaut is our *demeure* [residence]—eight of us from 93 Boul. Mich. And we've been here three days, preparing to put up barracks for *rapatrie sans terre* [landless citizens returning from exile], unloading some cars, and getting oriented. Me thought to flee the war when we came south but we have a bombardment from experimental cannons—(I mean new untried guns, no new kinds) from seven-thirty till ten and in the afternoon—it shakes the windows, and the shells shriek over off to their mark more than ten kilometres away. Aircraft are about almost continually . . . I had my first experience of the .075 the other day. It's the most nerve-rending concussion I have ever heard—a tearing, fierce, vindictive crash, not at all like the solid, rumbling thud of the .120s or the .240s.

The Chateau had been owned and abandoned by an Italian doctor named Casanova. The French Government is fixing it up a little and using it as a clearing station for some refugees who are to be distributed to farms. We eight have a room to ourselves—a room with a fireplace for which we are grateful on these cool evenings—but the rest of the house is pretty packed with people just now.

Tomorrow morning, Johnson, our *camioneer* [military truck driver], is going to drive a family of refuges thirty kilometres to *"la ferme Jojo"* [Jojo's farm], and the rest of us cast lots (that's my poetry for flipping a nickel) to decide who should be lucky or unlucky enough to go with him for a ride. It simmered down to Leslie—(Friday the Thirteenth was always my lucky day) and so I go.

We are enjoying this life thoroughly. Good hard country work is a pleasant change from an A.R.C. canteen at the Gare du Nord in the heart of Paris. My *ordre de mission* extends until the tenth of October—one month. We don't know yet how long this construction job is to last, but we're a happy chain-gang and strong for it.

The night is perfect and starlit—cool and calm . . . I can imagine thee <u>walking down</u> by the Charles. School will have long begun when thee receives this. Let us go forward and forget time—which is, as we have said, a small thing. *Nous nous entendons* [we understand each other] and what does time know about the human understanding?

Thy,
Les

Typical Red Cross ambulance
used during the Spanish flu epidemic

5

The Great Influenza

IN OCTOBER 1918, LESLIE RECEIVED A LETTER from Mary that left him stunned. Buried within her usual breezy news and encouragement for his work, she commented that she and Helen had been deathly ill with influenza. He had not been aware that the Spanish Flu was raising havoc in Cambridge.

The nickname "Spanish Flu" came from the large number of mortalities reported in the Spanish press during May and June 1918. By that time, flu had already appeared in the United States and France, but the press in most of Europe and America suppressed mention of the disease because of the potential effect on morale and on the war effort. As a neutral country, Spain did not censor the news.

The origins of this strain of flu are not known, although many scientists believe that it started in the United States in early 1918. The first outbreak of a particularly virulent form of influenza occurred at Fort Riley, Kansas, on March 11, 1918.

The first cases in Boston appeared in August among soldiers infected with the virus. The port was bustling with shipments of war supplies and troops. At the Boston Naval Yards, more than 7,000 men were in transit, living in overcrowded barracks and dormitory ships. Within two days, 68 men had reported ill. The flu spread quickly through the close quarters of the military units stationed in the area. The *Rochambeau*, the liner on which Leslie had sailed in July, had a major outbreak of the flu in August, and men were taken from the ship to St. Vincent's Hospital in New York.

By September 4, the epidemic reached the 16,000 men of the Naval Radio School living in the Harvard dorms and camped on Cambridge Common. The disease spread quickly to the civilian population. On September 3, the first civilian was admitted to Boston City Hospital. As people gathered in the streets for rallies and bond drives and as soldiers and sailors gathered to prepare to go overseas, they infected each other. The disease hit swiftly and without warning. A person who was seemingly healthy in the morning could be dead by evening. The virus caused the patients' skin to become blue, and they developed a cough with blood-stained sputum. Those who did not die quickly often suffocated from the buildup of fluid in their lungs. Nothing worked to cure the disease. Doctors and nurses could only hope to treat the symptoms. Survival was a matter of luck or some other unknown component of a person's constitution. Unlike other forms of influenza which strike mainly the elderly, infants, and young children, this strain was most deadly in young adults, ages twenty to forty, the very people who were crowded together in troop transports and living in dormitories at colleges.

Most of the doctors and nurses in this country had been conscripted or had enlisted in the military. Massachusetts was initially able to use medical students and to bring in medical help from surrounding towns and other states, but this source of aid soon dried up as the disease spread down the east coast to New York, Philadelphia, and beyond, and as doctors and nurses themselves succumbed to the disease. Emergency hospitals were created in a futile attempt to accommodate the growing number of patients, especially those arriving sick from overseas. The Red Cross formed a National Committee on Influenza to try to more effectively use nurses, volunteers, and medical supplies. This effort was insufficient to stem the spread of the epidemic. The dead were left in gutters and stacked in caskets on front porches. Trucks drove by to pick up the corpses. Public gatherings were forbidden. People hid indoors, afraid to interact with their neighbors.

In America, in October alone, more than 195,000 people died. For several weeks at Fort Devens, thirty miles west of Cambridge, as many as 5,000 young soldiers died each day. Before the war ended, more than 675,000 Americans had died from the disease. About half of the American soldiers who died in Europe died from influenza, not the enemy.[1]

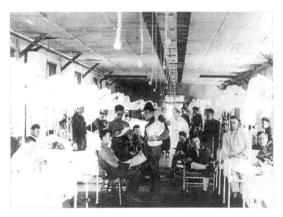

The infirmary at Fort Devens where infected soldiers and sailors were quarantined.

Mary, Helen, and their mother were among the lucky. They survived and were recovering by the time Mary's letters reached Leslie.

Leslie's unit was in the country and only mildly affected by the epidemic, but the influenza virus struck just as hard in France. The first outbreak of high-mortality influenza in France had occurred in July. In Paris, the government closed the schools but was unwilling to expand the quarantine, to avoid hurting morale. In October, at its peak, 4,574 people in Paris died of influenza or related pneumonia. In many French cities, more than half of the families had at least one victim.[2] Throughout France, the Unit workers, in their mission to relieve suffering, volunteered for hospital duties and provided services to the sick and dying in their neighborhoods. Fortunately, only five members of the Friends Mission died of the influenza.[3]

October 22, 1918, Mary in Cambridge to Leslie in Bourges

Dear Leslie,

I have three splendid letters from you—two of which came today, though one was written on Sept. 14th and the other on Sept. 30th—the one written on Sept. 25th came a long time ago. It certainly is funny—the perversity of the mail. I am so glad you are so busy and happy—new things must be happening all the time—I can see you speeding down the picturesque roads (now don't go too fast) to bring help to the grateful suffering people—how lucky you are to be able to help so specifically. I try to make myself see that I am doing my duty by sticking at college—but it is hard sometimes! Evelyn wrote us today that Ronald has been given permission to go with the Unit and will sail before very long—just think of it—you must get together in your work—I can just imagine your first meeting!

It is great when you write to have you mention things in my letters—then we seem to be really corresponding and conversing; and you make things so vivid with your colored descriptions. When you are working with the other "unit" men, do you talk French—or do you just practice your "r" on the natives? You really must be able to talk most fluently now.

I am beginning to feel that my love for mankind and ideals is too abstract—to love mankind as one must truly love all those with whom one comes in contact, universal peace must first be personal. The stars are my symbols, but they are very far away, and I am looking more now for inspiration in the eyes of everyday people. How can we help the world if we do not know the joys and sorrows of individual people—we must take interest—real personal interest—in the little things that mean so much to others. I think the person who can put himself in another's place has the secret of brotherhood.

It is that I feel hungry now-a-days to know what people are thinking about, and what their problems are—so that I get talking with people in shops and everywhere. Life is so intricate yet so simple, and you find everywhere the same hard work and loving sacrifice. On the other hand of course there is wickedness and suffering—but I have such confidence that good will gradually overcome evil—that I have no fear. You must see many, many lives with their problems each one seeming all important by itself and where the little things count for so much (the details of the Great Plan). Talk with the people sympathetically and intimately and you will learn more than there is in all the books in Widener Library [at Harvard]—then tell me about it—I am so anxious to hear and learn.

I had a chance to do a lot of thinking while I was sick. As I lay there, knowing I had a disease of which hundreds were dying, I seemed to see life more really than I had ever done before . . . and I realized the immense place that the little things of every day occupy. I looked at a clock and a book and thought how many generations of men had lived thru' all kinds of dangers to create those things that we take for granted. The sun shone into the room where Helen and

I lay, and we could hear the funeral processions clattering by at frequent intervals up Brattle Street—then the children in the next yard would scream and laugh with joy at their play. How strange it all seemed—an enormous vacuum filled with beautiful abstract truths and a multitude of tiny details. I could not make myself believe that if I were not there things would go on just the same—and when I went down to the Square the first time and saw the life and bustle, I was shocked that the world could be so heartless and carefree when hundreds were dying and being killed. Yet it is just this circle of life that keeps things going—any one of us is really of very little importance as long as there are thousands of others to take up the tasks and go on. How wonderful life is—so fragile and short—men must have opportunities to get more than the necessaries, the swamping details—these are not life—life is big and rich and full; and so few people have a chance to realize it. When I was up and around again I had the burning desire to stop people I met and tell them how happy they ought to be that they were alive in this beautiful world.

Now I have said enough about myself and my ideas. I must tell you about the others. Mother is all well again, feeling like her old self, and Helen after three weeks siege is beginning to study a little at home and go out for a short walk. It is wonderful to be all at table again together—we are mighty grateful people.

We have a colored girl to help with the work so that I can get my studying done instead of flying home between lectures to do the dishes, etc. I led an exciting life for about ten days and now feel like a lady of leisure. College work goes right ahead although the non-academic activities haven't started up yet. The first Idler [the play put on by the drama club at Radcliffe] was given up because of the "flu" and I don't know whether there will be one before Christmas.

Margaret Garrison[4] is living at the dormitories this year (and having a very healthy radical effect on the girls there). The other day was her birthday and one of the girls had a surprise party in her room at 10 p.m. for her. I went up just before 10 with some flowers and came into the room. Lured there on the pretext that the "News" editor wanted to see her about the Radical Club, she opened her mouth very wide and uttered not a sound. Then she held the cake while we filed by one by one taking a candle, wishing for her, and blowing it out. First we had a great discussion as to whether the wishes should be spoken or not—silence was decided upon—perhaps it was best as my wish was that peace come before Christmas based on the platform of the British Labor Party and that Margaret would marry a man like Scott Nearing![5] (She admires him so much.)

You say Mr. Briggs[6] is to be exchange professor—I had heard rumors to that effect too, but he doesn't seem to go, and comes to morning prayers every day as usual. Perhaps he is going second half—I do hope so as I have been trying to assemble some of my ideas for a little talk with him in one of his office "hours." Every year I do it and get great inspiration from him; he is such a great-minded and yet human man, isn't he?

Pipe down has sounded from the Radio School so I must go to bed. Good night—(I am pretending that you have been here reading a French play and are just leaving). We have had a delightful evening, have we not.

Au revoir, mon ami—As ever
Mary

P.S. I sang "O Solo Mio" all the time I was sick to keep my spirits up!

The Naval Radio school drilling on Cambridge Common

October 25, 1918, Leslie in Savigny-en-Septaine to Mary in Cambridge

Dearest Mary,

Day before yesterday came thy letter, mailed on the 27 of September. Don't they take ages to cross! I have read it five times, and thought a great deal.

Thy struggle is a peculiarly trying one, and I wish with all my heart that I might help thee in it. Yet, as thee says, the call must come, if so be, to leave all, and follow Him . . . in a little measure, I have felt thy struggle in myself at various times. Once, I remember, when there was a Fellowship meeting last June, in thy house . . . it was so strong upon me that I said something about a need for people to give up their home joys to work for the children and domestic happiness of others. And at that time I was applying it inevitably to myself. Whatever the call is, let us ask for strength to shoulder the task cheerfully, and though we have sorrows, sing it through!

We are looking for the same ideal, Mary; let us go forward, ever holding hands, and helping each other, being ready for anything that may happen. With love, faith, and courage, nothing can go wrong. May I be strong enough to believe this so as to live by it!

The work of carrying love into men's hearts is the hardest task I see, and yet the task of most beautiful promise. But how to carry it: in one's private life or to make such the chief occupation of one's activities? And suppose that the love for mankind which is in my heart is not real enough or strong enough to reach to them and do them good? I must develop it. That's my task, to get hold of myself, and let the Light of the World become my master. One has plenty of opportunities—and how often I fall far short of taking advantage of them!

The Spanish Flu! It has spread alarmingly, hasn't it, and become a menace. At first we here never took it in earnest—we put it down as a slight attack of grippe—I never imagined anyone could die of it. Thy words show that it is raging in America as in France and causing deaths! I hope that it doesn't touch any of thy family. Our *équipe* is congratulating itself on being out in the country, living in the open all day, and breathing good fresh air all night. But our health pride may be going before a fall.

The other day Arthur Fulton[7] and I dressed in our best after lunch, piled into the old Panhandle, and steamed out to try to get to St. Just, a little village across the Polygon (where the *tir d'essai* [test firing] takes place). We were told by the carpenter of Savigny that we could pass the sentries at three o'clock. After the narrowest escape from killing a hen, we jogged along the Savigny-St. Just Road till we came to the first sentry box. The noise of our motor woke up the ragged old army bird inside, who politely stopped us and in answer to our question about the probable end of the day's firing said "*Ah!— je ne sais rien!*" ["Ah!—I know nothing!"]

Foiled, we were forced to make a wide detour and came down through the lower or old end of the Polygon. The road was excellent and the old 'bus was doing herself proud when suddenly the good road ducked sharply to the left, and we bowled into the muddiest and vilest collection of shell holes a man not at the front ever saw. I don't know how that old boat paddled through them. Halfway through it (not along it) we met a *corvée* [soldiers on duty] picking up spent shells that had buried themselves deep in the ground. We gave them a nasty look, and went on without being stopped. Maybe they thought we were officers. Then the road, ameliorating, led us into Soye-en-Septaine, a nestling little village with a little monastery. St. Just, we were told, was first to the right and then to the left. The road that led us from Soye to the St. Just highway was the most beautiful country road, on the most beautiful day that I have seen. The road was just the right hardness— and smooth. To each side of it, the grass seemed to make a natural flanking carpet. And the wood was all around—with delicate yellows, reds, and browns in the most exquisite variety and profusion. There was not a soul on the road. No sentry. No war aeroplane was soaring in the sky. No gun was rumbling near—and no shells were whining along the blue. We could forget the war—and were childishly happy . . . What mattered is that the machine broke down utterly just then—because all the oil had leaked out? Leaving her in the road, silent, we walked on, in the afternoon sun to the parting of the ways . . . Arthur went on to St. Just, and I turned toward Savigny for oil. It was so like the parting of two of Robin Hood's men in Howard Pyle's story that the romance atmosphere had me enslaved for quite a while . . . .

Ronald, because of certain reports that have reached him about our work and its proximity to the military, had practically decided in his last letter not to come, even if he had the chance. I have considered carefully, tried hard to put myself in his place, and written to him, urging him to come! I'm sure it will do him good, give him valuable experience and some French. And I think we will be able to get work together!

Marie, ma mie, il fait tard . . . on me déblatère quand je veille de la sorte. Mais, sais-tu, ce n'est qu'en étant seul avec ta mémoire et ton présence que je puisse te dire ce que j'ai à dit. Et puis, j'aime à être seul avec toi, ainsi on peut parler du cœur et découvrir les pensées intimes. Je ne sens plus l'amertume de privation. L'amour est trop profond pour l'on le gâte par si peu de chose que le distance matériel. [Mary, my dear, it's late . . . I rant when I go on that way. But, you know, it's only when I'm alone with your memory and your presence that I can tell you what I have to say. And so, I love to be alone with you, when one can speak of one's heart and discover intimate thoughts. I don't feel the bitterness of the hardships. Love is too deep to be spoiled by little things as physical distance.]

À jamais, ton [Forever, your]
Les—

P. S. I was interested to hear that Frederick Eliot was surprised that the wounded were moved so efficiently. We did our best at the station, but at times were painfully aware of unfortunate changes in organization there. Altogether too much changing of leaders—until we were somewhat at a loss. But compared to the French system, it was quick—quick!

*A village in Verdun destroyed by the war
and a neighborhood after FRU workers built new homes*

6

Reconstruction Work

LESLIE WAS ASSIGNED TO THE BUILDING DEPARTMENT, one of the six departments of the Friends Reconstruction Unit. Other Unit members worked in the Medical, Manufacturing, Works, Agriculture, Purchase and Sales, and Relief Departments, or in one of the departments supporting the Unit itself.[1] His first assignment was in Bourges, Cher, in central France on the Yèvre River. He helped build barracks for refugees who were being transported to this region south of Paris, well behind the front line. Most jobs in the Unit were for skilled or semi-skilled manual labor, even though many of the men who joined the Friends Unit were college-educated. Leslie brought his experience from four years of carpentry classes, a year of machine shop practice, and four summers working on farms doing general work.

Many of the villages that were in the area of the fighting were barely more than heaps of rubbish. Farm machinery was broken. Farm horses had been taken for military purposes, and all young and able-bodied men had enlisted or been conscripted into the military. The men in Leslie's *équipe* brought help and hope to French citizens who stayed in their villages and were living in cellars or among rubble of former homes and refugees whose villages were still not safe for them to return.[2]

The materials for rebuilding the damaged houses and for new construction came from the factories at Dole in the Jura region and Ornans in the Franche-Comté region of eastern France. The factories were staffed by both British and American Quakers. The French government

French citizens in front of their underground shelter

furnished materials for two thousand houses. Using French timber, work teams made *maisons démontables*—houses in transportable sections designed to be dismantled and reassembled or repositioned. These were shipped by rail and assembled by the village *équipes*. The standardized house had two or three rooms. The exterior was stained dark brown, roofed in red tile, with windows and a dark green door with a knob of white china. Demand far exceeded the supply; the two factories could produce about ten houses per week. Before the Armistice, over seventy of the portable houses were destroyed by the bombardments. Still, by spring 1919, a thousand houses had been set up in the Auvergne region alone.[3]

Friends also assembled houses manufactured at French factories. As reported in the Unit's newsletter, *Reconstruction*, in October 1918, "Refugees are in some of the houses of the agricultural center being erected by thirteen Friends at Savigny-en-Septaine, in Cher near Bourges. These are French houses (not made at the Friends' construction camps), ten of them big 'Adrian' barracks, and fifteen of the 'Blocus' type, containing two rooms, each four meters by four, and a shed[4]. . . The refugees often come out to inspect the '*chateaux*' which are being built for them."[5]

With his natural curiosity and openness to other people and new experiences, Leslie did more than work on the houses. He served as an interpreter because of his fluency in French and came to know his French neighbors and the French workers in the area. He learned to drive a truck and was often called upon to ferry refugees and materials. These travels often took him over shell-pocked roads and through military checkpoints in areas devastated by the war. He also learned to drive tractors and was considering a position teaching French farmers at Buisson in an effort to re-establish and modernize agriculture.[6]

The work was hard and the living conditions primitive and sometimes under bombardment. Fortunately, no member of any Friends Unit was killed in these attacks.[7] For the most part, the Unit members were "glad in their work."[8] As one of the English workers told the American members, "At a time when people are thinking in continents, in millions of lives, and hundreds of millions of money, we have lived in small villages among humble people, doing unsensational though inter-

One of the trucks used by Unit members

esting work; we have come to see that personal sympathy and genuine understanding are all the more welcome at a time when individual personality is generally unconsidered."[9]

Leslie was finally doing the work for which he went to France, and his letters to Mary were enthusiastic. He had entered fully into the life of the French village, and he developed friendships with the soldiers stationed nearby. Mary, meanwhile, was recovering from the influenza, reporting on school activities, and contemplating her future.

October 27, 1918, Leslie in Savigny-en-Septaine, Cher, to Mary in Cambridge

Dearest Mary,

I have read thy seventh letter again, and it has made me happy ... contemplatively, wistfully happy; for although thee has a struggle involving the fundamentals of the future, yet thy attitude toward it is so courageous and high-souled that I am proud and happy. There was a time, I think, that the possibility of thy renouncing a future of marriage and home life should have filled me with apprehension. My faith has reached beyond the grave, I feel—and we can ever be comrades in service if we make our hearts high and full always. My backslidings are a source of weakness, which I must strive to overcome. Thy friendship, the reading of the Word, and the Christian fellowship here are doing wonders for me.

The day has been a beautiful one of late autumn. Golden yellow leaves have fallen, rustling and spinning in the wind. Shelley's "West Wind" seems written for just such a day. I love it—I love it all!

I am pretty sure that the war is virtually over—in spite of the newspapers and the militarists' savage attempt to prick humanity to blood-vengeance. This Sunday—though in war-time Sunday is treated as other days of the week—there was no firing down the Polygon, and very few planes were up. Let us pray that the sense-lessness of savagery has been grasped by many men!

Yesterday morning, I was taken twice for a flight in an aero-plane. My foolish spirit had been aching for the experience, and thee may guess how high my heart was when the chance came. My friend Trompier, the eighteen-year-old *mécanicien* [mechanic], was grateful for the cigarettes I got him (*"absolument introuvable à nous autres," "selon lui"*) ["ab-solutely not to be found for the rest of us," according to him], and told me to stop off at the *piste* [avi-

A Sopwith biplane from about 1915, probably similar to the one in which Leslie flew

ation field] on my way to work. I dropped from the *camion* [heavy duty military truck] as arranged, but my heart was rather forebod-ing, for the morning was foggy and only three machines were lined up outside the chic hangars.

Embarrassment for little Leslie—because the whole crowd of monitors, *élèves* [students], and *mecs* [slang, guys] looked at him cu-riously—at least so it feels. But Trompier runs up, shakes my hand and says, rather regretfully, that *"Il fait beaucoup mauvais temps."* ["The weather is really bad."] All hope is apparently gone. One mon-itor, encased in his eskimo or teddy bear, is ready in his plane. They swing his propeller. The motor catches with a spluttering roar, and he is off. Suddenly Tompier comes back and, jerking with his thumb, says *"Montez—là—Montez."* ["Climb on—there—climb on!"]. Hardly able to believe my ears, I walk over to the other Sopwith machine. How powerful and giant it looks from nearby, with its broad, gracefully tuned propeller-blades and the glistening rotary motor! I step upon the lower plane from the front, and climb into the front seat, directed by Trompier. The machines have double controls; but I am afraid to touch the *manche* [joystick] that stands before the seat, or to put my feet on the foot control. My eyes eat up the indicators and dials. There is a small windshield between my face and the propeller. The monitor, an old pilot, who teaches the *élevés*, clambers nonchalantly in behind. Trompier grasps the propeller, and calls "*Aspiration!*" ["Lift off!"] The pilot adjusts the gas and air levers and answers "*Aspiration!*" Tompier gives the motor a complete turn. You can hear the mixture sucked into the huge cylinders. "Contact!" The pilot gives her the spark and echoes "Contact!" One swift turn, and she catches with a roar and a gale strikes my face. The roar deepens and we start—we are off! Swiftly she skips along the sod—deafened, blown blindingly, I barely notice when we leave the ground. But here we are—climbing! Suddenly the machine seems to leap almost straight upward. What's he doing? Ah! That's great—but a serious thrill. We climb and climb and the fog cotton begins to race between us and the ground. I turn, exhilarated, and try to shout "*C'est chic!!*" ["This is great!!"] to the pilot. He sees me try and there's a twinkle and a tight-lipped smile. High and around we go—the squat hangars, the butterfly yellow planes, and the fields are far below. He cuts the motor, and, banking rakishly, we come around. We cannot plane down straight to the field, we are too high, I tell myself. Then like a flash, I hold tight—the plane has slanted deep down on its left wing—the right wing is almost vertical, and we are <u>falling</u>! The air rushes into my eyes, nose, and mouth. Stunned, I can't think; I just hold on and hope. Ah—when the ground seems dangerously near—she straightens, and whistles nearer the ground—he's going to stop . . . No—why! He gives her the gun full blast—and we tear along, a couple of feet above the soil, at eighty miles an hour, lift gradually, and then do that sudden bewildering upward leap again!

Around we go again, glide, and this time we straighten out to land—the wheels strike, we bounce along, the tail skid sticks in the ground more and more, and we stop. *Voila!*

I get out; the young *mecs* smile at me—at my inarticulate enthusiasm, and ask me if I have had *"des émotions"* ["some thrills"]. The *pilote*, who is *adjutant chef de piste* [chief warrant officer], by the way, asks me how I like the air. I try to tell him.

Then a crowd is watching another plane, skimming the row of walnut trees, almost hidden in the fog. *"Il va raccrocher une arbre"* ["It's going to hit a tree"], says one with a grin. Back he comes and lights nearby; he "taxis" his 'bus over to the crowd, and gets out. He is Lourme, I am told in a whisper—another monitor. *"Mais beaucoup imprudent, lui."* ["But he's really foolhardy."] So it seems, for Lourme, a ruddy, merry-eyed, full-faced fellow, begins to tell how he frightened an old peasant woman's horse *la-bas* [over there]. He imitates frantic bounds of the horse and the tense and despairing grip of *la bonne femme* on the reins. And how infectiously he laughs! Then he hears that Marot took me up *toute à l'heure* [earlier] and that he did a *chandelle* and a *glissade (sur l'aile)*—the leap and the slide I spoke of. I stand fascinated by the talk and the sights. At once, and very unexpectedly this time, they tell me to get in with Lourme! I'm ready for anything. That *beaucoup imprudent, lui* stuff couldn't hold me back for a fraction of a second. *"Aspiration!* Contact!" This time in the carefree accents of

Lourme. The roar and the gale, and we're off again! For my delectation he does a still more brutal *chandelle* than before and we're bound off across fields. *Tiens!* [How about that!] There's a little knot of artillerymen, pulling potatoes. We dive gloriously at them. The horses start, and the men, as we close over their heads, wave their hands enthusiastically and laugh.

We mount again—this is the sport of gods! *Voilà—une vache blanche, broutant seule* [Over there—a white cow, grazing alone]. By golly, we dive at her—and she gallops disconcertedly trying to hold her last mouthful without dropping it. The hawk-like swoop, dive, and climb is intoxicating. Turning, I laugh aloud to Lourme. We climb—up and up—flying towards the village of Crosses. There— there is Buisson—like a doll's house—and the barracks we set up. It looks like a house of cards! By gum, he'd better keep his eye out! It's no fun to get hung by the trousers to the church spire of Crosses! But he knows what he is doing . . . I see the peasant women at their doors, gazing idly up at us. Aeroplanes are everyday to them. We turn, and roar towards the *piste*. Only now am I confident enough to remember not to try to keep my vertical when the machine banks—but to lean with it. It makes you feel like part of the machine. We're flying rather low, now—what has he seen? Look—a wild duck flaps up out of the grass—we dive fiercely at it—and it barely escapes—this is hunting—with a 130-horse power engine and a propeller whirling 1200 times a minute!

Back high, around—a long, terrific wing-slip. I'm not used to it yet! For I hold on like grim death and am thankful that they put the belt on me this second trip—and we skim the ground, jounce, and slow to a stop . . . It's over—and I've experienced it! And my first rides weren't "plain sailing"—slowly up, soaring high above the ground for a few minutes and then gently down, either.

Sing the lullaby from "Jocelyn"[10] for me Mary—and I'll go to sleep in a minute.

Good night, *mon doux camarade* [my sweet friend]
Leslie

November 2, 1918, Leslie in Savigny en Septaine, Cher, to Mary in Cambridge

Dearest Mary,

I was deeply troubled, almost stunned yesterday when I read thy letter of October 4 and 8. How thee and thine have suffered—all while I didn't know—nor could know anything about it! The shadow which was so dark over thee in thy hour of trial and anxiety came down on me and has not lifted yet—though I pray that by this time Helen and thy mother are all well again. Of course thee must be, or I should feel it.

I followed thy urgent wish and burned the letter. In the high, black old fireplace were a few coals—I placed it on them and watched it burn, and it seemed that the warm breath of its burning brought me a whisper from thee—a whisper of cheer and hope. The ash of the letter was there partly intact, still holding a semblance of the form of the leaf—I picked it up and my eye fell upon two words "my tears," still discernable in shining black . . . Thy tears, Mary—my dearest—if I might have been with thee to help lift thy burden and share thy sorrow and hope! Who can foresee such things? We must be ready with strength and faith for any event, mustn't we? I confess, though, that the letter did give me a shock for the moment. The mere fact of its being down in black and white and from the hand of a veracious girl made my heart leap and stand still. Let her smile—I was stunned.

The flu is certainly in France, most of course, in the cities and towns; it spreads most rapidly there—so I am lucky to have left Paris and be living in the country. I certainly hope that none of us get an attack . . . .

Courage, mon amie, devant la catastrophe—t'en as du courage plus que les autres. Fie-toi a la miséricorde de Dieu. [Courage, my friend, in the face of the catastrophe. You have more courage towards it than others. Have faith in God's mercy.]

Good night, Mary—tomorrow I will write a real letter. We have been to town this afternoon. I drove the camion most of the way back along the road in the dark—we had no lights. Tomorrow morning, I am K. P. (kitchen police). I must be up to get our morning meal in from the other end of the house—how little insignificant cares and duties make suffering and sorrow lighter to bear!

Thy,
Leslie

November 6, 1918, Mary in Cambridge to Leslie in Savigny-en-Septaine, Cher

Dear Leslie,

There are so many things to tell you in the time I have to tell them in, that I don't know where to begin. I think I shall start with your letter written on October 6th—it was a splendid one—full of the spirit of work and *joie de vivre* from the certainty of beauty and truth. Of course it was not incoherent—just the interior of the wave as you say—now, Les, you mustn't write when you are tired after a hard day's work—promise me! I couldn't do it—that is why it is two weeks since I wrote last—I am so dead after rehearsals and studying, etc. that I can't write letters. But tonight I have the whole evening free just to sit by the fire and meditate and write . . . how one does appreciate a few moments of quiet when the days go by in one great whirl. I find as I write that my brain is more tired than I thought— so you will have to forgive me too if my wave is not as sparkling or so deep as it should be.

I liked so much what you said about the work over there making it impossible for the workers ever to feel at home again in a life of ease. The world has got to be entirely different after the war. I just hope and pray that [President] Wilson, and such as he, will not be drowned out by Roosevelts and Lodges. We are having our Massachusetts elections today for governor and senator and the Republicans are doing their best to give the Democrats a black eye. How foolish all the party squabbling is!

This morning came your letter written on October 16th in answer to mine written on coming home from Canada. It does not seem long after all between answers. To answer your letter—which was tranquil like the late hour at which you wrote. If you think now that you won't change your mind, it is only fair for me to tell you that the future is a great problem to me; and that I may feel that I cannot love one alone in order that I may love mankind the more. Now don't misunderstand me, Les—I know that you are saying that one love does not prevent all other love—but you see if I am called, I shall go—I do not know yet whether I am one of the chosen. Be sure that I shall let you know—for you are my dearest friend.

Just now I am thinking of going into a factory after I leave college—to see what life really is—to be one of the many and learn from them. My dream would be to go to France to help reconstruct, but somehow I feel it is romance and my love of independence that calls me there—and that the need is as great here as anywhere. Also there are many older more able and experienced women for reconstruction, and I don't think there are many who want to do what I dream of here.

And so, Les, since we know each other's thoughts as far as they can be known at present, let us be comrades as we agreed, and leave the rest for the future. It will be better for us both, that is all I can say. Don't think I am hard-hearted—it is because you are such a dear friend that I can bear to hurt you a little now for your own good later on. I have told you all this before, but I say it again "lest we forget."

Who do you suppose was here today—Packard.[11] He came to see if any of your family was in town who could look after your furniture. He is going off tonight to a Camp in Kentucky and didn't know what to do with some of your things (most of them he lent to a friend, but some things he will write to your mother about). He was anxious to hear all about you and said that Joe is now a very commanding figure as sergeant major at Harvard and will probably stay there all winter. He (Packard) said Baker was just holding out tempting bait now that he had to leave! Hard luck.

The symphony was glorious the other night. With Pierre Monteux[12] as leader of the remodeled orchestra (a great many Germans have left), they played César Franck's great masterpiece. The nuances of tone were most beautifully and delicately shaded and the ensemble playing was at once a whole and an intricate interweaving of tone. I seemed only to miss a feeling of sustained power—I can't explain it—a power that you feel even in the delicate touches when Muck[13] is leading. Perhaps it is the reflection of his personality as I saw it and not a real thing.

Another event of the past week was an interview with M. Mercier. He wants to start a Salle Française at Radcliffe, like the one at Harvard with a machine and papers, books, etc. I went to Miss Boody[14] about it, also visited the Harvard Salle—which is now in Seaver 9—and plans are afoot to carry out the idea. So many girls are anxious to learn to speak that I think it will be well used.

I must draw this conversation to a close now, *mon ami*, as I must rise betimes in the morning to give a last whack at the principle of diminishing returns in Ec. for a test. Good night, Les—(I wish you had been with me when I took a glorious walk by the river the other day; the colors were so lovely and I was so far from everyone that I sang to my heart's content.) On the other side of this page I am sending another poor poetic effort for your criticism—now please help me and say what is wrong.

As ever, your faithful comrade
Mary

A Dream

Far to the wind-swept meadows of the sun
I dreamed alone by shining corridors;
Already through the gates of dawn were flung
The banners of the day—when on the floor
A shadow darkly came to follow me.
It mocked my lonely dreaming, and my soul
Deep hurt with shame and grief I fled away
Back to the sunless places whence I came,
Losing in shade my all too-shadowed self.

The darkness heavy hung—'till hand in hand
Dreamers of dreams and workers of the world
Together braving nights of common sorrow
Won the bright dawn of love's immortal morrow.

*A common room used by the FRU workers
for meals and relaxation*

November 6, 1918, Leslie in Savigny-en-Septaine, Cher, to Mary in Cambridge

Dearest Mary,

Forgive me for putting off my letter to thee so long. Part of my reason for not writing sooner is that we have been augmented by five men ... we are now twelve—which makes difficult writing at the common table. And if I try to sit up to be alone with my thoughts of thee—the light is in the eyes of the would-be sleepers—and they object to having the windows remain closed after their retiring hour, which varies from eight o'clock to ten at the latest. I blush to tell thee how well acquainted I still am with the small and quiet hours of the morning. But I can't be satisfied to work all day at manual labor and not have any mental or imaginative stimulus.

The heavy shadow of anxiety for thee and thy family's safety still hangs before my eyes, although the cause or reason for it has, probably, disappeared long ago. Oh, I hope and pray that it has!

In looking over an August number of Life, I happened to see that its Book Review department had received two plays—prize winners for the Drama League's contest for patriotic place—one was Rachel Field's and the other was Doris Halman's![15] Thee may be sure I felt proud of them—as members of the Workshop, to have walked off with the blue ribbon.

Peace looks very near now. Pray God that it may please Him for us to have a merciful heart to our enemy!

This is a disgracefully thin letter, but yet it carries unseen and priceless sentiments.

From Thy

Les

Boston citizens celebrating the end of the war
on November 11, 1918

7

Armistice

THE WAR WAS OVER! After four years of bloody conflict, the Great War ended. On November 11, 1918, the agreement between the Germans and the Allies to end the fighting on the Western Front was signed in Compiègne, France. Officially, the war in Europe ended at 11 a.m. Paris time, the "eleventh hour of the eleventh day of the eleventh month."

Mary and the residents of the East Coast of the United States heard the bells ringing in celebration at five a.m. People celebrated all over the world, dancing in the streets, waving flags, shouting, and singing. In France and America, November 12 was declared a legal holiday for prayer and joyful celebration. On November 16, President Wilson issued his Thanksgiving Day Proclamation:

> "It has long been our custom to turn in the autumn of the year in praise and thanksgiving to Almighty God for His many blessings and mercies to us as a nation. This year we have special and moving cause to be grateful and to rejoice. God has in His good pleasure given us peace. It has not come as a mere cessation of

arms, a mere relief from the strain and tragedy of war. It has come as a great triumph of right. Complete victory has brought us, not peace alone, but the confident promise of a new day as well in which justice shall replace force and jealous intrigue among the nations. Our gallant armies have participated in a triumph which is not marred or stained by any purpose of selfish aggression. In a righteous cause they have won immortal glory and have nobly served their nation in serving mankind. God has indeed been gracious. We have cause for such rejoicing as revives and strengthens in us all the best traditions of our national history. A new day shines about us, in which our hearts take new courage and look forward with new hope to new and greater duties."[1]

For many pacifists, the conclusion of the hostilities was bittersweet. On November 17, a Mass for France's dead was held in the cathedral at Troyes. One of the Unit workers, Owen Stephens, wrote in his diary:

"The church was dim and dark; clouds covered the sky. Black hangings covered the lower windows of the apse and choir; a band of mourning hung completely around the walls; above it were lined thousands of motionless flags . . . A vast crowd of darkly clothed people filled the nave, the four side aisles, the transepts; it pressed against pillars and against walls . . . I was thinking of the ten million men who had been killed by men and the ten million women who were mourning, not that the men had killed men, but that their men were dead . . . How many war widows and war mothers are going to find their contentment in secluded mourning, and how many are going to find it in the long, long, hard, hard work of creating the laws, governments, customs, and religion which will eliminate war!"[2]

The terms of the Armistice required the Germans to evacuate the territories on the Western Front within two weeks. Allied forces were to occupy the left bank of the Rhine, with a neutral zone established on the right bank. German military equipment was abandoned; aircraft, railway wagons, trucks, and the entire submarine fleet were surrendered. The blockade remained in effect, and all German ships were captured. Limitations on shipping were removed. Allied prisoners of war were released, although German POWs were held until the formal peace treaty was signed. The Armistice was a compromise. The Germans saw the terms as punitive, but reluctantly accepted the conditions as they were in no condition to continue to fight. France was intent on punishing the Germans and saw the terms as too lenient. Wilson agreed to sign only after the German chancellor announced Kaiser Wilhelm II's abdication.[3]

The French also took to the streets, but Leslie's celebration was more subdued than Mary's. The work of the Friends Unit was even more necessary; the Armistice enabled more refugees to return to their homes in areas devastated by the war. Homes and businesses had been destroyed. Fields and farms littered with battle debris and poisoned by chemical armaments could not be used to produce food to support the returning citizens. Friends mobilized to provide food, clothing, and medical supplies and to help rebuild roads, schools and other public buildings, water supplies, and energy systems. They built community centers and schools to aid in reestablishing the social and community life of the villages. American Friends agreed to continue raising funds to support the members of the Unit and the work they were doing in France. To many in the Unit, like the soldiers who fought in the battles, the end of the war meant going home, back to colleges and jobs, and a return to their families. But those who were really committed to relief and reconstruction wanted to stay. The reconstruction work would be a continuation of the jobs they were doing during the war—plowing fields, restocking farms, rebuilding houses, repatriating refugees, and running maternity hospitals. Some of the absolutist COs, including Leslie's brother Ronald, now felt clear to join the Friends in France, which improved the morale of the remaining FRU workers. Leslie decided to remain.

November 10, 1918, Leslie in Savigny-en-Septaine, Cher, to Mary in Cambridge

Dearest Mary—

Tonight there came over me again, with renewed force, the realization of the blessedness and joy of helping others . . . Last night I dreamed that I was home again, and met thee . . . the realest Mary that I have yet seen in sleep: for when we walked together I had the deep sense of comradeship which I learned only from thy presence. When I awoke it was not a forgotten <u>phantom</u>; it really seemed as if I had spoken with thee, walked with thee, and sweetest of all, had kissed thy hand. Maybe that is why I did my best to be good to the other fellows today; I don't know—but the little I was able to do made me happier than it did them . . . and, best of everything, proving beyond a doubt that thee is the sweetest and best comrade and helper in the world, it made me think constantly of thee, and of thy natural love for such beautiful service . . . .

Six new men have joined our *équipe*; four of them have come through camp as COs. Fine chaps. And Mary—which following is no news to thee, but I can't help saying it—Ronald has decided to come over! It will be great for him and greater for me, if we get the chance to work together.

Mrs. Davis, although very busy, wrote me a letter on the 16th. She says that Dr. Dana brought thee and Marian around for a constitutional shortly before, that thee seemed well—oh, I hope that thee has not hurt thyself in any way by working too hard for others before thee was strong enough! And thy mother and Helen—tell them that I have thought often of them . . . if I might only have foreseen their illness I should have written them as best I could . . . In more ways than one this terrible, dragged-out crossing time is the greatest hardship I have to undergo.

Nov. 11

The war is over! How sweet those words sound in the ears of the French people . . . they are as happy as children—not that the Hun is beaten, but that war is ended. Flags flew this morning and work at the factory in Bourges was stopped—everybody came out to parade, drink, and rejoice . . . that suffering has reached the final post.

O for a real socialistic revolution in Germany!—For not only a republic, but a democracy—and what a democracy that might be! The Kaiser and Junkerdom[4] are mere incidentals in the face of such a rebirth. The great events which fall with the hours of each day— how eagerly they are watched by those vitally interested in world federation and brotherhood. I pray that our nation may not stain itself by putting any barriers in the way of universal brotherhood.

What will Harvard and the other militarized colleges do now? Will they hold on to their ridiculous aping of the Prussians for the rest of the year—or will they call it off at midyears?

My term of enrollment in the Unit is over with the war, but I prefer to stay at least until I have ended a year—perhaps two. I don't know yet—I'll do whatever I feel called to do. Almost all the other organizations will feel like letting down and slowing up—but the Friends just take a deep breath and go at it harder than ever ... May the Reconstruction period of France and Germany be dominated by a more humane spirit and less bitterness than that of our Civil War ....

The other day the chief of the refugee relief department of the Red Cross came down to inspect our work. The whole inspecting party seemed pleased ... Motion pictures were taken while we were setting up one of the houses—perhaps it will be shown in America in <u>Pathe's Weekly</u> or <u>Hearst's</u>—perhaps even some of our friends may see them, and so feel nearer to us and our efforts.

M. Leloire tells me that the Red Cross is in favor of establishing

Unit workers using tractors
to prepare the land for agriculture

that tractor school for French farmers here at Buisson—that it has furnished the necessary funds; in short, that the thing is going through, war or no war, for it will be a long while before means of living will be re-established in the devastated countries; and that they want me to stay on here with Chambers and Hanson, who understand the tractors, learn from them, and help to teach the farmers their use ... and to act as general interpreter. I'm not sure of anything yet,

except that the Friends want to concentrate their efforts on one district—Verdun—and make something visible and lasting. It may be
that I shall go there—no one can tell. But I hope, wherever I go, that
I may be with Ronald ... as I wrote to him, I don't like to think that
the curtain has been dropped upon our boyhood companionship ...
and I want to encourage him and study with him for Harvard ... I'm
certain that, catastrophes aside, he'll get to Harvard and through.

I'm thankful for the influence of Christian brotherhood that the
splendid Friends have on me. It's a precious thing, Mary ... but not
so dear as the assurance of thy loving comradeship and inspiration
... To recall any of the memories of thy friendship with thee is to
make me happy ... Time and circumstance cannot erase the tiniest
joy from my heart—and I pray to be kept true and made worthy.

Thy Leslie, who loves thee

*November 17, 1918, Leslie in Savigny-en-Septaine, Cher, to Mary in
Cambridge*

Dearest Mary,

I received today, after quite a period of what one might call eager
apathy, thy beautiful letter, the ninth. Apathy, because I have felt
that I have been living for myself. No happiness nor moment of inspiration has come of it ....

But thee doesn't know the joy and contemplative thankfulness
that thy letter gave birth to in me. The first letter after the heavy
shadow of sickness had lifted from thee ... To find it so urgent in its
generous call to love the individual, and its lease on new life!

I am sending thee a letter from Mme. Brocaille, who keeps house for us at 93 Boule Miche—I treasure it, and should like thee to keep it for me. It is a very touching letter when one remembers the terrible suffering she has gone through, under bombardment for two years—one of her two children killed, her husband a prisoner in Germany since the beginning almost—four long years. A woman that loved to sing with her husband in her own home, but who hadn't sung for years, until I begged her to. So grateful she was for the interest I was able to show and for the little words of kindness—the spirit of which I learned from thee.

How much depends on [President] Wilson, and on the British elections! If there is no League of Nations, all inclusive, after the greatest slaughter in the history of mankind, even the last paltry excuse or puny palliation of war's crime will be wiped clear.

America is in grave danger . . . she has won the war with practically no suffering . . . and put in enough fighting to make the people thirsty at the sight of blood . . . Now if the flu, or some war-plague, should really sweep the country, and sweep the foul realization of what war brings, into the minds of men—they wouldn't be so ready to foster that militarism which they were reported to be crushing on the Western Front.

I am glad for thee and for Harvard and Radcliffe that Mr. Briggs had not come over. An influence like his is urgently necessary when peace, savage joy, and swagger are to follow one another there.

The fire is almost dead—and the moon has been wrapped in the clouds . . . The night is passing, *ma très-chère*, and the darkness is falling from before my eyes.

Thy,
Leslie

November 19, 1918, Mary in Cambridge to Leslie in
Savigny-en-Septaine, Cher

Dear Les,

I have just been reading the flighty part of your last letter to mother and Helen—we all envy you your experience—how thrilling it must have been to be a giant bird for a few minutes. Your description is so vivid I can hear the whirring and feel the wind in my face . . . but you did such crazy things, I think you must live a charmed life to come out alive. The next time you go, I advise you to tour complacently through the sky and not try any aerobatic stunts!

I hope you observe how sanely this letter is written—I have calmed down somewhat since a letter I started to you a week ago and then tore up. When we had the false alarm that the Armistice had been signed—it was about noon on coming home from college that I saw a paper—it was too wonderful to believe—I thought it must be unofficial, yet great hope and joy kept surging within me, and I didn't know what to do—so I took my Oxford Book and went down to the river to collect myself. I was walking alone by the shore where it is quite lonely and I heard bells begin to ring and whistles shriek—then four boatloads of sailors came rowing in hurried disorder toward me—and when they saw me they all took off their hats and shouted and I heard one man say "Allelujah"—so I knew the great day must have come and I shouted back to them with all my might; the ground was like air under my feet, and I ran and ran till I found myself in the cemetery. There I sat down on a bench exhausted with alternate tears and laughter while the bells and whistles pierced through my brain. For once I could not read the Oxford Book and instead I tried to scribble an incoherent bit of my joy to you—it was mostly monosyllables and exclamation points, and when I found later that my joy was unfounded I threw it away. The disillusionment was terrible—when we had all pictured the quiet guns and the trenches no longer red with death. It seemed as though the world had begun again only to fall back into chaos. Then the days went by with lessons and work as usual and every morning the eager hope that the coming day would bring peace. At last on the 11th in the middle of the night I woke up and heard the air teeming with mysterious joyous bells. I was up in a second and waking Helen saying "Oh Helen! Helen! Wake up, and hear the bells! It must be peace! It must be peace!" Then we flew into each other's arms and ran to wake Mother. We all stood at the open window looking at the peaceful twinkling stars and trying to realize the joy that would spread over the world with the coming dawn. Then for the first time since war was declared we hung out our giant flag. Of course there were no more thoughts of sleep, and we dressed in awed excitement while the bells pealed on. When we were hardly dressed Margaret Garrison and Marian Svecinski came bursting in the front door and we all flew into one another's arms with shrieks of joy.

Oh, the glorious happiness at the thought of <u>no more war</u>—we just had to go in town to church to thank the Almighty. As daylight hid the stars and covered the earth, it seemed like a beautiful purifying and healing mantle for the poor suffering world. We went to St. Paul's—there was no service as there had been no time to arrange one—so we just kneeled in the great dark old church and gave thanks—we came out exalted but more quiet. As we went down Tremont Street (it was then still early morning) we met another bunch of Radcliffe girls full to the brim with joy and enthusiasm. We banded together and on the next corner were recruited by more

Radcliffe girls till we had a band of about twenty-five. People were beginning to collect in the streets with flags and beaming faces—before we knew it we found ourselves singing, and before I knew it I found myself leading, and there we were marching along singing the "Marseillaise" in ladylike but enthusiastic spirits. We went up and down the Mall perfectly joyous, and everyone we saw cheered while the men took off their hats. We met other little impromptu parades of working girls and men. We each cheered the other long and loud. Finally we found ourselves down in front of City Hall with a large addition to our ranks. We all climbed the steps and sang there while every hat was off in the crowded street below. We were all uplifted with a wonderful exaltation and everyone in the streets felt like brothers and sisters in their happiness. We kept up our parading 'till we were pretty tired (about 8:45) and there we suddenly thought of Cambridge and Radcliffe—now that Boston was roused (the streets were by that time jammed with people who were let off from work or who didn't go). I wish you could have seen the hundreds of joyous faces. We thought we ought to wake up our home town. So we all piled into the car and came out to the Square—it was dead! Not a sign of excitement anywhere—but we weren't to be daunted, we marched in formation into the Radcliffe Yard singing the "Marseillaise" and found that classes were going on as usual!!! Imagine it. We were still so tense from the excitement of Boston that we didn't stop where we should have—and what do you suppose we did? (Now Leslie don't be shocked!) We marched right into the theatre where there was a big Ec. Class (which I was cutting)—thru the theatre and out again singing. We never stopped to think that anyone would object—it was entirely spontaneous and thoughtless. The professor was furious—dismissed the class and went to the office. As soon as

I learned this (which surprised me greatly), I ran up to him and humbly begged his pardon. Then Miss Boody called him into her office and when he came out, I went in and said I felt terribly if in our enthusiasm we had disturbed the other people who chose to work. Miss Boody was awfully dear and said that Dr. Burbank felt very badly that he had lost his temper, and she asked me to write to him my regrets so as to rest his mind. This I assured her I would do, and I also offered to beg the class's pardon for disturbing them (it appeared that some of the girls were very cut up about it).

Miss Boody said we should have waited for the legal holiday next day to express our enthusiasm (as if spontaneous joy could be bottled up and preserved for later use!)—and she also said "Miss Peabody, if the college people do not keep their heads in a time like this what can we expect of others," and I said, "Miss Boody, if people are not going to show their joy naturally and in the heat of the moment at such a great thing as peace—then the world will more willingly tolerate war."

Of course we did not argue about it—I realized that we had gone too far and had unfairly disturbed others so I repaired the damage as best I could and it is all over. I am glad that it all happened because it was an experience in the crowds of Boston that I shall never forget all my life—and I also learned a lesson that personal emotion may be selfish if carried too far. (Also, a keener realization that the Armistice is not the end but only the beginning in the fight for liberty.) I think the college ought to have closed but it didn't, so we ought to have accepted it. I know however that I for one own the weakness of character of not being able to sit and think <u>economically</u> at one of the greatest moments in all the history of the world.

Of course the next day—the "legal holiday"—there were grand parades—mostly military. Mother, Helen, M. Garrison, M. Svecenski, and myself and others marched in the Socialist parade with red banners and cheered for the Bolshevicki—we did not go with the military parade but marched out to Roxbury to a big hall where they had a meeting. Oh Leslie, I was never so impressed in all my life as when that great roomful of men and women sang the "Internationale" in many different languages. Then there were pledges and gifts of money to start a Socialist newspaper in Boston. Men pledged $5 and $10 for whom you knew it meant giving their very bread. Oh, they are the heroes and the hope of the future. The vision and idealism at that meeting seemed to consecrate us all to the great work of freedom in the future.

In the evening there was wild hilarity in all the streets. I had a frivolous and jolly time—going everywhere and doing and seeing everything—sailors and soldiers threw powder in the girl's faces so that before the end of the evening our hair had turned white and our hats were covered with snow [a curious custom, but I can find no reference to throwing powder in girl's faces]. This belated celebration was so different in spirit from the exaltation of the morning before!

We learned today that there are not enough men to sing at Appleton at Christmas so the girls have been asked to do it alone. Another strange thing that the war has brought about is that ten of us from Radcliffe have been asked to usher at Cambridge Symphony—men are so scarce. Just think what an innovation—a great opportunity for us!

They say that Harvard will probably keep up its present regime all the year, as lots of men are getting opportunities for an education—those who want to will probably be let off, they say.

Appleton chapel on the Harvard campus

What are your plans, Les? How long do you expect to reconstruct? They must need you even more now. What you say in answer
to my struggles for the future shows what you are made of—you are
a splendid comrade—

As ever,
Mary

November 26, 1918, Leslie in Paris to Mary in Cambridge

Dearest Mary,

Thy tenth letter came tonight, finding me in Paris again, waiting
to be assigned out. Our work near Bourges—building sixteen *dis-*
mountable barracks for refugee use, seems to be practically in vain
now that the war has ended. They are to take down thirteen of them

sooner or later—leaving but three. The reason is, of course, that the refugees want to cultivate their own homeland, and that right early. Such a setting at naught of our sustained effort is disappointing— but what a small disappointment compared to the cruel setback of the earlier work, when the reconstruction work was repassed by the fiery wave of the front lines! I was prepared for disappointments, hardships, and disillusionment when I came to France, but my enthusiasm for the work is growing, not diminishing.

House being built by Unit workers

In spite of the frightful loss of sleep that I subjected my poor patient body to in writing thee letters through the silent watches of the night, I am in excellent health; I have put on weight and color ... But really Mary, don't think that I hurt myself by sitting up ... it was a labor of love and added to my happiness.

What thee says about my apparent aging in the picture makes me reflect. I remember Jim Norton looking from the picture (the passport one) to me and back again yesterday in the Provost Marshall's office in Bourges and remarking how much older I looked.

Besides, we had an unwritten law in our *équipe* that every man who could should raise a moustache and make and carry a cane back to Paris. All of us but two were able to carry out the first requirement; and that two made valiant efforts . . . but their lips were not fertile. Every one of us had a cane made from some beautiful straight hawthorn or wild cherry shoots . . . Garfield Cox[5], one of the new men (who, I think I told thee, reminds me so much of Clarence), aged 24, thought at first (I suppose because of the moustache) that I was older than he! *Ma mie, je vieillis—il ne faut pas me faire perde ma jeunesse, et la fraîcheur de ma joie et de mes efforts.* [My friend, I am aging—it's not necessary to lose my youth and the freshness of the joy of my efforts.] It is true that I don't feel so young as I did . . . that in this short time experiences, physical and spiritual, have left their effect. How like an old stager I talk!

It was hard to leave Buisson Farm; in spite of having to read and write by candlelight, we had a splendid big old fireplace, warmth, real comradeship, excellent country food, and good hard work in the open air. To enter Paris after two months and a half in the country gives one a strange effect. One is dazzled by the bright lights and bewildered by the movement. But you feel so strong and healthy— that you are wearing clothes and that clothes are not wearing you.

Nov. 28, Thanksgiving

Thanksgiving night! We have had an excellent dinner and games after it—about fifty of us. I met fellows I have never seen before, but whom I was anxious to know, and Donnell, one of the fellows from the CO barracks where Ronald was at Camp Dix!

Our bunch leaves tomorrow morning early for Sermaize. It is possible that I may get the job of Secretary of the Works Department up there—to handle dealing with the French, etc. I shall be glad to get there, because all of the Friends' efforts are to be centered on reconstructing the Verdun region—and we shall be moved from Sermaize to Verdun . . . But another possibility arises. Horace thinks he'll have to go up and report to work in the Verdun area, and wants someone to take his place, meaning me, if I am found able. And then,

if practicable, he would like to get into other work, if I could continue to edit <u>Reconstruction</u>. I see advantages, great physical ones, in the outdoor reconstruction work; again I see the advantages of learning more French and meeting more cultured people in Paris. I can't decide yet.

Garage at Unit headquarters in Sermaize

Oh, I'd give anything to be there for Christmas carols! Last time's was the most beautiful choral singing that I ever was in. When the performance comes off, picture me over among the first basses, putting my whole soul into it, for I shall be there in spirit.

Thee won't forget last Christmas, and I wish thee a happy, happy Christmas and the rich joy of a great dream of love and service.

Thy,
Leslie

November 29, 1918, Mary in Cambridge to Leslie in Sermaize

Leslie, my dear comrade,

No one could have more beautiful letters than I have had from you this week. I realize more than ever how ideal our friendship is—I think we understand one another better now than we ever have before; and we are rich in understanding, for there are not many people whose ideals coincide so exactly as ours do. How often I, too, dream that I am struggling toward my hopes—and always when I am discouraged I feel that my comrade is not far away. When I am happy, too, I feel your sympathy.

I hope you will have a very, very happy Christmas. How much that great day grows in meaning when we realize the immortal beauty of the life of Jesus. This year we can sing "Peace on Earth Good Will to Men" without a great lump in our throats, and with the fire to make it come true, in our hearts. We are rehearsing the carols for Appleton—I think I told you that it will be just girls this year—how strange it will seem.

I am so very glad that Ronald has decided to go over—I didn't think he would be able to resist your encouragement. A year ago this time, who would ever have thought that you two would now be over tilling the soil of France. What do you suppose—Professor Hoernle[6] became so interested in the COs through some letters that Margaret Garrison showed him in connection with Phil. 18 [a senior level philosophy class at Radcliffe] that he has formed a CO Committee in the Harvard Liberal Club—isn't that great. They are going to look into the conditions of the men at Leavenworth about whom we have been sending telegrams to Sect. Baker. We are also getting petitions filled asking for their release. The Harvard

S.A.T.C. is to break up in a month and we are hoping then to get into communication with Liberals over there and help put struggling Y.D. [Young Democracy] back on its feet. At present we are giving what extra time we have in at the League of D.C., the Women's Trade Union League, and the Consumers League[7], and we hope in the course of winter to get many recruits in the way of Radical Clubs started in different places as branches of Y. D. This organizing work is fascinating, and I find it hard to know when I ought to study—I have filled out my application for honors and really ought to study all the time if I expect even a humble "cum"—as you know, the great college problem is how to divide your time best among all the things you want to do, *n'est-ce pas?*

I am afraid I shall have to say farewell to Dramatics for the year, tho' Aime Martin says they will surely have a French play in May (just when I shall be studying hardest—oh dear, oh dear!). Martin is probably coming to speak at our next Cercle meeting at Radcliffe—won't that be fun. I think he will just love it, in the midst of so many girls!

We had such a nice Thanksgiving Day yesterday—a lot of us young people went for a walk in the morning. My cousin Tom Homer was leader of the party and where do you suppose he took us—to Prospect Hill in Waltham. It was perfectly beautiful—we rambled over the hills getting a gorgeous view and then wound around down into the valley toward Watertown. We were splendidly hungry when we came home to the table laden down with good things. I never felt so gratified in my life as when we all bowed our heads in a happy circle around the home table and thought of all those we loved the wide world over. It was a memorable day. In the afternoon we played games and danced. I was full of spirits but somehow they were put-on spirits, for although the young people were splendid fun, the boys were so superficial that I felt no really common interest to enthuse about. Unconsciously I measure all my friends to your measuring stick, and they don't bear the test very well . . . the result is that in the midst of jollification I suddenly felt as tho' I would much prefer to write to you, than struggle so hard to find something worthwhile in my partner. But we must keep at our tasks, and by comparing notes we can encourage each other. How often one's imagination comes to the rescue too, doesn't it?

I am so sorry that you worried about us and the "flu." I meant to make my first letter on getting well plainly cheerful and certain of the recovery of all, but my optimism probably (tho' great to me at the time of writing) had not seemed so to you in proportion. I worry about you with all the "flu" over there—now <u>do</u>, <u>do</u> take care of yourself—how thankful I am you are not in crowded Paris.

I was so interested in your saying that it was peace the French seemed to celebrate more than victory. Here at first too it was peace that made us laugh and cry at once, and later the cry of victory tried hard to drown it out. Although I try not to believe it, things seem more conservative than ever—and the socialists are suppressed on every hand. There was a dreadful riot in N. Y. when the soldiers and sailors forcibly broke up their big meetings in Madison Square Garden where Scott Nearing was speaking. Mrs. Davis was at the meeting, but had left before the attack was made. The papers are full of "Red Flag Riots," Bolshevicki assassinations, etc.[8] I almost am willing to lose what little real news there is by not reading the paper at all. Wouldn't it be glorious if Germany could find her own feet in a real democracy—and I have faith she will if we let her alone politically and just sent relief in the way of food, etc. Wouldn't it be thrilling to help reconstruction in Germany along the President's splendid lines. We will feel like a lost country when he goes over— but I am mighty glad he is going—his presence will have great influence I should think. Your plans for tractoring and interpreting sound most interesting. If you stay over there until college next fall, you will have a good long time to work with Ronald and could be in Harvard again as a regular junior in 1919. Probably lots of your friends shall be back then too. Harvard has sent out a sort of proclamation urging the boys to come back and finish their education.

I am going to keep track of the movies in town for Reconstruction pictures—I am bound to see you building a house! Every board your Quaker Unit puts up is a monument to your splendid idealism and spirit of brotherhood. Mrs. Davis and others (Fellowship groups in N. Y., Phila., and elsewhere) are planning a sort of brotherhood of gospel workers for the COs when they are all released later. There are no definite plans but the men are to go out like the Disciples and preach the brotherhood spirit.

Leslie, I think I am becoming a Quaker—it is so simple and beautiful. It is a great compliment to say that with them I inspire you. You too inspire me, *mon ami*—and you are living your beliefs. While I am still only seeing visions and dreaming dreams, you are doing both.

Joyeux Noël, mon camarade. May the light of our Christmas candles stream across the sea to you and yours to us. Get some friends together and sing "The First Noel" (you sing tenor in the chorus). Oh isn't it great. The Christmas thrill goes all through one at the thought of it. It was last Christmas after the carols that we got to know each other wasn't it? Merry, merry Christmas and the happiest of new years, *mon cher ami.*

Marie

Thee and Me

When I am gay and dancing in the sun
I seem to see thy face alight with smiles
And to my laughing song tho' half begun
Thy voice comes echoing over sunny miles.

When I am sad I think of thee as so,
A sharer in my momentary pain;
Yet when in sympathy thy dear eyes glow,
Smiling to make thee smile I laugh again.

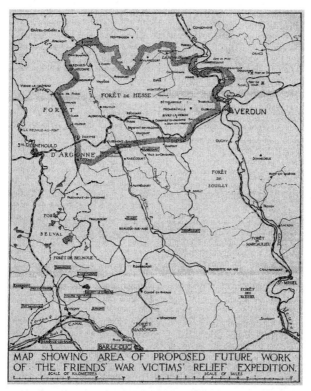

MAP SHOWING AREA OF PROPOSED FUTURE WORK
OF THE FRIENDS' WAR VICTIMS' RELIEF EXPEDITION.

Map showing the work of Friends relief in Verdun,
published in Reconstruction

8

Still More Work to Do

THE WAR WAS OVER, ending Leslie's contract with the FRU. However, he was offered the opportunity to remain in France and felt called to stay. The need for the services of the *équipes* was greater than ever. Now that refugees and *émigrés* could return to their villages, Friends would be able to provide vital support in helping to repair houses, distributing furniture and bedding, supplying seeds and farm tools, loaning out heavy agricultural equipment, and providing medical services to the French people.

In November 1918, shortly after the Armistice, the General Committee of the FRU met to decide whether to continue the work in France. Since the end of 1917, the Friends had begun developing plans to concentrate the work of the Unit in Verdun, in the Canton of Argonne in northeastern France, the region that was hardest hit by the German invasion. The Committee, after long discussion, adopted the following statement:

> "The principal obligation of the Mission is in the area west of Verdun which has been assigned to us; the work of all departments should develop with an increasing concentration in that area as the primary consideration and no new work should be undertaken

which in the opinion of the Executive Committee is likely to conflict with that increasing concentration. The sense of obligation felt by our former workers in the Somme to their former fellow-villagers must also be taken into consideration. Work in the Châtillon district or elsewhere outside our special area in the eastern Marne and the Meuse should be undertaken with the full understanding that such work is secondary to the Verdun work."[1]

Lewis Gannett summarized the necessity for such a decision:

"We have not unlimited resources in men, women, or money and with the end of the war in sight we must reckon with the loss of many workers. Our minds must control our hearts; infinite as is the destruction and need at Châtillon or Varennes or any one of a thousand other points, they are but pin-pricks on the map of invaded France, and if we permit our sympathies to drag us left and right in response to every urgent appeal we should never achieve the profounder results for which we strive."[2]

Starting in November 1918, the Allies advanced northwest of Verdun. As soon as the area became safe, Quaker workers moved in to help clear and rebuild houses and community centers in the villages. In December 1918, only twelve men were serving in the Verdun area. Over the next few months, the staff grew to over one hundred Friends to meet the needs of more than ten thousand refugees returning home. The fighting had been almost continuous in this area. Only about five percent of the houses were left standing and these were badly damaged.[3] One British worker described the battlefield in his assigned area:

"On all sides can be seen the debris of an army: shells, cartridges, rotting clothes and boots, and rusty food tins by the hundreds. It is these last which give an air of everyday reality to the scene which otherwise (so bare and blasted as it is) might be taken almost for a freak of the imagination or the work of some supernatural power. When one sees a 'Skipper' sardine tin amongst all this chaos, then with a jump one is brought to the astounding fact that all this destruction is the work of modern civilisation and that all the resources of civilisation are behind it."[4]

With financial assistance from the French government, the Friends established their headquarters at Grange-le-Comte in the Argonne region. The area had been used as the divisional headquarters of the French and American armies, and most of the military buildings had survived the war. This center included accommodations for the Unit workers in barracks no longer needed by the American Army, as well as extensive outbuildings to store supplies to support the Mission workers, goods to be sold to the villagers, and agricultural machinery. Barns were used as stables and for breeding livestock. Electricians from the FRU installed a local area telephone system and wired the dining hall, medical barracks, post office, and stores. The American Army provided trailers and fuel for distributing agricultural tractors to the villages and for moving pre-fabricated house sections.[5]

The goal of the project was to help the returning residents in this region become independent so that they would only rely on the government for a limited time.[6] Friends established canteens in each village to feed the refugees until they were able to provide for themselves and hostels for people who had no other shelter. The French government provided repatriation money to the residents of the villages, and the Friends set up cooperative stores to limit selfish profiteering, selling building materials, furnishings, household goods, food, and other necessities, all at or under cost. Eventually each village store was handed over as a viable business to a local society, the Meusienne Co-operative, and shares in the shops were given to the families in the village.[7] Friends also prepared large communal gardens for every village and provided vegetable seeds to all families who asked for them, so that people would be able to plant food crops as soon as they moved back.[8]

Friends unloading supplies and household goods
to help furnish the houses and cooperative stores

Relief workers, under the direction of British Friend Sophia Fry,[9] also aided in the reestablishment of community life by opening libraries and community centers and reviving lost industries, including pottery, basket making, spinning and weaving, needlework, mattress making, and boot making. These goods were sold in the local stores and overseas to raise funds for the community.[10] Friends set up kindergartens and schools for children, many of whom had never attended any formal classes. Workers even had to teach children games; as one worker said, "At first the children seemed scarcely to know how to play, and it was explained that they had forgotten their games."[11]

FRU workers accompanied families to homes to provide moral support and to help them make decisions about what was needed to rebuild their houses and farms and what equipment, implements, and furniture they lacked. The Unit workers then initiated steps to obtain the necessities for each family and, if warranted, arranged temporary housing.[12]

Village children running to get supplies for their families

The French government encouraged villagers to do the reconstruction work through the cooperative societies run by the French citizens so that community life could begin to return to normal. The refugees were employed as helpers in the work, partly for wages and partly in exchange for the services they received. On some properties, farming was no longer viable due to the poor soil, trenches and shell holes, and the possible presence of unexploded bombs. The FRU workers encouraged those families to raise sheep, goats, pigs, chickens, and rabbits, and they often supplied a small amount of livestock. When barns and stables were needed as winter set in, the Friends negotiated with the military for permission to use army buildings in the district for the village livestock.[13]

The Friends also brought medical services. The maternity hospital at Chalon was reopened, and health centers were established in many of the villages. District nurses coped with localized epidemics of measles and diphtheria and administered first aid. Doctors affiliated with the Friends and other organizations traveled among the villages, providing dental and optical services; during March and April alone, over one hundred French people were furnished with glasses. Leslie's Unit worked to construct improvements to sanitation and water supplies.[14]

Through the efforts of Henry Scattergood, the American Army gave Friends access to five depots or "dumps" of material and supplies. Rufus Jones reported that "this material covered many acres at each dump and consisted of lumber, bar-iron and steel, farm and road implements of every sort,

The Army gave the Friends material and supplies from several dumps.

miles upon miles of barbed wire, and an almost indescribable mélange of all material which might be useful in a modern war."[15] Among the indispensable items salvaged from the dumps were building nails—an abundance of them. In just a day and a half from a dump near Langres, six mechanics salvaged three tons of new and used parts for repair of the FRU vehicles. Even Leslie found the dumps handy, finding paper and inks that he could use in setting up a new publishing operation for the Unit. The French government also allowed Friends to salvage from some of the German abandoned materials. As Leslie reported in the FRU newsletter:

> "Being badly in need of railroad transport to move cars loaded with Mission property from Souhesmes to the East line at Clermont, for shipment, the transport chief made acquisitive, inquiring gestures in the direction of the *Militarischeeisenbahnmotorwagen* [German military railway motorcar], which had

caught his eye. The French army, which was guarding the dump, said, "*Mais oui, nom d'un chien, emporte-le!*" (meaning, "But yes, name of a dog, carry him off!") or words to that effect. The Transport Department, never needing to be told twice to salvage something, hitched a three-ton Liberty[16] to the *Militarischeeisenbahn-motorwagen*, whom we have called Jerry, to save space, and rolled in the direction of Grange-le-Comte . . . Jerry stood for days in the court at Grange, having his dirty weather-beaten coat of *feld-grau* [field-grey] exchanged for the Mission silver grey, and being decorated with the Mission's name and star, and his internal workings were arranged inside the garage . . . Great and glorious was the day when Jerry ran down to the railroad under his own power, climbed onto the track, and thuttered off, clanging his bell, and tooting his whistle."[17]

Much of the material in the salvage dumps was used by the Friends in their work; the rest was sold at very low prices, and the railroads agreed to carry it free of charge. The money from the sale of surplus supplies was used to help finance the cooperative stores and set up permanent cooperative businesses for the French people in the war zones. In the spring of 1919, the officers in charge of the liquidation of army supplies in France gave Friends the free loan of nearly forty cars and trucks needed to finish the work. This offer improved the efficiency of the *équipes* and enabled them to reach more villages in the region.[18]

In Verdun, the Allies offered the Friends the labor of German prisoners of war to help sort and load material from the dumps. The Friends accepted their service on the honor system by telling the Germans that they would no longer be able to work with them if any tried to escape. One prisoner did escape and, as a consequence, no prisoners of war were allowed to work with the Quakers for a while. One Friend noted, "We were sorry to lose him; he was the best decorative painter we've had." Eventually, the German wrote a letter to the Unit, apologizing for his actions.[19]

December 3, 1918, Leslie in Sermaize to Mary in Cambridge

Dearest Mary—

This time I have a great deal to tell thee. From the heading thee sees that I have arrived. We passed through Chateau-Thierry on the way here. Some parts of it are badly damaged, and shell holes, trenches, barbed wire, and cemeteries are thick about it. After it, we passed several villages, more or less demolished. Stopping at Vitry-le-François for lunch, we came into Sermaize after nightfall. The town of Sermaize was burned in 1914. Some of the walls of the houses are standing; others are grass-grown ruins. It was in German hands only six days—then they were driven out. The Hindenburg line[20] is only a few miles from here; but the Verdun drive did not reach this far. Many of the inhabitants have begun to live in temporary houses, many of which have been erected by the Mission; for here the greatest part of the Friends' work was started.

There are two main *équipes* in Sermaize: La Source and Le Château Hospital—about forty at the first and twenty-five at the second. La Source is the name of a hydrotherapic bath establishment and casino, which was not destroyed. The bath-edifice is garage, store, and machine-shop for the transport service, while the casino acts as headquarters for the personnel. Those who cannot be accommodated in the large building are housed in several Friends' *baraquements* or huts in the vicinity. The Château Hospital is at a certain chateau, used in 1914 as Headquarters by a German general, and so not destroyed. It is augmented by several large *baraquements*, and has electric light, generated there. I have been lucky enough to be sent up to two isolated

One of the ambulances used by the FRU at the Le Chateau Hospital and nearby villages

baraquements . . . which (because we have our own cook and don't eat at La Source except at noon) is a separate *équipe*, under the chiefship of Geoffrey Franklin, a young Englishman—who by the way, has been over in the Mission longer now than anyone else (even than Harvey—for he came with Harvey who has been home since), over four years. Here, too, I met Francis Birrell—secretary, initiator, and editor on Reconstruction's staff. He is the moving force of the Mission, I understand. Very unassuming and quiet, but a powerful, fertile mind. He is about thirty, a son of Augustine Birrell, former Cabinet Minister and essayist. It was a privilege to hear them discuss things—Birrell, Franklin, and Walmsley.[21]

I am a member of the Works Department—newly created—whose duties, besides construction, are to keep things in order generally. My work thus far has included carpentry, plumbing, electric wiring, and dirt sweeping—not to speak of dismounting tires from an old automobile. Besides work, Mary, I have a dilemma. It is thus—(maybe I have told thee already—my memory is wretchedly

Unit workers relaxing in their common room at La Source

poor) Horace Davis, who is Lewis Gannett's lieutenant in the office of Reconstruction, has held down the job for more than six months now. He would like to come up and report the opening of the Verdun work, and get someone to substitute for him and perhaps take the job permanently, if the sub proves adequate. I have been asked (first to hand in a sample of my writing, though). Pro: It will be first-class experience. In Paris, with plays, Sorbonne, and the probability of becoming acquainted with cultivated French people . . . and, best of all, some leisure in which to study and write. Con: The country life is ideal—manual work has built me up remarkably, and would do more; the close touch with the forwarding of the Mission—the view near to hand of the returning refugees and their cultivation of the torn fields. Although the fields call me, the desire to learn to write is stronger, and I am sending in soon an article to Lewis Gannett. What I hope is, that if I am to be sent to Paris for paperwork, that I may first see the district we are to work in—and hear the plans and see the personnel & the Mission. Although if I am not for Paris—so much the better for my lungs and muscles.

This letter may or may not reach thee by Christmas. My heart yearns to sing a Christmas carol—to be in Cambridge—in Harvard Chapel—to be with thee . . . Oh, I am thankful, more than thankful to God for thy friendship . . . it will do more to make of me some good than anything in this world—Mary!

Leslie

December 9, 1918, Mary in Cambridge to Leslie in Sermaize

What a sunset! Les, I have just been down skiing by the river and it was glorious—glorious beyond description. At first the sun was crimson in a nest of golden clouds—all the snow flushed with pink, and the steel blue water reflected again the red and gold. Little by little the pink tinted snow grew colder and colder—the sinking sun turned to Burgundy wine and the water changed to ink and blood. I skied along against the wind, singing—my soul filled with joy at being alive. It seemed as though I were watching a great changing symbol of life as I watched the brilliant colors grow richer and darker and melt into the night (a night only of mystery, not of death). Oh, how can men sit at their books and counters when the world outside is so beautiful—of course I know they could not all leave if they would, and I felt doubly happy to realize how free I am. I had been studying in the library when I saw the golden light, and I could not stay another minute. Out there alone by the river I was unutterably happy, for it seemed as though all my ideals were possible and not far away after all—and that always, always, through joy and sorrow, nature would be there to inspire me with her beauty. I could not live without beauty, and feeling myself a part of nature is a step nearer God—If you had only been there—someone who understands—I was stifled with happiness, because there was no one to share it with, and self-expression is necessary to man, isn't it. How dependent we human beings are on sympathy. Loneliness must be the most awful state—how much better to die than live a lonely life. And the world is full of sympathetic loving people if we only look for them.

Dec. 11

Again today it is snowing, and now the river is frozen over. Your letter with Mme. Brocaille's enclosed came today. How she appreciated your sympathy and kindness—Indeed it is no small talent to be able to gain people's confidence and give them sympathy in return. You know the secret, *mon ami*, and it is very precious. I shall take good care of the letter with the pretty branch 'till you come back.

I am wondering how you keep warm in this cold weather and what work you do when it snows. Last Sunday we had a cozy afternoon chat around the fire at Mrs. Davis's. She said Horace is sailing for home on Dec. 29th (on the Rochambeau) and expects to return to Harvard for the new term. (January–August will be a whole year.) I think he is a bad boy to run away from you—or will that put you in the same class after all? I don't remember how long he has been away. Our talk was mainly about COs—Mrs. D. was hoping to have a reunion party before Bob and Ronald and Bill Bowen go off but it doesn't look as though it could be arranged. The conditions of the COs at Leavenworth are being investigated, and now there are wonderful plans in the air for the released COs. We can't say anything definite yet—but our big radical men feel that the COs must prove their public spirit by service to the community. There are thoughts of buying farms in different places to be run by those agriculturally inclined, and where others can live who go out to preach. Then in the cities there will be the Fellowship House Centers. The idea is for all kinds, socialistic or religious, to be loosely bound in a sort of great brotherhood to spread the message of truth and good will. It may sound like a kind of utopia now—but if something of the kind could be started, I think it would solve the problem for a great many of us who are not satisfied just to go out in search of a successful career. I am exultant and yet lost to think that I shall be out in the world next year. What will I do with the French literature that I have studied so hard to master—how am I in the least prepared for service—and what am I practically going to do? I ask myself these questions a dozen times a day and never find the answer; perhaps this new scheme will bring a solution, tho' it seems so far only for the men. What do you think of it?

The Christmas carols are going very well—only we miss the men so <u>terribly</u>. It all sounds thin and weak, especially "Break Forth"—which positively hurts without the tenor and bass. There are to be no [paper] programs this year so we have to enunciate most carefully. I come home from every rehearsal in a kind of Christmas ecstasy. The music is so beautiful—if we could only do it justice! There is "The First Noel"—"Good King Wenceslas"—"Saint Nicholas" (French)—"Bring a Torch"—"Come All Ye Shepherds"— "Break Forth" and a little lullaby that is exquisite whose name I have forgotten. We are to sing for the Radio School, too, in the Drill Hall, the Sunday before Christmas. The whole Radio School is to be moved out to the Great Lakes in April.

We are all rejoicing because we are to have two weeks' vacation at Christmas instead of ten days—Harvard has to have some time to get the new term started—and we are thankful enough. I shall spend most of each day in Widener working on a thesis.

Oh, I wish you could see our Salle Française—it is all furnished now and open to the college. It is great having it in the library because we can have all the French books we want. The tentative *Causerie* [chat] groups that I proposed have been so popular that there have got to be various divisions in order to make conversation possible. A member of the Cercle directs each group (my pet is the play-reading one), and they meet in the Salle. We have a Victrola, which really helps a lot. I tried repeating after it this morning—and I find that the girls are using the room a lot. It is furnished in blue and brown and golden yellow—and is really very cozy with easy chairs and cushions. M. Mercier is very anxious for it to give the spoken side of French that the courses lack.

We had such fun at our last Cercle meeting—Eva LeGallienne,[22] who is acting here with Ethel Barrymore in "Off Chance" and who went to school in France with one of my friends, came and recited from Hugo and Verlaine to us. She was perfectly charming, so unaffected and direct. She is only nineteen and has supported herself and her mother for three years by her acting. She came in her riding habit looking like a young boy, and between poems talked "shop" about her stage experiences. It was charming and in spots very funny, as when she said "*C'est un peu ennuyeux néanmoins, quand vous vous querellez avec le jeune premier derrière la scène et puis devant l'audience il doit vous faire la cour.*" [It's a little boring, nevertheless, when you quarrel with the leading man behind the scene, and then in front of the audience, he has to woo you]. She invited us to come and see her behind the scenes, and we are crazy to go. You know,

CERCLE FRANÇAISE

OFFICERS

MARY PEABODY, '19	President
MARY REED, '19	Vice-President
MARY TAFT, '19	Secretary
MARION HARRIS, '21	Treasurer

The officers of the Cercle Française,
the French language club at Radcliffe

Les, sometimes I have the wild desire to go on the stage, myself. Who knows, perhaps that is where I will end up!!!

Now I was to converse with your last letter—Your feeling of "eager apathy" I have experienced, too, at times—it is very unsatis-factory—I am sure you could not have had it for long tho' the necessary routine of your work must diminish the moments of enthusiasm. Then it is that spontaneous inspiration counts. I must say I dread going into any work such as a factory—that would be very monotonous. I think it would kill all my enthusiasm. Yet if my idealism couldn't stand that test, I don't know what it is worth.

Do you know that our philosophy of love and service is rather individualistic than socialistic? I have been trying to think out a

204 We Answered with Love

complete idea of life for a thesis in philosophy, and my conclusion is a "Cooperative Christian Individualism."—That sounds very ponderous—but it is really very simple, and I think it is what I believe now. How do you reconcile the centralized power of the socialistic state with the moral laws and freedom of the individual? Isn't the ideal the development of the individual so that fewer and fewer laws are necessary? I was talking the other day with a man who calls himself a Christian anarchist, and his philosophy interested me immensely—it seems to me more idealistic than socialism.

I wish you would send some pictures of what you are doing and your bunch of men. You haven't sent that other picture of yourself you promised either. No, I haven't taken mine yet—perhaps I'll wait and send one of my regular senior pictures that will be taken soon. In place of the promised snap-shot I enclose one of the artistic achievements of my Italian friend sent to me on recovering from the flu—I thought the touches of realism would charm you. Sometime in the future, i.e., on your return, you can return it to me for my scrap book.

Bonne Année mon ami—que Dieu te garde toujours [Happy New Year, my friend—May God protect you always]

Ta camarade,
Marie

Hand-decorated envelope sent by Anthony Fraioli to Mary
(original is in full color)

Leslie at the piano entertaining his co-workers in the community room

9

Documenting the Work

LESLIE FULLY INTENDED TO WORK in the Verdun *équipes*. His plans changed, however, when Horace Davis decided to resign from the Unit and return to finish his education at Harvard. Lewis Gannett had already resigned to work as a newspaper correspondent for *Survey*, a journal of social reform. Horace recommended that his position on the Unit newspaper, *Reconstruction*, be offered to Leslie. Leslie did not dither long. The opportunity was ideal, and he was excited to accept the job. He loved to write, was naturally curious and boyishly enthusiastic, and the work would get him back to Paris, where he could once again bask in literary pursuits.

Reconstruction was started in April 1918, under the auspices of the British Friends War Victims Relief Committee (FWVRC). The initial staff was mostly British and headed by Francis Birrell, who had been with the committee since 1915. Two Americans from the Friends Reconstruction Unit were early staff members: Horace Davis and Lewis Gannett, both Quakers from Harvard. The intent of publishing the newsletter was to stir up "a becoming interest in our international experiment." *Reconstruction* also served as a centralized publication to foster communication between the various *équipes* and projects and to give the field workers a forum for expressing their opinions.

The early issues of the paper focused primarily on the work in France, but the organizers also hoped to include reports of Friends' work in Russia, Holland, Greece, Africa, Corsica, Armenia, and other places. Francis Birrell stated that:

> "Our purpose then is twofold—moral and historical: to make us realize, in spite of ourselves sometimes, the real width, diversity and interest of our work; and at the same time to form a historical aperçu, [from the French, a glimpse or understanding] which may be extremely useful in the future, of what we are doing month by month . . . It should truly be a 'mirror of Quakerism' and of everything that the Society of Friends does and stands for in these times of misery."[1]

In *Reconstruction*'s early issues, the reports necessarily focused on the work in France. Lewis Gannett wrote, "The editors have been in France, able to bully their fellow-workers there into writing. There are nearly six hundred of us in France—the overwhelming majority of all our workers, but even in France, we have been widely scattered."[2]

Circulation for the early issues was one thousand copies. One year later, twenty-three hundred copies were printed, with many going to Friends and Quaker meetings in America and Great Britain, to explain the work to those who were funding it.

Shortly after arriving at the *Reconstruction* office, Leslie became the publicist for the Friends Units. The editors noted that:

"'Publicity' is one of the penalties of democracy . . . When a few people are doing a thing for a lot of people, they have no right not to tell the many what they are doing . . . We cannot tell them what they want to know with a cut-and-dried fiscal statement and annual report. They want their annual report to come out in installments in the Friends papers, in the daily papers, in letters from their sons and their neighbors' sons. We cannot ask people at home to keep on giving without telling them what we have done with what they have already given."[3]

Being a publicist gave Leslie the freedom to travel around the areas where the Friends worked, to collect new information, to talk to the workers, to report on developments in the field, and, most importantly, to record the spirit undergirding the effort to bring aid to the French people. For a time, he went to headquarters in Paris only when necessary to look after the printing of the newspaper.[4] He told Mary, "It is a blessing to be up here in the area where work is going on. One can't picture the life and spirit of it until one is in it. My job up here has been to collect material for Reconstruction and to take photographs of the work."[5]

This work was very important. There was a constant demand from London and Philadelphia for pictures of FRU's work. Initially Edward Horner, a British Friend working at the factory in Dole, collected and passed on pictures sent from workers in the various *équipes*. Leslie soon obtained a camera and took on the tasks of documenting work and organizing pictures for publicity.

Leslie also took on the responsibility of gathering and organizing information for a future book about the work of the Friends in France, to be published in America when the FRU concluded its work. The book,

The new houses in Sermaize,
one of the publicity photographs used in America

eventually written by Rufus Jones in 1920, was entitled *A Service of Love in War Time: American Friends Relief Work in Europe, 1917–1919*. Jones did not attempt to give the complete history of the work; he said he used only a "fragment out of a vastly greater mass of material." His goal was "to interpret the effort which the American Friends have made to express their spirit of human love to a part of the world—an innocent part— caught in the awful tangle of the tragedy."[6]

December 15, 1918, Leslie in Paris to Mary in Cambridge

Dearest Mary,

I came down to Paris yesterday. The day before that, Friday, they took me along on a trip from Sermaize up fifty kilometres towards Verdun—to the edge of the Argonne, into the area to be the scene of the concentrated effort of the Friends from now on. We visited Grange-Le-Comte, a large cluster of buildings evacuated by its owner because he was a pro-German,[7] and projected as the probable field headquarters of the Unit.

Thy letter, the eleventh, was handed to me just as we were starting from La Source at Sermaize—so I read it while the Ford was skipping madly along the road leading northwest to Verdun. I have mixed impressions of the Radcliffe damsels parading the early-morning streets of Boston and desolated, smashed villages in the Marne and Meuse. You girls did have a wonderful celebration! And marching into the Ec. Lecture! Thee's right in not regretting it—it's a great deal more original and appealing than to sit yawning at outworn creeds of coin and platitudes of pelf. I confess a feeling of inadequacy of ability to overflow spontaneously with joy at the Armistice. Was it because I had not entered into the war, sufficiently felt the pains and longings of others? I hardly should say so. But I had been preparing my mind for it so long—that it wasn't news when it came; but principally I didn't kick my heels because I wasn't confident that this was a veritable war to end war. Had I been sure of that, my joy would have known no bounds. But any peace, I suppose, is better than war . . . .

I have been called out of the field work to replace Horace Davis on Reconstruction. He is going home, I understand, at the end of the month. So thee sees that I shall be installed in Paris for some months at least. It will be rather hard not to be able to work with Ronald; but the mail service here is good and we can carry on conversations and lessons by post. Let us hope that he got my letter in time before sailing so that he will bring my Underwood machine with him. To learn to write fast—to compose on it—is what I am anxious to learn to do.

Lewis Gannett is to be busy with newspaper correspondent work, but will not sever interest entirely with Reconstruction. However, the main work, according to Horace, will devolve upon Francis Birrell and me. I am expecting great stimulation from working with Birrell—he has a brilliant, fertile brain and is an inspiring initiator. Horace is going to break me in on the routine and duties of the work.

Probably I shan't stay on after the end of next summer—maybe come back to Cambridge then. I can't tell, though—so many things may happen!

I am rather surprised that Harvard will continue its military program on through the year . . . .

I loved that part of thy last letter where thee tells how thee ran to the cemetery and heard the soft clangor of the bells floating across the plain . . . It makes me remember how far I am from that sweet cemetery on the ridge of the hill—and how I have wandered physically and mentally from it! But whatever happens, I'll not lose my hope and faith. The look of trust and sympathy that thee gave me once has stayed in the visioned room of my mind as its dearest possession.

Thy would-be comrade,
Leslie

December 22, 1918, Leslie in Paris to Mary in Cambridge

My dearest Mary,

I was moved to the bottom of my soul to read thy Christmas letter. It was so true, so feeling, and so comradely—a message of supreme friendship; it gave me a pang of grief that shook me and a sense of unspeakable joy—both so strange, so strange that I may not describe them. It was a grief that I never knew in Cambridge: pain in the soul for my sins and ingratitude and shortcomings . . . and joy at the wonderful blessing of a true friend and comrade. It never seems possible to me that thee can have any such moments of sorrow, that sorrow must always be with others and for others!

Mary, thy poem of "Thee and Me" brought me near to tears . . . What a strong tender friendship thee is capable of—which would be mine if I might only rise to it. I shall treasure those verses.

Doesn't thee feel the great sense of wondering, delighted freedom at casting out temporal aspirations for service for mankind? Isn't it like stepping from a narrow, high-hedged lane into a gracious countryside—full of everything that is real and fresh—because it is God's? What a blessing to be freed from the desire of comfort-getting!

The most beautiful letter I ever got from my brother Clarence came the other day. He has received an intimate experience of the Lord's power and presence—it has made a new man of him; I can read it in his words. Oh, I am so thankful for it—his power for good will be strengthened a hundred-fold. His letter is loving and powerful . . . it gives me hope and faith each time I read it.

Shall we be much changed when we meet each other again? Remember how thee said once how much older I would be when that time came? In experiences and firmness of ideals, I feel I have grown; but I still love to sing and dream and imagine as a child. Let's not lose any more of our childhood joy and sincerity than we can help, Mary! When I think of thee it is most often with the simple trust and affection of a child. To be free from the emptiness of worldly things and uncharitable tongues from calculating men!

Back in Paris to take Horace's place. He will be starting home on the 29th, if all goes well. Just now he is up at Sermaize, visiting the *équipes* near and in the Verdun area.

Picture me in a little white-walled, tiled-floor room, formerly a dispensary, in the court before the Student Hostel. Here we edit Reconstruction. Notice that I say "we"—although I'm all at sea—having been in the country at manual work so long that I hardly know a mail-box from a typewriter. This work will teach me method if anything will.

I'm so sorry that thee will not be in the Cercle's histrionics—but lessons is lessons! The people at home have sent me "Bright's" Anglo-Saxon Reader.[8] To save a half-course at Harvard I'm going to try to learn it here. 'Twill be *assez difficile*, but I'll do my best. To begin it makes me sympathize with Ronald, who's going to begin French. He may be over very soon, now. Men are arriving every now and then who knew him at Rosedale . . . I doubt that he will be here by Christmas, though.

We shall have candles here—they'll burn down during our Christmas supper and as they go out, their light and warmth will go from me to thee as trust and affection. Before, Mary, I was seeking thee for myself—now, I am seeking thy hand that we may walk together through darkness and day towards the Holy City. My faith was in myself, and now it is in the Lord. The future has no fear except that of losing light, beauty, and love out of my life.

Has thee thought any more of going into a factory on getting out of college? I think it is a great purpose. Nothing can give one the real fellow-feeling for a worker like being a worker. And not to be a dilettante—but really to break away from the supports of home and live on one's own earnings as a wage-slave—that's real and priceless. I am not the man to try to shield you from the suffering of the world and its grime—the inner light and love is what we live by, and not the comforts of a padded existence. Nothing has made me prize thy friendship more than this evidence of thy love to suffer with others and to serve.

Think of it! A CO committee in the H. Liberal Club! It rises in my estimation by leaps and bounds. That is a beautiful purpose of the COs to become latter-day apostles. Heaven knows that we need men to live their beliefs.

I have been singing our old Christmas carols again. What a sweet, deep recollection they call up! The mysterious joy—so great as to be almost unrealizable—in the singing of "Noel" throbs in my heart. "There Were Three Ships"—"Listen, Lordings, Unto Me." Has thee forgotten that afternoon when we walked on the frozen Charles—the thin, feathery mantle of snow that flew up as we ran?

Happiness and the love of others be ever with thee and thy loved one. *Je remercie le bon Dieu pour la flamme quil a mises dans ton ame. Que la flamme d'amour et l'etoile d'esperance brillent plus claires et pures dans l'ame humaine!* [May the flame of love and the star of hope shine very clear and bright in the human soul!]

Thy friend forever,
Leslie

December 29, 1918, Leslie in Paris to Mary in Cambridge

Dearest Mary,

Thy letter of the 9th and 11th—the sunset ecstasy—was superb and touching. How often I too have felt the overflow of joy dammed up by loneliness! Behind the farmhouse at Savigny, nearly over to the brook there was what I imagined as a cathedral of trees—the autumn dress of quiet yet profuse beauty—the exquisite hush of the wind's whisper through the foliage—the carpet of sturdy but gentle grass—all filled my cup to overflowing and in longing for someone to share my joy; it turned to thankfulness and I felt mysteriously closer to God.

Yet there is an emptiness, a hunger for love and beauty in me that almost hurts. I long for a religious experience like those of my two brothers. To feel near something—the vital something of life and yet not grasp it!

I rejoice in thy renewed joy in life—in thy exuberance of strength and love which makes everybody happy around thee. Thee always seems to me as reaching out a hand to ease people's suffering and as eager for learning the truth about a person or a thing—the truth, which is its beauty. Love—of which thee is my symbol—says "Rejoice with me!" and at the same time "Let me bear part of the burden!" Oh, how ideal, how perfectly formed is thy character! All my sense of what is of love, service, and truth—the idealist in me—comes to rest on thee. Where would I be without thee, Mary?—Perhaps I ought not say these things—but what harm is there in speaking a truth that will be expressed?

I am in as much uncertainty as thee is about what the course is that the Lord would have me follow. The plan of the CO brotherhood thee speaks of sounds true and right. Isn't there as much or more service possible to women in a work like that? But besides spreading the Gospel in the manner of the apostles, it is also possible to lead a Christian life for service in one's own community—if one only has the strength to stand free from the throttling hold of latter-day civilization. And we must not forget that Christianity has never been and is not "respectable." I have a strong human desire for approbation, to be friendly and well looked upon by all; "<u>Woe unto you when all men shall speak well of you!</u>" And I believe that it is the respectable class that is most bound by heathen and evil tradition and is more likely to be wrong in the eternal values than the simple folk. Happy, and three times happy should we be, if we found that in acting towards the humble as Christ would have us, we should be evilly spoken of by the "upper" class! Thereupon should we be offered the supreme trial and opportunity of a lifetime—to love our enemies. <u>There</u> is a career more marvelous, and yet more humble than anyone ever dreamed. Let us lift up our hearts!

Tolstoi says somewhere that all man's moods and his good or evil desires arise from the things and amounts he eats—in brief, from the state of his stomach. Mary, I've eaten altogether too much candy and chocolate. By all the rules I ought to be sick and pessimistic. But no! My head is up and the world is rose! Joy and gladness are in and around me . . . Oh, if we were walking together today—what a talk we should have! "Samson and Dalila"[9] at the Opera the other night was superb. Several of the duets charmed me—and the bass was excellent. After the end of the opera, there was a pantomime ballet of bewitching whimsicality and daintiness. Hungry for gossamer and gold, I hung on every color—every movement—every fancy.

Last night Tatnall Brown[10] and I, at the instance of Mrs. Rhoads (the wife of the head of the Friends Bureau of the American Red Cross) went down to a settlement house (<u>neighborhood</u> is a better word) and helped to entertain them—an audience of about five hundred. The rest of the program was piano music and a lecture (illustrated) on Alsace; I was told by one of the ushers that our act had been advertised in the quarter and that the bigger part of the crowd was for us—possibly that was *bourrage de crane* [brainwashing], but they gave us an enthusiastic welcome. We sang "Oh Mister Moon," "The Long, Long Trail," "In the Evening by the Moonlight," "The Bulldog," "One, Two, Three, Four," and several others—Tat accompanying on the guitar, as well as singing. Then he did a clog and a little "Queen of the Nile" stuff—what he calls "synthetic dancing." After we'd taken our last call, they kept on clapping and stamping and when we shambled out again, they gave us a regular cheer— *Vive! Vive!! Vive!!!*" I never heard an American audience cheer so intensively or so well. What made us feel good was that apparently they enjoyed it, and went away happy—I'm glad we went.

Mme. Marrault, who works down there sometimes for them, says she puts on plays and asked me to do a little one with her. It sounds excellent—an opportunity to entertain those poor people, and incidentally to learn more French and acting myself. What does thee think?

Our Christmas evening was beautiful, but not so filled with the Christ-day thrill and *élan* as I could wish. Nothing like the ecstasy of the carols that thee knows and that was mine a year ago.

Que Jesus soit ne dans nos coeurs comme dans la creche de Bethlehem il y a mille neuf cent ans! Un flambeau, pour eclairer et chauffer les fonds de nos ames! [That Jesus is in our hearts as in the crib of Bethlehem nineteen hundred years ago! A torch to illuminate and heat the depths of our souls!]

Ton camarade a jamais, [Your friend forever,]
Leslie

Barnard Hall and Bartram Hall on the Radcliffe Campus, 1914

10

Mary's Senior Year

COLLEGE LIFE AT RADCLIFFE AND HARVARD began to return to normal in the spring of 1919. The young men who had left for military service, ambulance work, and other projects in support of the war effort were coming back. Mandatory military training for all men at the university was discontinued. The Naval Radio School closed, and the sailors left the campus and removed the tent city from Cambridge Common.

Mary was determined to make the most of her last semester. She had health problems, which she attributed to stress and the lingering effects of the influenza. After taking an enforced break from her studies, she moved on campus so she would not be distracted by the work involved in maintaining the household and running her family's small boarding home. She also gave up her dream of graduating with honors.

Mary entered into campus life with gusto. She enjoyed the freedoms and the social side of dorm life. She attended dances and concerts. She participated in her many clubs and organizations and acted in small theater productions.

But senior year was also a time of great introspection. Mary anguished over her career choices and whether or not marriage was in her future. She

MARY MAY PEABODY

13 Hilliard Street, Cambridge, Mass.
Born September 29, 1896, Dorchester, Mass.
Prepared at Cambridge School for Girls.
Concentrated in Romance Languages.
　　Choral. German Club. French Club. Music Club. International Polity Club. Suffrage Club. Socialist Club. Radical Club. Poetry Club. Servant of King's Dog in "King Argimenes." Mr. Nagle in "The Manoeuvres of Jane." Ferdinand Gadd in "Trelawny of the Wells." Duke Frederick in "As You Like It." Countess of Remenham in "Cassilis Engagement." Tawots in "The Arrow Maker." Le Barronne in "L'Aventurier." Mere Bernier in "Mystere de la Chambre Jaune." Dramatic Committee 1917-1919. Chairman Sophomore Luncheon Committee. Treasurer Socialist Club 1918-1919. Chairman Class Constitution Committee. Freshman President. Secretary French Club 1917-1918. President French Club 1918-1919.

Mary hopes to aid in the establishing of Trade Unions, and to have a hand in the coming Industrial Reforms.

and Leslie discussed how to live a life of service. While they agreed that giving to others was important, they had very different ideas of what that meant. Mary was politically motivated, having worked with her mother in many causes, including women's suffrage, the rights of workers to unionize, and assisting conscientious objectors. Mary envisioned a future of service as an organizer, perhaps helping to start a school for working class people, promoting trade unionism, or some other radical project.

On the other hand, for Leslie, a life of service meant giving to others as a teacher, helping individual farmers, or working at a settlement. His idea of service was more personal, built on a foundation of relationships with people and communities. Leslie greatly admired the married couples in the FRU and hoped that Mary would join him in this work. On some level this vision appealed to her, but she also saw a path more in line with her own dreams. On February 10, she wrote, "I hardly think now that I shall go across; things are so exciting here, changes so unforeseen are coming I think and there is certainly much, much to do—organizing industry is the great task today, and labor here in America is so far behind."[1]

Marriage was an important topic of discussion among Radcliffe seniors. These young women from the middle and upper classes expected to make good marriages and become full-time wives and mothers. Social activities revolved around meeting suitable men—dances, dinner parties, group activities. Many of Mary's friends were announcing their engagements; she was truly happy for them, but was not at all sure that marriage was for her.

Mary did not have a good role model for marriage. Her parents divorced when she was young—a very messy, very public divorce. Early in their marriage, her father, Frederick Peabody, had gone into debt and had run through his wife's small inheritance. He became increasingly abusive to his wife. By the time Mary was five years old, her mother, Anna, left him and took the girls to live in Cambridge. In 1908, the Peabodys were granted a divorce. Much of this played out in the newspapers because of Frederick's notoriety as a vocal, sometimes violent and obsessive, opponent of Mary Baker Eddy, the founder of the Christian Science Church. By 1912, he had remarried and had two sons, Richard and Alexander. He closed his law practice and moved with his second family to Ashburnham, Massachusetts, leaving behind a trail of debt.[2]

Anna Peabody had sole support of her daughters and took in boarders in their house at 13 Hilliard Street in Cambridge to help make ends meet. Mary did not want to find herself in such a position and was determined to forge a career for herself. Starting in the late nineteenth century, led by reformers such as Jane Addams, more women of means were finding careers in social work, as labor organizers, and working in settlement houses. These women, for the most part, were single and self-supporting. Mary saw herself following in their footsteps, and she threw herself into activities that would prepare her for this work.

December 18, 1918, Mary in Cambridge to Leslie in Paris

Dear Les,

I have just come home from Appleton where the singing went as well as it could without you men. How we missed you! It didn't seem the same at all—the chapel was garlanded in green and the tall red candles in a row across the chancel flickered and shone their brightest, but somehow nothing was the same. Oh, if you had only been here this Christmas of Christmases, when peace has come at last to the poor world. Oh, that Jesus could come again to the earth and the beautiful star lead us to find him. Would that we were simple like the shepherd of old and could follow the vision that should bring peace and good will upon the earth. As I sang tonight, many times a mist came over my eyes so that the candles shot out strange long beams and the music seemed far away, as if the angels were singing in the clouds—and I thought of the sorrow there is in the world at this beautiful time—the candles will have strange long beams for thousands of eyes and it will be very hard to rejoice— but oh, now we must begin all over again—and as Dr. Davison played the great final chords of the Hallelujah chorus, I felt as though I had received a flaming consecration and I prayed with all my soul for power to follow the great star unwaveringly. As you see, I don't know how to say it—it was one of those big minutes of our lives that are beyond description, but I know you understand, Les, and so before I go to bed I want to sit down and write to you. I tried to pretend you were sitting right over on the other side of the choir tonight—but my imagination played me false, and I will just tell you plainly that I missed you terribly. Next year you will be back again, and I shall not be there! I can't believe that these were my last Appleton carols. How I have loved them—loved everything connected with my dear old colleges, for Radcliffe is my *alma mater* and Harvard is my *almus pater*.

I had a beautiful talk with Mr. Briggs the other day, and when I said that I have loved every day of my college years, but that I felt very unprepared for service in the world, he said, "You may be sure that everything you have learned in college will help you, though you may not know it." When I left his office I felt more strongly than ever that what we do is really very little—and that it is the spirit alone that counts.

(He is sailing in January, he says—Mrs. Briggs and Lucia hope to go with him.)

December 30th

I didn't post this that night because it was too late and the next day I thought there would be much to add—so the busy days have followed one another and now the Christmas celebrations are over and I can sit down quietly and tell you about them. It is more than two weeks since I heard from you last so you seem very far away— I have been afraid you might have the flu, but have tried to think you have written and the mail is delayed. I thought I would wait and send this letter when I heard from you—but the things to tell have grown so numerous that I must send them along to you and trust to hearing soon.

This Christmas was full of carols. Some of us sang at the City Home (Poor House) and then in all the wards of the Brigham

Hospital. It was real pleasure for us and the others seemed to enjoy it very much. On Christmas day we had our own home fun—I couldn't bear not to have some celebration so I dressed up a little tree with real candles and little packages from the 10¢ store. Quite a lot of people were staying with us so we had a great time and I wish you could have seen Helen's face when she saw the bicycle I had smuggled in. It was decked with holly and red ribbons, with a card bearing the words "Sister H this is for you—so that you no more'll have the flu"—beautiful verse, *n'est-ce pas*! Now she will be able to go off all day sketching, which is her delight—and not have to ride in the germy cars!

On Christmas night, we all marched in the League of Nations pageant. We wore liberty caps[3] and carried red lanterns and appropriate standards. Mine said "A United World." We marched around Beacon Hill singing "Adeste Fidelis," and then gathered on the State House steps and sang a lot of carols. It was really very nice though poorly managed—it might have been glorious if more time and thought could have been given it. As it was there were great crowds watching, and Mrs. Davis, who saw it, said it was very effective.

The day after Christmas, Helen and I went up to Ashburnham to see Daddy. They are having an awfully hard time up there so that it took all our joyous Christmas spirits to keep things happy. Oh, Les, *la vie est bien difficile* sometimes, *n'est-ce pas?* [Life is very difficult sometimes, isn't it?] But the country was glorious in the winter weather and we had lots of skating. Coming home on the train I sat with a girl who looked hopelessly uninspired—Her hair was all in her eyes, her clothes showy and cheap, and she chewed gum continuously. I feel like a pig to eat candy alone, so I passed her some of my chocolate—that started a conversation that lasted for an hour.

She talked eagerly about her work in the shop, her husband at war, and her ideal of friendliness to everyone. When I got out of the train I thanked her with all my heart for her friendliness to me. I learned a mighty lot from her about the power of ideals!

When we reached the house, we had just time to eat a hasty lunch before meeting Hal, George Hallett, Ralph Cathrall (spelling wrong) and others at Symphony Hall where we heard a beautiful concert. Sally, Esther, and Frances Townsend were there too. Afterwards we all piled into the long-suffering flivver [old, decrepit car] and went to "Franty's" for tea and games. It was great fun. Then we flivvered out to Cambridge up the dark river drive singing all the way. Once Sally said "Do you remember the time we were coming home from the Wayside Inn how John Leslie sang those funny songs!" Did I remember—I was just wondering what you were doing, that very moment.

We still have five more days' vacation in which I must get started on my thesis. I have a permit to study in the stacks at Widener— and I intend to make the most of my opportunity.

You know, Les—the more I think of it the crazier I am to go over there next summer—I must use my French a little and I am sure I could be useful. Of course they may never take me—but I am having such a hard time deciding what among the thousand things to do here that I think I shall end by sailing away from them all, to France. I don't know really at all yet, but at moments the desire is so strong that I think I must go; and at others I think I am adventurous and romantic and that common sense tells me to stay at home.

J'attends de tes nouvelles—soigne toi et ne travaille pas trop fort. Un chaque jour contienne bien de moments d'inspiration—c'est le souhait de ta camarade. [I await your news—take care of yourself

and don't work too hard. That each day has many moments of inspiration—that is the wish of your comrade.]

Mary

January 4, 1919, Leslie in Paris to Mary in Cambridge

Dearest Mary—

Time does pass quickly in spite of everything, doesn't it, Mary,
when there are many things to take it up. It is a blessing to be busy
in useful, loving work; the curse is to allow one's time to be stolen
by petty, ephemeral incidents. Think of the opportunity—rare!—
that we have, possessed of an ideal of love and service to God and
man on which to build friendship and a marriage of hearts and
minds, which might be as lovely and rare as an orchid. Marriage in
the civil, terrestrial sense is an incident, not of vital importance. The
jewel, the pearl, is the friendship, the concord of ideals, the harmony
of struggles against self and for the right. Consider the joy of together helping others to eternity! Think of the freedom of love and
the bondage of self! These are my best thoughts—when I express
them to thee I feel it. It is thy comradeship, friendship, and inspiration that keep me at my best and bring my poor erring mind and
heart nearer to God . . . .

Sunday

This morning I went to the Russian Church.[4] We stood in the dim, round-arched Byzantine temple and heard the Mass . . . intoned by a wonderful bass voice—noble, resonant, and full. The choir—all male—was hidden from me. They sang unaccompanied, and their crescendo and diminuendo were mysterious and exalting. The bass, of course, was their best part—it vibrated through the vaulted hall like an organ tone.

Today at lunch I had a fine talk with T. Edmund Harvey,[5] an English Quaker M. P. and the head of the Mission in France. He was interested to hear about Swedenborg, and let me run on quite a little. It is an inspiration to converse with that man—same feeling that one has in speaking with Mr. Briggs . . . .

What are my plans? Probably to come back to school in the Fall—I'm not sure, yet. Bill Southworth, Horace Davis, and Carroll Binder[6] are returning almost immediately.

Are thy plans still to learn for a while the mechanics and misery of a working-girl's life? One of the most reprehensible qualities of our education is the attitude of indulgent superiority attempted to be bred into us toward the working class. Laurence Plank of our Unit, feeling the need of understanding their pains and troubles, used to spend his summers away from college in factories and lumber camps . . . and he's a better man for it.

My hope is still to be able to write; economics isn't in my nature—it's an awful pull for me to interest myself in schedules and formulas; lives are what appeal to me: lives, struggles, problems. Much as I feel I ought to know the politics, economics, and science of society, and money and systems, my mind doesn't crave it at all.

Has thee a similar trouble? I envy people—like Lewis Gannett—who are *courant* [up-to-date] with all the tendencies, and the significance of every move . . . To me it seems that the pulpit or the stage are my gates to the company of men working for the social revolution, or deeper yet, the change of heart.

Que Dieu te garde toujours. [May God protect you always.]

Thy comrade,
Leslie

P.S. *Merci mille fois pour les "Crimes" et les "News." Tu as l'envie de me donner la nostalgie cantabrigienne? Il ne faut pas lever en moi ces doux souvenirs-là ou je prendrai le prochain bateau pour mon pays!* [Thank you a thousand times for "Crimes" and "News" [Harvard Crimson and Radcliffe News]. You want to give me a nostalgia for Cambridge? It isn't necessary to raise those sweet memories, or I will take the next boat for my country.]

Undated—Mary in Cambridge to Leslie in Sermaize

Dear Leslie,

How I wish too that we could talk together—we will have many things to tell each other when you get home. When I read your letter I felt reproached that I have not written to you more often lately. It is easier for me to write than for you, and if it really helps you any to hear from your old comrade she ought to do that much at least for you. I am not at all capable of helping you, *mon ami*—but I expect <u>great</u> things of you and trust you <u>entirely</u>—just remember that it is your faith in the big splendid things that is the real help.

I think it would be perfectly great for you to be on the Paper in Paris. You are needed there just as much as for building houses, and because you love to write you would be using your best abilities. Of course you will make it—your next letter will be from Paris probably!

Jan. 8, 1919

Yes I was right. Two letters came from you today from Paris— one written on Nov. 26 (where can it have been all this time?) and the other on Dec. 15. I knew you were to be on Reconstruction anyway. Mrs. Davis told me that Horace said you were to be—several days ago. You are seeing all sides of the work—it is a great experience. Now, Les, I think you make a mistake in thinking that you must abandon all ideas of becoming famous because you want to serve. Why can't you do both? Haven't the great dramatists like Brieux[7] done untold good by showing up injustice and wrong? If a person is given a talent he has no right not to use it to its utmost for others. You love to write and you are going to write; that is your field of service, and as I said before, I expect great things of you.

Oh I am crazy to get out into the world, though I am tempering my expectations of what it has in store. What I want now is something real and living—that part of my education has not begun! You know you are awfully lucky to see all that you are seeing—and what a Frenchman you must be by this time. I shall be ashamed to try my small vocabulary again with you when you come back!

I laughed when I thought of your reading my Peace Celebration letter as you flivvered along the desolated region—a wild letter in wild surroundings—happy coincidence. I knew you would sympathize with our enthusiasm! As you say, you realize much more than we what the Armistice meant. We rejoiced because the firing was over but you thought of the future. I know we were very excited and short-sighted for a while—it didn't take me long to see that.

I think it is dreadful that they can't leave up all the houses your *équipe* built. Why couldn't they be used still? Anyway they served their purpose while they were needed, and what more does one want.

Harvard is not continuing its military program thru' the year as you suppose—they are all settling back into the old ways and uniforms are fast disappearing.

Ever your true friend,
Mary

[With her letter, Mary enclosed a postcard of the Widener Library. She had written the following on the reverse:

"I've come to a jumping off place in my studying, so I will take a few minutes recess to write this card to you. (They are on sale in the Treasure Room—looks natural, *n'est-ce pas!*) I have been studying all day in the stacks for my thesis—just stopping long enough to eat some sandwiches. (It is now 4:45) I have a desk in a cubby hole all to myself—it is great. My window looks out toward Pres. Lowell's house and the Union. Today the boys register to start the new term; and on the stairs and everywhere you hear discussions of courses, rooms, etc.—much enthusiasm!

WIDENER LIBRARY, HARVARD UNIVERSITY. GENERAL READING ROOM

I feel like a barbarian outsider down here in the sacred stacks—but they treat me splendidly. It is awfully funny to see a man go by, suddenly see me, a girl, down in the sanctum sanctorum, he starts and stares—then passes on wondering. I chuckle to myself and go on studying. There is a serious looking man writing a thesis at the desk next to mine—I hardly dare breathe for fear of disturbing him. Guess I'll go home now, I feel rather hungry."]

January 12, 1919, Mary, to "Leslie, Kindness of Ronald,"

Dear Les,

For a brief and exciting hour this morning, we have been trying to see how many words a minute we could talk all at once. Ronald called up early on the telephone and said he was in Boston for a couple of hours before going to Portland to sail, so we have been having breakfast together and talking COs and reconstruction with all our mights. Now Ronald has gone in to meet Evelyn and I am going down to the Portland train to surprise Ronald. How I should like to send thee something nice by Ronald—but he is laden down with baggage so I shouldn't want to give him anything more. So I thought he could slip this note in his pocket, and he will give it to thee when you meet (probably thee will have had other letters from me written after this because Ronald goes to England first).

Oh, I know thee shall have the socks I have just made—Ronald will stick them in somewhere. I made them in odd moments and they are very poorly done, but now thee shall have them and not any old Red Cross. If they don't fit, give them away—but let's hope they will be of some use to thee in the frosty winter weather in Paris.

What a time thee will have when thee sees Ronald. I wish I might witness your meeting!

Au revoir, que Dieu te garde toujours, mon amie [Goodbye, may God always keep you, my friend]

Ta camarade,
Marie

January 13, 1919, Leslie in Paris to Mary in Cambridge

Dearest Mary,

I long for a walk and a talk with thee! Thy presence has been very close to me, very real, very sweet of late; I have communed and meditated, and no call came to me to write until now.

Thee will soon be in the midst of those terrific midyears, *n'est-ce pas?* College studies of the type offered to us seem hardly the best way of training ourselves to love and serve, but since we are in them let's do them up brown and clear the way for new preparation—what opinion has thee of such of philosophy? I certainly shall pray for thee and be with thee in spirit during each exam . . . to encourage and hearten—but there will be no need! I do hope both Helen and thee are feeling strong and well enough to hit those exam papers and knock them into cocked hats.

You know, I did some typing the other day for our old friend, Norman Angell.[8] He is currently in Paris, living in a hotel very close to Place de la Concorde. Sunday at ten o'clock in the morning he gave me two pieces to copy and <u>to deliver before three hours</u>. So I did my best, but on the horrible French Smith-Premier there was nothing to do. He wasn't happy, you understand. But, finally, he's a very nice man, though nervous, which gives him a fairly brusque air.

Twenty-seven new young people are coming to France this week for the Mission. Maybe my brother and Bob Dunn! How I would love to see them! We need such men in the Mission.

Madame Davis told me that she sat between the two "Ms" at a conference with Professor Heoernle. That was good for all three, I bet. And I accompanied her son on the Metro to say good-bye. He did a lot of good here in France. It'd be great if we could say the same for everyone!

Mary, the eyes of my heart follow you always. You are and will always be my ideal, unto eternity. No man has ever had such a friend; and Woman has never had such ideals, such a heart, such a soul—such a capacity for sacrifice and service! Good night, my comrade! Forever,[9]

Ton,
Leslie

January 19, 1919, Leslie in Paris to Mary in Cambridge

Dearest Mary—

Yesterday evening I heard by cablegram from Father that Ronald is on his way over! He left on the thirteenth and ought to be here Wednesday or Thursday. How happy I'll be to see him— and I'll try my hardest to make everything as pleasant for him as I possibly can . . . so that he won't have the slightly lost feeling that some of us experienced in the first days. Think of it, Mary! Put thy-self in my shoes—or imagine Helen rejoining thee after seven months of being alone. There won't be a happier boy in France than little Leslie! And perhaps—perhaps we can get work together part of the time! Rejoice with me, my dearest, dearest friend, in my love for my brother. The Lord doesn't give everyone such a brother—in this world, at least.

At a beautiful meeting tonight Rufus Jones spoke. He is inspired—a man ruled by the love of God and of man. In the silence afterward I prayed and saw the love in our hearts as a beautiful portal, on which shone the pure rays of God's life . . . and I saw that through this door should pass every thought of reflection or action—before it issued into the lives of others—and be purified and sanctified in passing by the light irresistible . . . and I seemed to feel that every unkind or base or selfish purpose stole out misshapen and evil from some dark door of our minds upon the world.

Thy desire to come over into the Mission interests me greatly—more than anything else in the world as thee knows . . . and it goes without my saying that thee could do a wonderful service . . . .

We have been taking it for granted that I shall return in the fall to go on with college, agreeing that it is important that I finish. But—I don't know whether this spring and summer can give Ronald enough start in his work of preparation for Harvard, or not. I am not sure that he shouldn't be coached longer—for thee can realize what a struggle it is to try to study while giving one's best effort for the sufferers here—and what encouragement and sympathy one needs—even one with Ronald's iron will. I can't tell yet.

Reconstruction and publicity work have been crowding me of late . . . I have had no time to write—and taking thy advice, haven't sat up much past one . . . .

Bonne nuit ma chère, chère Marie—Dieu te garde dans tout. Que ton étoile brille toujours. [Good night, my dear, dear Mary—God protect you in all. May your star shine always.]

Ton camarade à jamais,
Leslie

No date, Mary in Cambridge to Leslie in Paris

Dear Leslie,

Thy letter in answer to my Christmas one made thee seem very near—in spite of the distance that separates us, we are closer friends now than ever. Leslie, thee must not dwell on thy shortcomings as thee calls them; they are so few and so easily conquered. Thee makes me feel so small to think that thee should worry about thy "sins" when I say nothing about mine which are so great. But we must not get introspective—just work hard and be happy, and as thee says keep young with dreams and songs. As I go along the street, I sing all the time or hum old tunes and ones that I make up to fit my mood. Dost thee feel every day, when thee goes out and looks up at the sky, how glad thee is to be alive? *Oh, la vie est bien belle!* [Oh, life is very beautiful!]

Now, I will tell thee a little frivolity. The other night when I was all dressed for the Senior Prom in my new green and silver dress with silver slippers—I stood in front of the mirror for a final inspection. Mother said everything was all right, but I somehow knew it wasn't, because I wished thee was here to go to the dance with me. (What fun we had last year.) Victor was just as nice as he could be, but he was Victor all the time. He is a splendid fellow and we have much in common *mais toi et moi nous nous entendons et ca fait tout le difference au monde* [but you and I understand each other and that makes all the difference in the world].

By the way, has thee heard that Bob Dunn has decided not to go after all? He was intending to sail in a week or two but has had so many interesting offers made him in the Radical Movement on this side that he has decided to stay. Young Democracy is rallying to its feet under flying colors—we had a meeting here last Sunday afternoon and the parlor was just crowded with young men and women, all eager to get into the new movement—each one represented a different group of radicals and they are going to tell others; so that at the next monthly meeting, we expect a big crowd. There is a central "Service Committee" made up of reps. from different groups (I rep. Radcliffe), and we send members of our groups to organizations or meetings in town as they are needed. The League for Free Nations,[10] which is having a big campaign for membership, seems to be very glad of our help—and we learn an awful lot just by doing the scrub work. Lewis Gannett has consented to be the foreign correspondent (that sounds grand, doesn't it) for the Young Democracy paper.

Is thee able to get in touch with any radical young people's organizations over there? It would be so interesting to compare notes. What are they going to do at the Peace Conference when there is such a difference of opinion about territory between Wilson and Clemenceau?[11] I'd give a lot to know what the opinion of the great French public is— Do the masses sympathize with Clemenceau or Wilson? I suppose it is hard to tell, and the Socialists are probably kept pretty quiet. But what do the liberals think?

I haven't decided yet, but instead of working in a factory, I may get into some kind of work among the Italian immigrants. I should so like to use something I have learned in all this time if I could. Perhaps working with them, I could work for them, too. Harry Dana wants me to teach in a Workingmen's College[12] he is hoping to start. I imagine it will be something like the Rand School,[13] tho' not for socialism or any kind of propaganda—just a free college for all. It exists only in the idea as yet however. If it does really come

into being, I may go in for that. Thee is right there is a wonderful
sense of freedom in the thought of future service. I can't wait to
begin! Tell me what thy ideas are for after college for thyself.

Thy comrade in service,
Mary

January 26, 1919, Mary in Cambridge to Leslie in Paris

Dear Les,

I have just come home from the most thrilling lecture by Harold
Evans about the Friends Reconstruction Work with lantern slides.
He gave it at my uncle's church and there was a big crowd of young
people—How familiar the pictures all were—and the ones of Sermaize—I could hardly sit still I was so excited. I hunted hard for
thee in the group pictures—but the faces were so much in the shade
that I could not have recognized thee. One picture of Mr. Harvey I
thought was thee at first. What was my astonishment (for I did not
even know that he had landed) when Mr. Evans said that Horace
Davis wished to say a word. He got up, and for a minute stood in
the bright light of the lantern with darkness all around him. I felt
as though I knew him already, thee has spoken so much of him in
thy letters—but I was eager to see his face and I think it is a splendid
one. When Mrs. Davis introduced me to him I called him Horace
before I could stop myself, and he said he was glad. He says he wants
to see me soon, and I guess I know why. I shall make him tell me all
about thee, thee may be sure. His eyes were so kind. I think thee

must have told him of our friendship. How glad I shall be to get all his news and local color!

That last letter came just in time to cheer me out of a little fit of depression. I will tell thee about it though I was very weak and foolish. We had our red-tassel[14] senior elections the other day and though I was nominated for five different offices I was defeated every time by a more popular girl. I had hoped in my secret heart to be class poet, because I felt that I had something to say in the class poem but Ethel Kidder[15] was elected. She will do it much better than I, I know—I was only disappointed because I was burning to write a poem full of my ideals.

After the elections, we all had supper together and as they had previously asked me, I made four or five toasts in verse to girls who are leaving at midyears. Thank goodness I could control my feelings and give the toasts in fine spirits (but it was hard). The girls seemed to like them very much, for they laughed heartily at some and were very serious at others as I hoped they would be—then we all sang the class song (the words of which I wrote) and then went home. Several girls spoke to me afterward and said that the toasts were splendid, and I smiled hard until I got home. Then I cried, yes, Les, I was a baby and nothing else. I had thought the girls were fond of me and that I had done some services for my class, but then I felt that after all I had made a terrible failure. I went to bed and thought calmly and before I went to sleep I laughed at myself for being so silly as to care. I know the girls do love me because I love them, and it is only because I have been so busy with studying and other things that I have dropped out of the popular circle in the last year and others have taken my place. If they care for me they care for me, and red tassels mean nothing; or else I am not worthy of their affection and must work hard to show my worth. I shall study harder now than ever and put less trust in outward signs. If I do each day the very best I know how toward my ideals, I will need no tassels or symbols for reward. After all, I think it was very good for me to have this disappointment; it taught me to care less for the outward show of the world and more for the invisible rewards.

In the real struggles of existence there are few rewards, are there, Les?—and I must not be discouraged—no, I <u>will</u> <u>not</u> be. Thy letter helped me come to this, for I said when I read it, "Oh what do I care for recognition or popularity when I have such a friend." No matter what happens, we will go on and up toward the bright dawn.

Thee is right about economics, Les—I am not made for it either. Ec. A. is awfully hard for me, and depressing too because Dr. Burbank is such a pessimist. He said in class the other day when I objected to some remarks he made about men being ruled by the almighty dollar, "Miss Peabody you have too much faith in human nature"—but that is just what we glory in, isn't it, Les—and no one can take it away from us!

Au revoir jusque qu'après les examens [Good-bye until after the exams]

Thy comrade,
Mary

January 26, 1919, Leslie in Paris to Mary in Cambridge

Dearest Mary—

At supper we had Oswald Garrison Villard (M's cousin) who came at Charles Rhoad's[16] invitation. He is a splendid man—I liked him at first sight . . . He told us what a generally fine bunch of men the newspaper correspondents are here—but how discouraged and despondent they are at present over the suppression and secrecy. The American correspondents are worse off than the English— Lord Cecil talks quite freely with them, but neither Wilson nor anybody else who knows anything will open their mouths to our men. No correspondents are allowed in Germany. The government has twenty-five State Dept. spies in there now, seeing that nothing in the way of intelligence gets out. O.G.V. has had 1,600 words of one of his cables suppressed by the censor here in Paris. The worst is, he says, that the conference delegates are doing nothing, and that a self-appointed committee composed of Cabinet and Foreign ministers and others, meeting no one knows where and absolutely secretly, are running the whole show. The small nations are getting up on their ear, too, and being promptly sat on by Clemenceau. O.G.V. thinks that unless the League of Nations is started with real purpose and deed as a league of peoples, it may be an instrument of reaction and worse than nothing.

T. Edmund Harvey again spoke in meeting tonight, and I derived spiritual cheer and strength from his words. He spoke of our struggles and trials and how in our search for truth and good we come upon evil, troubled waters at first—but if we persevere, we come upon the deeper well-spring of Divine Love springing up into everlasting life. "Let us not fear or distrust the 'divine discontent'—

it is that by which we eventually find life, in love and service . . ."
Such thoughts spoke right to my heart, for I am seeking—finding
first the meshes of selfishness and idleness which would hold me
back from further search—and which I am praying may be loos-
ened. I feel on the verge of experience—I feel capabilities within me
which might be brought out to some use if I succeed in turning the
center of my life to God. I feel the need of Him—a longing which,
when I am not doing my best to satisfy it—burns me.

I hope—and I think maybe it will be so—that Ronald may be
allowed to work with me for a while, at least. Thee was right in thy
conjecture about the back work: there's plenty of it—and if I translate French labor articles for American syndicalist publication, I get
up to my ears—and without robbing myself of sleep, I have no time
to write or meditate. Francis Birrell thinks I better keep Ronald,
too. He (FB) won't be able to do much more at present for the Paris
office, because he isn't well, and later is going to tour England and
lecture for the work. It's great fun on the paper . . . only I must write!

Ronald is in England now, at the Friends' Ambulance Unit's former camp at Jordans,[17] twenty-five miles from London, waiting for
passage into France with twenty-three others! I'll see him soon! Tell
Helen I couldn't write her as good a letter as I wanted to . . . Luck
for the thesis!

Thine forever,
Leslie

Dearest Mary,

The American Army must have known how anxious I was to hear from thee (or rather, must at last have realized it) because thy letter of the twentieth came today—making extraordinarily quick time.

Ronald arrived Friday last, having had a splendid time in England, seeing the sights of London. Quite a crowd of COs—fine caliber—some of whom I had met at Dix—and two chaps, whom I had just met slightly, from Harvard.

What a joy it was to meet Ronald again! I couldn't be at the Hostel when they came; they were eating when I arrived—Ronald was at the nearer end of the table, talking to someone farther down, so I was able to sneak behind him unnoticed (by him) and put my hand on his shoulder. The boys' happiness in our joy at being together again made us gladder still.

We have been rambling around looking at a little of Paris, but he is a stranger, naturally, to it, and hasn't yet got the *goût de voir* [sightseeing bug]—it will come.

Thee may imagine how I plied him with questions about thee and thine, and Evelyn, and the family and a thousand and one things. And he had a surprise for me—my typewriter came with him! That blessed boy had carried that thing, in addition to the enormous suitcase or rather, hand-trunk, he groaned under. Then it was that he gave me thy note and the pair of socks, and told me how thee went especially to South Station to give him them. Thee shouldn't take so much trouble for me, Mary—but now that I have them, thee must know that they came at a most opportune time,

just when sundry yawning holes were appearing in the socks I
brought from Philadelphia, and Leslie was looking about in a
hunted sort of way for some way out of the difficulty. Thank thee,
Mary!—Certainly they fit and will prove a godsend.

Mary, let me tell thee and not another soul about my trouble,
which has arisen since Ronald came. Thee knows how he sacrificed
his education for the family and for me—what a wonderfully loving
brother he has been. After his visit to Harvard last spring, he expressed a strong desire to go, if possible. I know he'd do well there,
if his heart was in the work.

I asked him by letter to find out what studies he needed to prepare for entrance, and to bring books; but he never got it, or got it
and forgot, for he is sans books. Now, since I hear from thee that Bob
Dunn is decided not to come, Ronald may be stationed in Paris for
some time with me—and we might study . . . But when I mention it,
he answers rather semi-interestedly—as though he felt that perhaps
it was a good thing to study and to go to Harvard; but he doesn't
seem eager; and if one is not eager and whole-hearted in that sort of
difficult preparation one will never get through the preliminaries. I
think he is not interested enough. Perhaps a call or so on Dean Briggs
here in Paris will help him, especially if I drop a word first.

'Tis thus: is it worthwhile for me to make myself furnish all the
enthusiasm—try to create eagerness which does not exist now and
continually keep it up? That, for me, is almost a superhuman task;
yet if it is really for the best, I'll do it. If, for the present, while working with the Mission, he doesn't want to look forward eagerly and
solely, for the moment, to a college education, what and how can we
do to help him? It's so hard to know what he does want.

I'm perfectly capable of staying here till a year from this summer if it is to be my greatest use to go on with publicity and tutor Ronald. Otherwise, as I thought when Horace went back, I should return to college next Fall, and not entirely lose my class. There's no doubt that I'd be willing after thirteen months over here to return, if it were for the greatest good.

What I'll do is to go on studying Ronald and see what he really does want. There's a job for a tactless person! If he ever suspected for a moment that I was staying over here simply to see him through, he wouldn't hear to it! I must wait and watch until his desires crystallize into something I can see.

Feb. 8

I'm appalled at the way time has slipped by since I wrote the foregoing. But maybe it is for the best, because I have talked some more with Ronald. He is not interested at all in going through a regular undergraduate course at Harvard for a degree.

He wants to help the social revolution—apparently at present, by going to Russia and interpreting their more advanced and socialistic methods of living to the rest of the world. He wants to learn French and then Russian and learn to write. He was extremely interested when I told him that there are good Russian courses at Harvard. I believe what he plans now is to stay here, working and learning French for about fourteen months, and then either go back to Cambridge for special work in English and Russian, or go direct to Russia if the way is open.

This may mean that I'll come back to school next Fall . . . .

I am overtaken sometimes by the cynical thought that after all we are not much different from other young people—that lots of them have high ideals and radical principles when they are young, yet rarely or never hold on to them through life—(Or what is nearer the truth, keep their minds young to be able to appropriate and assimilate the advancing thought of the next generation.) The only test I can see is whether we are sacrificing, whether in fact we love others more than ourselves, whether we are out in the fire, or watching interestedly. We both realize the great joy and freedom of such an opportunity—and some of the finest things we may do for each other are to fan the fire of the other's devotion and to catch, nourish, and foster the more Christ-like sparks in the other.

I see thee now in thy gown of green and silver—and the mental picture is poor food compared with the reality—I must live on the sweet quaint dishes of memory . . . the Junior Prom is there—a perfect little cake, as white as snow, with sparkling heady wine poured over it.

Last Wednesday I went to the Opera. They played "Castor et Pollux," an opera by Rameau first given in 1734, and which, before its revival in 1918, had lain dormant for 133 years. It was charming—the Spartan characters were dressed in the hoopskirts and ruffles of the eighteenth century, and the ballet was, too. The music is entirely different from the grandiose effort of the Italians; it is restrained and more melodious than over-wrought. Between the acts we went for a promenade in the magnificent salon—and then out to the dark balcony, overlooking the Place de l'Opéra. The circumstances of the splendid room, the brightly dressed people, and the transition to the dark, cool balcony poured into my brain memories of the Class Day dance in the Union—and all the happy thoughts that are attached to it. Sometimes memories are just as real as actualities, and much sweeter . . . .

Thy future looks much brighter than mine at present; I do hope that Harry D. can put through his dream of a Workingmen's College—it is a great conception of the real step in the right direction of educational equality of opportunity . . . .

Has thee seen Horace Davis? I believe that his work here has done him a great deal of good, and that he is becoming a first-class radical; I hope he will be articulate in the Harvard papers from time to time if any opportunity offers.

Lewis Gannett dropped in tonight. He is a splendid fellow—with a remarkably gentle disposition coupled with a brilliant and fearless intellect. He has been working pretty hard of late, writing articles and interviewing people and attending Socialist meetings.

We're sorry that Bob Dunn is lost to our reconstruction work, but our loss is your gain. A new crowd of about nine COs from camp came in last night—among them Cope (one whom I'd met in Dix) and Henry Stabler[18]—who is an extraordinarily intelligent lad. These COs from camp, as we've often said, are tempered in the fire of persecution of what they believe.

Que l'amour de Jésus Christ soit avec toi. [May the love of Jesus Christ be with you.]

Ton,
Leslie

February 10, 1919, Mary in Cambridge to Leslie in Paris

Dear Les,

Hurrah! Hurrah! Hurrah! Midyears are over! And in fact the second term has begun. I have not heard any of my marks yet, so I am still happy. I enclose our Philosophy 18 exam, which I am sure will interest thee—how I wish I could have done it justice. Thee couldn't have timed thy last two letters better—the first came when I got home from my Ec. exam and I needed cheering very much; and the other I found on the mantelpiece when I returned from an afternoon of selling Suffragists[19] down-town. I never did anything so discouraging in my life—crowds and crowds of painted women and uniformed men seethed by me and either paid no attention at all or else turned up their noses in disgust. I was bound I wouldn't leave my corner 'till I sold all my papers and I finally succeeded, having learned several lessons in human nature! Thee can imagine I was glad to get a bit of thy optimism on returning home and to hear all about thy <u>secret</u> show (it must have been a great success) and thy work for Norman Angell. Really I don't see where thee <u>ever</u> gets the time to do so many things—yet perhaps I do—When we were coming home from a Young Democracy meeting yesterday afternoon in the good old flivver we were going up a steep hill, and I said to Horace, who was driving, "It is still a mystery to me what makes this car go up this hill," and Horace said, "Well if you know John Leslie Hotson you ought to know what a lot of energy there can be in a small space." Wasn't that prettily said? Horace is mighty fond of thee. He said the English Quakers are perfectly splendid but not a bit demonstrative, and that thee had so much spirit and enthusiasm it was refreshing—

oh, there is so much to tell thee. Horace and I have had some fine talks; I wish I could tell thee all about them. He told me about the Friends work and Reconstruction; it all seems so real to me now. He says thee will be able to speak French like a Frenchman when thee comes home. I really must keep in practice or thee won't be able to understand me.

I have many things to tell thee but somehow my mind feels powerless to recall any thoughts or express them—I studied very hard this year and accomplished very little. My exams all came in a bunch so that they seemed to use me up—or perhaps it is because the "flu" took more strength than I realized. I worked on my nerves and am just beginning to calm down.

In the few days' vacation after my exams, I went to several meetings—one at the Fellowship House about the "Comradeship," as the new order is called—it is the thing, Les, the very thing that we are looking for—a chance to serve without thought of self, and its principles are love and fearlessness. I could go on talking about it forever, but thee will learn all about it when thee comes home. We talk about thy return as tho' it were coming very soon, don't we? When in reality thee hasn't decided just when to return. I don't see how with all the work both of you have over there that Ronald and thee can study, too. I should think he would have to wait until he comes back and do some concentrated cramming in the summer some time, tho' of course he might get a good start over there.

I shall probably take a while to rest after college is over in June and then later in the summer go into a factory for a while at least, and start in some more definite constructive work in the fall. I hardly think now that I shall go across; things are so exciting here, changes so unforeseen are coming, I think, and there is certainly much, much to do—organizing industry is the great task today, and labor here in America is so far behind.

How I wished thee could have been here Sunday evening—we had such a lovely party. Hal brought his mandolin, Horace his clarinet, Victor his banjo, and Hood Van den Arend[20] (Harvard Freshman active in Y. D.) his violin—Helen and Virginia and I added our voices and we had a great old concert around the open fire. We played and sang all the good old songs to our hearts content. Thee would have loved it if thee had been there—but I'm sure thee was—wasn't it fun! We think we must get up a Y. D. orchestra to make money for the organization.

When thee gets this, Pres. Briggs will be over there. How glad thee will be to see him. He sailed on February eighth, I don't know to what port. Before he left here (this is a secret of course) I suggested to our Student Gov't President that it would be nice to give him a little sum to spend for others on the other side of the water as he liked. The girls took up the idea and each giving what she could we raised $100 and gave it to him. We wished it were ten times more but perhaps it will come in handy to do some little thing that he would like to very much. How we shall miss him! I hate the idea of getting my degree from anyone else (Professor Robinson is to be acting President while Mr. Briggs is away).

Today we had our first meeting with Captain Morize for French 7. He is going to conduct the course about as differently from Allard as possible. There is to be class discussion; once a week a student is to conduct the class; frequent reports are to be written in French; and the reading is to be of texts and almost no histories or literature. He is going to study romantic poetry minutely with us in class so that we will really know what we are talking about.

His attitude is perfectly refreshing, he is so alive—he wants our criticism and asks our opinion on conducting the course. M. Mercier is just the same in French 10 (Social background of Fr. Lit.)—it must be the French way of teaching—whatever it is, it is great. The students are forced to keep alive and interested.

Now I have something very strange to tell thee—be prepared for scandal! The Harvard Cercle Français of which Dick Bassett[21] is now the President has asked Boston Society girls to act in their play this year instead of Radcliffe. Moreover without a word to any of us, they published in the paper the interesting little fact that two of their performances would take place in Agassiz Theatre. Miss Boody saw this in the paper and called me to the office to see what it could mean. When I told her I was as ignorant as herself she said, "Well of course the boys must be told that if they do not invite you to act in the play they cannot have our theatre— because it is not a public theatre, and the only reason they have used it in the past is through Radcliffe's courtesy." Now Leslie did thee ever hear the likes. M. Mercier told me today that the boys this year haven't consulted the professors at all about the Cercle, and they are perfectly disgusted with this behavior. I am sure I can't make it out—Bassett is restricting the Club very closely and evidently wants to get in with the Boston swells. He is making a mistake, I am sure, because it will cause much hard feeling where there has always been great friendliness. M. Mercier says we ought to get up a rival play—and I think we would if Radcliffe rules did not forbid any more dramatics.

What a time thee and Ronald must be having together—thee can show him around Paris as though thee had always lived there and make him feel at home at once.

I loved the picture of thy thoughts during the Quaker meeting, Les, the contrast of the shining portal of Love and the dark evil spirits that had to shrink away from the searching light.

Like thee, I often wish that we were off together for a walk and a talk, and I look forward to the time when thee will be back again. But oh, I don't know, I do not know. Will we be able to continue seeing each other as comrades when thee comes home again? I should ask for nothing better, but I cannot help feeling that it would not be fair to thee. Anyway we cannot decide now, so let's be happy in our splendid friendship and not worry about the future. Perhaps we can find the path of lasting friendship (which so many people say is impossible) and always be comrades in service. Anyway that is our great ideal, *n'est-ce pas, mon ami?*

It is wonderful to have such a sympathetic ear for all my tales of joy and woe, as thine. When things go wrong or when I am thrilled with something beautiful I say to myself—I must tell Leslie about it. And thy letters are so full of inspiration and idealism—they strengthen and encourage me, thee doesn't know how much.

Bonne nuit—la lune est si brillante ce soir que tous les toits semblant être couverts de neige et nos étoiles sont tout près, comme si l'on pouvait les prendre dans la main sans difficulté. Mais c'est justement parce qu'elles sont si loin, je crains que je les adore! C'est leur beauté mystérieuse qui m'attire. [Good night—the moon is so brilliant tonight that the roofs seem to be covered with snow and our stars are very close, as if one could take them in our hands without difficulty. But it's only because they're so far, that I believe I love them so! It's their mysterious beauty that attracts me.]

Bonne nuit encore de ton camarade,
Mary

February 15, 1919, Leslie in Paris to Mary in Cambridge

Dearest Mary,

I have read thy letter over and over—each time we exchange thoughts and feelings we come to realize more how deeply and completely we understand each other; and how at one we are in hopes, ideals, and aspirations . . . how steadying and uplifting is such a friendship! It is meaning more in my life than ever before, and spurring me on to be better than my best self.

Thee must have been interested in the Mission lecture—and what a surprising way of seeing Horace! Thee is bound to realize his fine qualities if thee can see through his reserve and diffidence. I certainly hope that he is getting what he wants to out of Harvard. He has gone back with finer ideals than he had two years ago.

Mary, thee doesn't know how deeply I felt about thy trial on red-tassel day—it was as if I were in thy place and knew some of the bitter momentary disappointment. It was splendid of thee to keep hold of thy spirits for those toasts—I'll bet there were few who realized just how much courage it took. I know I shouldn't be able to control human emotions like that, superbly. Of course thee won't be discouraged by such a thing; our ideal, which we are struggling for, conquering for, lifts us far above heart-burn. It is just that freedom of all-inclusive love and untiring service that we are willing to sacrifice for; we know what strength and serenity it brings; in our more inspired moments we can feel the élan that it gives . . . If, for example, thee had received the mark of popularity, thee would have been happy and would have thought thee loved the girls deeply— but how much more real and precious is thy love for them now that it has been tried in the fire! The difference is a little like that between the affection of a popular hero for his supporters and the love of the Savior for those that rejected Him . . . no matter how humanly weak we feel we can always see our way clear to our ideal if we reflect. <u>That's</u> what makes us friends!

Lewis Gannett told me this morning that for the first time, Wilson came and talked frankly with the newspaper men. He told them a lot of anecdotes, not for the public, but calculated to cheer them up; by his general attitude and answers to their questions he put their minds at rest on many things that had been festering there. If he had only had the sense to do that a month ago, Lewis said, a great many nasty telegrams to newspapers would never have been born. He says that General Bliss,[22] when Foch gave out that stuff about Germany's ability to raise three million soldiers, said, "Marshal, did I understand correctly that you said that?" "Yes," said Foch. "Well, would you mind showing me your data?" "I have no data," said Foch! Bliss, according to Villard, is almost a pacifist—<u>in private</u>. He is of the opinion that universal military training is the worst thing that could happen to America!

When thee gets this letter, the stress of midyears will be all over; thee will have started on the last lap of college. What college can be for thee and me is a place to work out under most adverse circumstances the high ideal of a loving, serving existence, as a preparation of real life.

After once tasting the value of our new friendship, I cannot be satisfied not to have it grow in inspiration and idealism. To have it a fruit-bearing tree—of use to everybody because we foster it and nourish it. If I can but do my share—heaven knows I want to be worthy.

Toujours!

Les

Workers in the mills in Lawrence, Massachusetts,
on strike for better wages and working conditions

11

Political Activism

AS WINTER SET IN and the excitement of the Armistice waned, Americans grew more fearful for their own country. Always a joiner, Mary became politically active in the Radcliffe Suffrage Club, the Radical Club, the Socialist Club, the Liberal Club, and the International Polity Club.

Mary and Leslie had become involved in anti-war activities soon after war was declared. At the beginning of the war, a group of American students, led by Robert Dunn, formed the Collegiate Anti-Militarism League (CAML), which opposed all systems of permanent universal military training, especially military training in colleges and secondary schools. CAML worked for a world based on the principles of industrial and political democracy, accompanied by international disarmament. It also worked to influence public opinion to promote a peace by negotiation at the earliest opportunity. And it stood for preservation of freedom of speech, press, assemblage, and liberty of conscience.[1]

At the time Leslie and Mary became involved in CAML in early 1918, Anna Davis, Roger Baldwin, and Emily Greene Balch[2] served as advisors.

Leslie was the student representative from Harvard, and Mary's sister Helen represented Radcliffe.

After the Armistice, an extensive network of government intelligence organizations recruited thousands of volunteers to search for draft dodgers, critics of government policy, potential German allies, immigrants, socialists, anarchists, African Americans, and others who were deemed unpatriotic, as well as those who even associated with them. The Espionage-Sedition Act of 1918 expanded the types of dissenters seen as potentially threatening to the security of the nation at war. Radical students at Harvard and Radcliffe challenged the limits of the act by protesting conscription, not buying Liberty Bonds, and distributing leaflets opposing American intervention in Russia.[3]

The new Bolshevik government resulting from the Russian Revolution pulled Russia out of the war in March 1918. Mary and other student radicals supported the Bolshevik government, which they understood was ruled by workers and peasant councils ("soviets") with the ultimate goal ensuring of workers' rights and establishing democracy in its purest form. Many Americans feared that revolution in America could bring down the economy. "Red-hunting" became a government obsession, creating a bridge from wartime fears to postwar hysteria.[4] Towards the end of January 1919, the Overman Committee, under the leadership of Senator Lee Overman of South Carolina, began to probe into pro-German activities and propaganda and, in the process, stirred up widespread fear of Bolsheviks in America. The committee believed there was a link between the Bolsheviks and the postwar radicals and developed a watch list of two hundred names, including Jane Addams and Roger Baldwin.[5]

Mary's mother, Anna Peabody, was active in the League for Democratic Control (LDC), and Mary and Helen often helped in the league office. Anna served on the Civil Liberties Committee, which focused on free speech and conscientious objection to military service, as well as other efforts to maintain constitutional rights. By February, the LDC in Massachusetts adjusted its work to meet peace conditions: making known the labor strike situation at Lawrence, Massachusetts, and in other industries, continuing to fight the Espionage Act, working for the release of every man imprisoned for his religious or economic convictions in regard to war, and educating the public about the necessity of the League of Nations.

In April 1918, Charles Francis Phillips, a draft resister, had formed a new organization, Young Democracy (Y.D.). The Harvard chapter was active from the beginning, and Mary enthusiastically joined the effort. Phillips envisioned agitators and organizers travelling far and wide to rally the youth of the country in support of the radical labor movement and to champion the cause of the conscientious objector. He called for a national conference combining delegates from all the various pacifist and radical societies in the country, declaring:

> "If militarism and military training are to be beaten, they must be beaten by the young . . . We demand that the youths of our generation and of all generations to follow shall no longer be compelled to bear arms at the behest of old men, to submit to laws imposed by old men, to toil under the frightful conditions fixed by old men, or to accept an educational system decreed by old men."[6]

The first executive committee included two Quakers: Henry Cadbury of the AFSC and Harvard student Robert Dunn. They issued a statement calling on all young people to become involved:

> "Its purpose shall be to awaken the youth of America to the consciousness of their power and their responsibility to humanity;

to fuse the energies and ideal of the young into a co-operative unity, to the end that they may have a voice in the construction of their own future and the determination of their own destiny; to invite the cooperation of all existing young people's societies, in order that the youth of America may present a united front on problems vital to us all; and to establish bonds of international good will and fellowship between young people of all nations."[7]

Mary also joined the movement to secure women's voting rights. Her mother had been a suffragist since she attended Radcliffe in the 1890s, and Mary joined her in trying to sell copies of *The Suffragist* newsletter. Politically, suffrage became a war measure when President Wilson heard from the National American Women's Suffrage Association that women would withhold support for the war if their right to vote were not granted. In the fall of 1918, Wilson recognized the contributions of American women to the war effort and expressed his support for giving women the vote:

"We have made partners of women in this war; shall we admit them only to a partnership of suffering and sacrifice and toil and not to a partnership of privilege and right? This war could not have been fought, either by the nations engaged or by America, if it had not been for the services of women—not merely in the fields of effort in which we have been accustomed to see them work, but wherever men have worked, and upon the very skirts and edges of the battle itself . . . I tell you plainly, that this measure which I urge upon you is vital to the winning of the war . . . And not to the winning of the war only. It is vital to the right solution of the great problems which we must settle, and settle immediately, when the war is over."[8]

Suffrage was seen as more important for working class women than for those from the middle class. Once women secured the vote, they could push legislation regulating women's employment, assuring women of equal pay and enforcing regulations.[9] Some socialist women felt that suffrage alone was not enough to liberate women under capitalism, however, and that unions, including union leadership positions, needed to be opened up to women as well.[10]

On May 21, 1919, the House of Representatives passed the Nineteenth Amendment which granted the vote to women. On June 4, the Senate passed it and sent it on to the states for ratification.[11] Mary was able to vote, for the first time, in the national election of 1920.

While Leslie was participating in what Rufus Jones called "a service of love in war time," Mary envisioned service on a broader scale—she wanted not just to help individuals caught up in the sufferings of war, she wanted to change society. Like many intellectuals, she envisioned a new world order, an internationalism in which countries and peoples worked together for mutual good and for the good of the workers.

During the 1880s and 1890s, an increasing number of middle class women, including Mary's mother, turned their attention to the plight of the women working in factories, shops, and tenements. Mary grew up in an era when well-educated women used their training in economics and sociology on behalf of the poor by inspecting factories and visiting workers in their homes. They saw mothers who worked in factories for twelve hours and came home to a full evening of housework. They saw men injured or maimed in industrial accidents with no insurance or worker's compensation to provide for their families. And they saw children working and young girls drifting into prostitution because they could not survive on meager wages.[12] They published reports filled with hard data about such working conditions.

Trade unions were seen as the most promising vehicle for improving economic status according to middle class advocates of social justice who had seen firsthand the need for labor organizers.[13] The Women's Trade Union League (WTUL), founded in 1903, encouraged women to join existing unions or to start new ones. Through the suffrage movement and the support of labor, women hoped to improve their own lots, and, at the same time, to humanize industrial America for all.[14]

Because of the war, women working in factories and arsenals were often paid relatively high wages.[15] Both men and women workers made many gains, including better working conditions and a sense of participation in something important. After the war, as soldiers returned, there was a glut of labor. Women, immigrants, and African Americans were forced to leave their good jobs so that their positions could be offered to the men who served their country. Because workers were so plentiful, wages began to fall and the newly achieved protections were abandoned. Food shortages and high prices continued after the war, fueling worker discontent. Hoping to build on wartime gains in wages and working conditions, men and women workers staged more than three thousand strikes in 1919.[16]

The Fellowship of Reconciliation (FOR), which included many Quakers as members, became active in Boston in June 1918. FOR established a fellowship house on Massachusetts Avenue, and A. J. Muste[17] and Harold Rotzel moved there with their families. These two men were instrumental in organizing support for the labor strikers at the textile mills in Lawrence. Nearly 32,000 mill hands working at the textile mills in Lawrence, Massachusetts, went on strike on February 3, 1919. The strike lasted sixteen weeks. Mary sided with the workers and supported the work of FOR, and her sister and mother attended strike meetings with Rotzel and Muste.

Protest was not the only way to effect change. Henry Dana resigned his Harvard professorship to establish the Trade Union College in Boston.

Mary felt teaching in this school would be an exciting opportunity to put her ideals into action. She sent Leslie a copy of Dana's pamphlet, "Preliminary Announcement of the Trade Union College Under the Auspices of the Boston Central Labor Union," an advertisement for the first term from April 7 to June 14, 1919.

Labor unrest in the spring of 1919 was not limited to America. In Paris, there were riots on May 1, International Labor Day. Workers shut down nearly every activity of the city, including street-railways, subways, shops, and theatres. The labor syndicates had arranged for parades and celebrations, but Prime Minister Georges Clemenceau prohibited any such demonstrations. Fearful that the French would follow the lead of the Russian Bolsheviks, he ordered great numbers of troops into the city. Leslie accidentally got caught in the melee that resulted but was able to escape unharmed.

February 20, 1919, Mary in Cambridge to Leslie in Paris

Dear Les,

Yes, here I am up at the dormitories in the prettiest little room thee ever saw. I will tell thee how it happened. One night last week Mother surprised me by saying that I was taking life too seriously and that she wanted me to get away from the home responsibilities and finish the year at the Halls. I wouldn't hear of it at first because I thought we couldn't afford it, and also I knew it would make more work for somebody else to take over my little odd jobs. Besides when I am at home, I can keep an eye on the family and see they don't get too tired, etc. Well, Mother and Helen just begged me to go, saying that they could get along perfectly well without me and that I mustn't have other duties if I am going to study so hard. The result of our discussions is that I am here. I feel horribly selfish, and I run home every other day to see how Mother and Helen are. We are such a united little family that we miss each other terribly. Helen caught a bad cold as soon as I left, and when I say I ought to be there to look after her, she says it is about time she learned to look after herself. The college life here is certainly fun—and one can waste a great deal of time playing around in different people's rooms if one has the time to spare. The girls tell me it isn't the thing to study and tell me I am setting a very bad example when I retire betimes to my room to do my lessons—I have just been sitting in my west window watching the sunset—all red and purple—behind the pine trees near our Hall. Every evening there is one beautiful star that brightens as the sunset fades and I can't keep my eyes off it 'till it disappears beyond the horizon. I call it thy star because we both love stars so much.

So many things have been happening lately. The Lawrence strike of the textile mills for an eight-hour day with no reductions in wages has been causing great excitement. A group of Fellowship of Reconciliation people, Mother and Helen included (I had to teach Sunday School or I would have been there too), went down to Lawrence last Sunday to attend a strike meeting and show the strikers that they considered their demands just. They were met at the station by mounted police who drove their horses right into them, even up onto the sidewalk. Several people were hurt and the party was scattered, only getting together much later at the strike meeting under great difficulty. Helen says she will never forget in all her life the clatter of those horses' feet as they came down upon them. But she said the quiet, determined faces of the working people at the meeting repaid them for all their trouble in getting there. Of course the papers wrote it all up as much to the Fellowshipers' discredit as possible—it was positively funny what tales were told, and Mother has been getting letters from dear old respectable members of our family saying that she is disgracing the name. Oh Les, Les, the struggle is on—how crazy I am to get out of college and get into it. Industrial Democracy[18] is bound to come—I only hope that by education and the spirit of love it may come without violence and hatred.

[President] Wilson is due here in Boston on Monday and great excitement is brewing—there is to be a huge meeting in Mechanics Hall,[19] but only dignitaries will be able to get in I believe. What a task that man has taken on his shoulders and how perfectly horrible it will be if the League of Nations is not ratified. I don't see how it can fail to be, but I have heard much pessimistic opinion on the subject.

On Sunday afternoon, Mrs. Davis is inviting quite a few of us out to her house to hear Horace talk about the Friends work. I am so anxious to hear him, tho' he has told me a lot about it already. I ran into him when I was at Widener this morning. What a calm, unruffled disposition he has, hasn't he? Helen says that when the police horses were almost on top of him down at Lawrence he marched on with great dignity—his mother on his arm—never looking to right or to left!

This afternoon I have been having a great old talk with Harry Dana about my thesis. I am writing on the "Social Significance of the Plays of Molière," and he has given me some very valuable hints. I never saw such a man—he seems to be familiar with all the literature of all the nations! He spoke to the Harvard Socialist Club the other day (which has revived most flourishingly under the presidency of Hood Van den Arend) on "Socialism and the League of Nations." Arthur Fisher spoke to the Radcliffe Radical Club last week and made a great impression. Girls who had no idea of being Radical and who were induced to come out of curiosity went away saying they would never again be blindly conservative—that they would begin to find out! Dana's plan for a Workingmen's College here in Boston is progressing by leaps and bounds—we'll all end up by teaching there. Bob Dunn is probably going to run the executive part of it.

As far as I can make out thee seems to be commander-in-chief of Reconstruction—has Birrell left? And how can thee <u>ever</u> do it all. Don't forget thee must send me the paper as it comes out—I am crazy to see it. By the way, I am going to have my picture taken next week for the Senior Book. I do hope Ronald persuaded thee to have thine taken, Les—thee is growing much faster than I am because thee is really out in life—Thee will find when thee gets home what strides thee has taken. I have been thinking that perhaps thee did not understand what I said in my last letter about our being comrades when thee comes home. Thee sees that we have both changed greatly in the past year, and thee even more than me. If I have not yet decided what the future has in store for me, I don't want it to make any difference for thee. Marriage is about the most beautiful thing in the world, and if I should be keeping thee from it, I should never forgive myself. We can always be dearest friends even if thee marries someone else. I don't want thee to answer this—just think it over and thee will see that I am right. I am not going to write about it anymore because I leave it to thee—but I wanted thee to understand that I believe in marriage with all my heart, and I thought from thy last letter that perhaps thee didn't—you said, even if I may never have it—and thee deserves a splendid wife, a much finer woman than I. Don't forget, I don't want thee to answer this, Les— just remember it.

Ever thy true comrade who wishes thee the best things of this world and the next,

Mary

February 20, 1919, Leslie in Paris to Mary in Cambridge

Dearest Mary,

Horace wrote me a card, dated Feb. 3; he said that thee and he had a long talk—and that he had come to the (very judicial!) conclusion that I had done well to make such a friend! Quite a dictum from Horace, *nest-ce pas?* Also, he says it is surprising to see how nearly normal things are at school, and how little people know what war is ... Somehow, when one's in France and seeing the people and conditions every day, one forgets that America was hardly touched by the destroying hand.

You're not going to work too hard—take care of yourself, will you?

Thy comrade forever,
Leslie

March 2, 1919, Leslie in Paris to Mary in Cambridge

Dearest Mary,

After having given up hope of hearing from thee for quite a while on account of the exams, thy letter yesterday, written on the tenth, was a joy and a surprise. Long before this, thee must have got thy grades and be still more happy. And the Phil. paper—thee must have just blossomed on it—the very questions that have been close to our hearts.

I have an admiring, hopeless sort of envy for people who can sell things. For my mental constitution, it's the hardest thing I have ever tried. So thee can see how profoundly I can appreciate thy efforts and discouragement with The Suffragist. But I'm proud that thee stuck to the finish.

Thy talking with Horace means so much to me—to have two dear friends of mine meet and become each other's friends is like a warming drink to my soul. And as for the good old musical evening, I'm pining for one. I was there in spirit all right, but I could not take part: nobody ever taught me to pick out a spiritual tenor!

Here I am in Paris doing office work. Ronald is helping me some, but is beginning to take over the duties of the library—the mission one, which will move later up to Grange-le-Comte. The reason I called thy attention to the office work (which thee was well aware of) is that feeling the need of physical exercise to react upon the nervous mental work, I am starting to take fencing from a *maître-d'arme* [master of arms] right around the corner. I find it excellent and fascinating—sorry that I didn't do something of the sort at school.[20]

A young woman who worked once in the office of the American Friends Service Committee arrived recently; she tells me that correspondence concerning the coming of Harry Dana to France is resuming. Is it that he can get a passport? I'll be happy to see him.

Professor Briggs came a few days ago. I'm waiting until he's a little more established before visiting him. You can be sure that I will tell him all the news of our work.

A lot of officers and select soldiers have arrived here now to study in the schools and at the Sorbonne—some say two thousand. I wonder how many among these brave military men will understand a conference in French. I doubt that they will study the language first!

Please give your mother and the charming Helen many friendly wishes from me.

Your comrade,
Leslie

March 4, 1919, Mary in Cambridge to Leslie in Paris

Dear Les,

Spring is in the air and the crew is on the river. I couldn't resist so I went for a good walk along the old Charles, breathing in hungrily the soft sweet air. Soon everything will begin to change to a dress of green and how—how can I make myself study then!

The clipping from the Crimson explains itself tho' it does not give any names. It was Hood Van den Arend's room that was raided.[21] We have gotten to know him very well this winter and he is a splendid fellow. The Liberal Club was mightily indignant about the affair, and Harry Dana wrote this letter to the "Crime"

[The Harvard Crimson] about it. We were all delighted when the editorial column came out so splendidly—But just think of such a thing happening at Harvard! Speaking of raiding—Victor Heatherston's quarters out at Devens were raided the other day and all his literature taken away from him (including Nations, New Republics, etc.) He was called up and cross-examined by the officers and threatened with a court martial. Nothing has come of it yet, however, except that they watch him closely and do nothing about discharging him. Tell Ronald he has almost given up the idea of going across and will probably try for a Fellowship at Harvard or Columbia to get his Ph.D. in Education.

I was so glad to get thy fine long letter telling all about Ronald's arrival. What a good brother thee is to be so willing to give up thine own plans for him. It would be a great task with all the other work to tutor him, too—he would have to be mighty ambitious to make it a success, for thee couldn't do it all. As thee says if he really doesn't care, it isn't much use to try to put it through. If he stays over there a year or so, perhaps he could enter without exams? But I don't know what the rules really are. Thee will decide what is best. I am mighty glad thee has got him to help thee on Reconstruction now. Oh I was so glad to get those numbers thee sent and to see thy name on the editorial staff! That little article thee wrote was splendid; thee certainly sees beyond the outside of things and thee has a "sympathetic" pen. I am waiting eagerly for the next number!

The Lawrence strike is still going on and now Cedric Long[22] and Mr. Muste have been arrested. The story of their arrest is thrilling and unbelievably cruel—the police followed them from street to street—or rather drove them by hitting them on the shoulders and backs with clubs which were discarded a year ago as being murderous weapons. They kicked them and called them vile names. Finally one heavy blow knocked Mr. Long senseless and soon after Mr. Muste fell and couldn't get up. Think of it, Les—oh it is horrible, horrible—if these splendid men are treated so, what do they do to the workers? Mr. Muste told us all about it in his quiet voice at a Fellowship meeting the other night (where Frank Keddie,[23] just returned from reconstruction work in Russia, spoke)—he was so firm yet so forgiving that it seemed as tho' Christ himself were speaking to us and had come to earth to suffer and be mocked at again. And he has—I believe that Christ is in every one of these splendid men who give their lives so fearlessly for what they know is right. Mr. Rotzel has been at Lawrence, too, trying to help the strikers to keep dignified and peaceful—he did not happen to be there that day, so hasn't been arrested yet.

It was strange that night, after I came home from that meeting where Mr. Muste spoke—I suppose I was more wrought up than I realized—for several times in the night I flew out of bed to help somebody who was being beaten—and then when I found myself on the other side of the room and no one there, I realized that it was a dream and went back to bed so excited that I couldn't sleep for a long time. It is utterly foolish to get this way and I am going to try to cure myself—it only remains to find a way, and I think that is not to go to any more meetings while I am studying hard—there will be plenty of chances after June. I feel selfish and wicked to close my eyes and ears to what is going on in the world even for three months, but Radical Club work is all I can get in with my studies. Oh, Leslie, how I wish I were blessed with brains, real brains. It takes me so long to accomplish anything. I really mean it when I say that I know I am going to make a great fizzle of finals. I can't seem to keep my

heart and mind on my work—I study hard and only get B, B, B—
But I must stop rehearsing my troubles; it must bore thee terribly
and thy letters are always so bright and courageous.

La nuit passe. Bonne chance et bon courage <u>toujours</u>. [The night is
moving along. Good luck and good courage <u>always</u>!] I am so sleepy
that I don't know whether I am writing French or English. I just
know that I am thy true friend,

    Mary

March 8, 1919, Leslie in Paris to Mary in Cambridge

Dearest Mary,

    If we are to be pacifists, we must be prepared to be pariahs—
that is, the reactionary governments naturally have no use for anyone who won't fight for his glorious country, and the revolutionary
working class, in death-grapples with the capitalist system, thinks
a man a traitor to his class who will not lift his hand to help. We
are to get it going or coming, which is natural; Christ tells us to expect it. Our task is to prepare our characters and consecrate our
lives that we shall be able to see the vanity of temporal things and
love our fellow-men in spite of shattering trials and disappointments. <u>There's</u> a hope and an aspiration in which one can never be
cast down. I haven't lost my desire for that great path, so I think
there is still hope for me. But I need to tear my thoughts away from
selfish hopes and pleasures which never lift me a particle. I am like
a plant growing in the bottom of a pool—my thoughts and desires
are the long green leaves, waving sinuously in the water, which I

send forth. They tend to wrap themselves around a stick next to me—and I have to tear them off to give them a chance to reach upward toward the light at the surface.

It's all very well to say that "it isn't what you do, but the spirit in which you do it"—Just the same, if you get the right spirit there aren't many things you can't do. I'm groping still for a field of activity in which I can do my best work, and yet, always for others. How I wish I had, as Bob Dunn has, the practical command and pleasure in facts of political and social development and events. That to me seems the most wonderful and helpful, but I don't feel drawn to it: don't feel gifted to handle matters for it. Disappointment. But one can't change one's brain formation, and after all, our usefulness in the next world will depend on how much love we have in our natures for our comrades and for God. Why repine, Leslie? We'll always have, if we keep our faces to the light, a more marvelous and amazingly beautiful hill to struggle up, which will take all our powers.

This morning I went to the Russian Church again. The music, I felt, by the unaccompanied choir was more spiritual than ever. There is a tone of love and faith in those voices, which is very uplifting. I just closed my eyes and drifted far into the unknown on the changing tide of harmony that swept my soul along.

An American sergeant has dropped into our pension. (There are a great many Americans studying this or that now in Paris—it's a good thing.) This fellow has been three months in Germany and learned to speak the language fairly well. He went to Newton High, then to Framingham, then to Mass. Aggie—and he's a next-door neighbor of Guy Beetlestone, my old roommate in Gore! What queer chances. He has an extraordinarily good report of the German people.

Tu as toujours du courage, ma mie! Tu sais ce qu'il nous faut pour être de vrais camarades sur notre grand pèlerinage. Ce courage devient de plus en plus fort quand nous l'échangeons entre nous—ce courage provenant de l'amour désintéressé. [You always have courage, my dear! You know it's necessary in order to be true comrades on our great pilgrimage. This courage becomes stronger and stronger when we share it with each other—this courage from selfless love.]

> *Ton camarade,*
> Les

March 16, 1919, Mary in Cambridge to Leslie in Paris

Dear Leslie,

The rain is pouring down outside while I sit cozily toasting myself by the fire, and write to thee. I would be at church with the others if I were not pretty tired and thought I would try to get rid of my cold. We will have a nice afternoon chat—*n'est-ce pas?* That was such a sympathetic letter thee wrote to me about red-tassel day. Thee understands—yes, I am happier now than I ever was before. Life is so rich and full and beautiful!

Next week spring vacation begins, just think of it—how the time flies. We have ten days, 'tho Harvard only has a week—(they are having midyears now.) I am planning to get the rough draft of my thesis done if possible during vacation so as to have any extra time after vacation to study Italian literature which I have to do by myself. My thesis is great fun—did I tell thee the subject—"The Social Significance of the Plays of Molière"—I try to prove that his fearless free thinking and satirical attacks on authority paved the way for the spirit of the French Revolution.

The 47 Workshop gave three one-act plays last week. I only got there in time for the last one, which was very good—tho' nothing remarkable. As I was coming out from the 47 one of the monitors said to me, "Mary, your mother has just called up. She says there is nothing to be frightened about, but to go right home." Thee can imagine I flew down Hilliard Street—and found Helen and M. Garrison and Hood Van den Arend in the study, sitting around talking about an automobile accident they had just been in. They were not hurt but looked as though they had been through everything. It was <u>terrible</u>, Leslie. With Mrs. Davis and Harry Dana they had all been down to Lawrence for the day, and coming home they were run into and the Ford was upset, throwing them all out. Mrs. Davis was thrown quite a distance and had to be carried home in an ambulance. Helen got her arm bruised and Garry her face badly scratched. Harry Dana hurt his neck and Hood got generally banged up. It happened out in Reading. The description of their various feelings as they crawled from underneath the car or from the gutter sounded like a novel. Each one thought he or she must be the only one alive at first, and the joy at finding everyone else alive made them feel as if they were walking on air. It was a fearfully narrow escape.

Mr. Davis and Horace don't show their feelings very much— they are very much alike I guess—tho' I think Horace is like his mother too. I can't make him out exactly. He came to the Harvard Radcliffe socialist meeting the other day, at which Harry Seidler spoke. He asked for the last news from thee and I told him that the Friends wanted thee to stay another year (thy mother told me so in a letter lately), but that I didn't know what thee was going to do. We both agreed that we thought thee had better come back to Harvard next year, tho' we wanted thee to decide for thyself and do what thee thought was best.

What thee said in thy last letter about Lewis Gannett, Foch, and Wilson is all terribly interesting. There are two great forces in the world today—the conservative and the radical—and here they are becoming more and more distinct. There is a nation-wide campaign on, against the Bolsheviki—the newspapers have huge denouncements—half-page things like ads with pictures, etc., telling of the horrors of Bolshevism, and the other day Mother received in the mail a disgusting anonymous pamphlet claiming to be a copy of the Bolshevik laws about free love. They say they are sending these out to "parlor socialists" to let them know what they are tolerating, or rather advocating. Keddie said that it is absolutely false and spread purely to discredit socialism (K. is the Russian Friend I told thee about.) In our discussion group with Prof. Lake at college, he says we must make it our business to look into Bolshevism and search everywhere to learn the truth because the papers do not tell it. Prof. L. says socialism is advancing by leaps and bounds and we have got to meet it intelligently, not ignorantly and passionately— he is great!

I don't know what I would do if I couldn't go home over the weekends—the dormitory life is so unnatural and institution-like. Its only advantage is its carefreeness and opportunity to study.

Good night, fellow traveler—how fresh the wind is from across the moor; it means a bright tomorrow.

Thy comrade,
Mary

March 17, 1919, Leslie in Paris to Mary in Cambridge

Dearest Mary,

Letter nineteen comes from the dorms! A beautiful message from a beautiful place. Thy removal there shows wisdom. For though the actual time thy home duties required was not much, thee certainly must have felt freer to concentrate when the intangible sense of responsibility was removed. I'm glad! Or at least I shall be glad when thee promises not to kill thyself with cold-blooded over-studying.

I should not go against thy wish for no answer except reflection to a part of thy last letter, did I not feel bound to set thy mind at rest upon a possibly troublesome doubt. For nearly a year, I have thought things over and over; and thee can tell what the result is when I say that the mere suggestion of thinking "if thee marries someone else" hurt my whole being. My ideal of marriage is not ordinary. Recently my feelings towards marriage have been distilled, and I see more clearly: as a course to be taken in this world, or merely postponed till the next world . . . it is certain in the end—a part of God's plan. As thee knows, the few years we spend here are very short. Just because I love, revere, and long for marriage to the bottom of my heart is not a reason why I should make a *mariage d'occasion* [marriage of opportunity] here on earth, if I may not have the perfect one—does thee think so? I feel that any marriage below an attainable ideal is in some sort a desecration. There are men, I know, who say that they need a wife, and even seem to—Longfellow and Lowell both married twice, I think—but as far as I know, I am able to renounce a second-best marriage. But because this is true, don't let me sway thee in thine own judgment in thy difficulties,

Mary! Thee must not think that the hurt to me of one of thy possible courses would be cruel; it was for this that I was given such a faith of conviction and sure hope for a next world. And as thee says, it is also because of the ideal as well as the faith we have that no matter what happens, we shall always be the dearest friends.

Last Saturday, I went to the Sorbonne to hear Mr. Briggs lecture. Arriving just before he began, I found his *auditoire* [audience] to be at least half feminine; the rest were French officers in many and varied uniforms, several old men, and four Americans.

His subject was "History and Principles of English Versification." It was perfectly great—a real spiritual feast for me to watch his face and hear his voice, and the quaintly-repeated first syllables. I shut my eyes and was back in a twinkling in old Sever 2! He seemed to be looking at me all the time, though I was in the back of the room. In reality, the first he saw me was after the lecture when I went up to talk with him. He took another Harvard man (Burlingame, '12, a lieut.) and me into a side room and told us a lot of news about school. Then Burlingame had to go, and I walked with Mr. Briggs down to his hotel near the Seine bridge of the Carrousel—and he invited me up for tea. There I met Mrs. Briggs and Lucia. It was delightful.

Thy subject for thesis interests me a great deal—I can't think of a better one for folk like thee and me in French literature. To me there is a sense of freeing in his plays—not an individual shout for liberty, liberty, and still more liberty, but a common-sense, humoring removal of various baleful, long-worn chains from the social mind . . . Harry D. is a brick—there's no other word for him!

Thee has said it, Mary—the struggle is on; the world must go forward; tyrannies must give place to brotherhood. But in the struggle, we pacifists have almost the most difficult role of all. We cannot take our stand simply and squarely with the revolution, to fight and fall for it. By being with the revolutionaries we are "traitors" to the governing class of the existing order. By refusing to help the liberators with our arms, and even discouraging their use of them, we are traitors in their eyes too. We can plainly see what is ahead. "Rejected of men" may be just as true in a short while for a modern pacifist as it was of our Master. Yet I fancy more tolerance will issue from the hands of the poor than from those of the rich . . . It is a great age, Mary—many things are going to happen: our opportunities for service are manifold and appealing—and we call each other to them!

Spring is opening my <u>Oxford Book</u> again for me; somehow it can't stay shut at the opening of God's perennial inspiration to the soul of man. If I can't be on the bank of the Charles in flesh and blood, the glory of the sinking sun will seek out my heart there, and the whisper of the wind across the ruffled water will meet my spirit. May we not meet there sometimes on the fairy-soft spring days? Then if thee thinks I'm not there, how mistaken thee'll be!

Ton camarade,
Les

March 25, 1919, Leslie in Paris to Mary in Cambridge

Dearest Mary,

It's now my turn to protest—but without tirading. Formerly (before thee came to Barnard) thy letters usually said in closing "Mother's sending me to bed" or something similar. Now they say

"*La nuit passe!*" [The night passes!] What can this mean but that having left Mother's care, thee is staying up to unconscionably late hours? Ah, Mary, I am talking to no purpose for thee has already seen the impossibility of it.

But do not be troubled about apparent difficulties of accomplishments in study. The great thing thee has accomplished is the centering of thy life in the ways of Christ, which is a thousand times more wonderful than the highest honors in any college. If thee finds that hard study isn't developing thy best desires, I shouldn't worry about it. It isn't worth it. That is quite a statement for me to make, considering what a fetish learning was for me (and tries to be still). It was comparatively easy for me to crowd religion out of my head while I was studying during the week. The only time it came up, disquieting my false living from the very bottom, was on Sundays in the New Church in Cambridge, making evident that my life wasn't turned in the right direction.

Learning, music, art, poetry—if they are done only for themselves—are not creative of love, and in that case are far from the road we long to travel. But insofar as we can gain added power of giving from them, they are precious.

One of the favorite war-time expressions over here was "*Faut pas chercher à comprendre, c'est militaire*" ["Don't try to understand, it's the military"]—a sentence produced by war, which tends to take even man's power of understanding away. On the other hand, we know that a man governed by love can understand more things than the greatest individualist or selfish brain the world could produce . . . .

The story of the raids on Van Arend and Heatherston are significant of reactionary forces. How small people betray themselves to be when they persecute those whose freed thought might tend to destroy their cherished unjust privileges! Rowdyism of that sort isn't new. Think of William Lloyd Garrison! For the first time, I feel the deep conviction that these are momentous days. And Mr. Muste! Wasn't there a cry from the Young Friends or somebody about that treatment? Or are they still for capitalism and think he was misguided or indiscreet in his actions? I think the Young Friends are waking up. It is high time!

T. Edmund Harvey, the President of the Mission, gave a talk with slides at the Settlement House I told thee of before. It was a wonderful evening. One could feel the hungry yearning of the people for relief from their hardships, and the generous joy in the help given to others who have suffered even more than they. They are brave *gens* [groups of families]—one can get so near to their hearts. As a rule you are miles away from cultivated persons when you are talking to them, with a barrier of artificiality and dissembling staring you in the face.

By the time this reaches thee, Oswald Garrison Villard will probably be home again. He turned up the other night from Germany, having disappeared in there some time ago to see conditions for himself. See if thee and Margaret can't get near enough to him to talk sometime—he has very interesting experiences to recount. I didn't hear him the other night at Lewis Gannett's—it was the night of Harvey's talk at the Settlement House—but they say it was great.

News from Hungary! The forces of darkness seem to be losing ground. Carleton MacDowell[24] just came in. He's in rather a bad way wanting to get home, and facilities for getting home on transports have been abolished; no French liner sails until April 4.

Thy,

Les

March 26, 1919, Mary in Gloucester, Massachusetts, to Leslie in Paris

Dear Les,

I am sitting on the rocks looking out to sea. The gulls go circling by and the air is fresh and salty. I feel as though I were beginning all over again—and I really am. Just before this vacation I had a sort of nervous collapse. I had been going on my nerves for more than a month, and I suddenly found that I couldn't go any more, so Dr. Whittemore has sent me down here to the ocean and made me give up the idea of honors entirely. I am so disappointed and so angry with myself. It is all because I didn't know how to manage my time and tried to do nothing but study intensely, which I have found I cannot do. Now I shall just finish college getting the most out of my studies and pleasures and forget my ambitions.

I am just happy that I am alive in the sunshine and shall wait until later for other things. This letter probably won't sound much like me because I haven't really found myself again yet, but oh, I am glad that I can write at all—for I thought—yes, Les, I thought that I should never write to thee again. Dr. Whittemore laughs at me when I say that I thought I was losing my mind, but, Les, it really was terrible, and I only wanted to die and have the nightmare over. The great thing that helped me was faith in God. I would put all my trust in Him and become more peaceful knowing that the future was in His hands and that He would do with me as He thought best. I am so much better now, though I don't think thee would know me, I am so thin and drawn. Oh there is nothing like religion, it takes us outside of ourselves—I pray that mine may be always strong and true.

About thy coming back, we will decide all our problems when thee gets here—it is so hard to say just what one means, or rather be understood, by letter when the intervals are so long. Thy friendship means so much to me, more than thee knows. In these days of anxiety I have felt thy sympathy and strength, and as I have just now watched the white ships sailing out of the harbor to the open sea I have thought of thy great confidence in immortality, and life seems more than ever only an instant in eternity. And yet how precious that instant is; as I get well I cling to it more and more. Yes, spring is coming, but I cannot realize it yet—I seem to be bewildered like a person waking out of a dream—soon I will be really awake and find myself in the midst of a blooming world—my only hope is that with my returning *joie de vivre*, I will find that I am some use—I have been profoundly discouraged by my failure in my studying—I just can't talk about it—but I still have faith that someday, somehow, I shall do something worthwhile for others. Tell me that thee thinks so too, I need encouragement—oh very much.

Take care of thyself, Les—we must be strong to do our part, and now I know that it is the most unselfish thing in the end not to overdo. I must stop now as I can't seem to think coherently any more. It has done me so much good to tell thee all my troubles, forgive me—don't try to understand this letter—I know it is incomplete and I would like to say so much more. When the sea air has blown my mind all fresh and new I'll write to thee again. *Que Dieu te garde toujours, mon cher camarade* [May God protect you always, my dear comrade]—

Mary

March 31, 1919, Leslie in Paris to Mary in Cambridge

Dearest Mary,

The swift and full message I just got from thee is like a reviving draught that brings me back to my best self—to the ideals I'm bound to live by and to the comradeship which is as dear as life.

The accident!—ah, the accident. It looks like a special dispensation of Providence that no bones were broken. But how about the car that threw the Ford? I'm convinced that it belonged to the mill owners and the "accident" was a cold-blooded attempt on the lives of the influential strike sympathizers! They followed the folks to quite a distance from Lawrence to avert suspicion. Ah hah! It's a great life. After having once been a radical, does the comfortable career of a respectable "social worker" ever attract one? The question is its own answer.

I had an experience last Thursday that means much to me. The children from the Settlement House "Union des Familles" wanted to go on a hike. The twin daughters of M. Eugène Burnand were to go with them. I vow I can't remember whether I've told you about them or not; at any rate I'll repeat for safety that their papa is one of Switzerland's greatest modern painters; that his series of about eighty heads of typical warriors of all nations and colors is to be exposed at the Luxembourg gallery as soon as it opens (in May, I think); the girls had twin elder brothers, artists, who were so alike that even after they were grown their mother used to make mistakes in them; and the two girls are twenty-five; they are Swiss, speak German and Italian as well as French and are learning English; they are Protestant and very serious Christians. Well, since the director of the school wouldn't promise to go, they asked me. I was only too glad to be able to go out with those lads, who are great companions, and to have the chance to exchange ideas with the girls. We started out bright and early: went to the school and got the kids, walked out to the wall of Paris with them, took a tram from there to Clamart, and then walked out through the woods. Snow began to fall, then hail, and then honest rain, and cold wind blew. Those poor girls and some of the kids were very thinly dressed for such weather, but the spirit of the whole crowd was just great. We sang and laughed at the rain, and all shivered in chorus. And we jumped over "pud muddles" and waded through with great glee. The soft blue-gray mist that hung over the distant trees was just softening into Spring ... And as we walked, we talked—mainly about conscientious objection. I told them as much as I knew about it, and they seemed very interested—most especially at Ronald's history. And then they told me that their oldest brother had the same idea and would have been a CO if mobilized—and that they know of one case of a soldier (an old farm-hand of theirs) throwing down his gun and turning CO ... he was finally persuaded to get into the *Section Sanitaire* [Health Section]. They said they were glad they weren't men, for if they had been confronted with a call to war they don't know what they would have done. According to their statements, I was the first one in France they had ever talked to about this thing—apparently it doesn't exist in France. At least folks can't understand it. I believe that the few COs France may have had were either put in an insane asylum or shot—mostly the latter.

Then we talked about the theatre—I told them about 47 and they seemed highly interested at the things that are apparently possible in America. Then we shifted to the problems of careers of men and women ... they called my attention again to the greater difficulties besetting a woman—how it is hardly possible for her to have both a family and give herself for social service. They think that either one or the other must be sacrificed . . . .

April 8

Experiences have come thick and fast in the time that has passed since I wrote the above. I have been up to Grange-le-Comte to attend General Committee (semi-annual) and to visit *équipes* in the neighborhood. It was like a wonderful draught of fresh water to me. My health and spirits had been rather low, but, as luck—or rather Providence—would have it, just before Committee, the rains stopped and fine weather prevailed.

Joe Marvel and I were delegated from the Student Hostel *équipe* to be present at the Committee. Grange-le-Comte certainly looked different from what it did last December when I first saw it. Then mud and dirt and American soldiers were everywhere, and the *équipe* numbered only some twelve men. Now the Friends are over one hundred in number, the electric light plant is in, and the place fairly hums with activity. The Chateau has mostly offices and common rooms in it; the new dining room is a large barracks (wooden) very near at hand, with excellent arrangement for feeding a large number of folks in a short while.

But what I got from my visit was not just that collecting of new information so interesting in itself, but the "feel" of the greatness of the spirit being put into the effort to bring aid to the French people. Jim Norton talked it over with me. He says, and I realize the truth, that I ought to be up there most of the time looking about, being with the work—in the game; only coming to Paris when necessary to look after the printing of Reconstruction. That's what I'll do! I'm free to do practically anything necessary to the job, and I'm convinced that that's necessary.

A little "aside," Mary—Marion Norton, Jim's wife has been working in Paris as stenographer in the Friends Bureau of the Red Cross ever since they came over last May and has just been allowed to change her place of work to the new headquarters at Grange, where Jim is the head of the Maintenance Department. She is overjoyed, naturally; she loves the work, and it has been a revelation to her to get into the middle of things up there. They have a room in the tremendous old stone farm building, and a huge fireplace. And just imagine—they get <u>into</u> this fireplace and seated on stools in the opposite corners, they look at each other and talk with the fire between them! I never knew the full meaning of "chimney corner" until now. Those two young people are taking a beautiful journey on this Quaker mission to the unfortunate, and they have an inspiration and a consecration to happy, devoted service which is beautiful to behold. If all our young people could be like that, the working class would come into its own and there would be no oppression and cruelty. There are several young couples in the Mission now—and they have a peculiar contribution to the general spirit of the Mission because they are so fine. In every case, both husband and wife are efficient, active workers and have high spirits. Their presence lifts the spiritual being of the large number of young men. Their comradeship and close association in work is an incalculable benefit to most of us.

The discussions in Committee were of intense interest, as showing what the Mission is thinking about. One of the most interesting points raised was on the question of using the labor of German

A few of the German prisoners
who worked for the Friends after the war

prisoners, which has been offered us. At the time of Committee, we were using about 190 a day. The situation was this: the prisoners (*Prisonniers de Guerre,* or P.G., taken by French) were almost starved to death. When they came to work for us, they could hardly lift a shovel—and, seeing a barrel full of old axle-grease in the courtyard, they surreptitiously scooped out handfuls and ate it. Well, we gave them a good meal and tea at four o'clock and some to take back to the rest, where conditions were terrible: sickness was rife and the men were sleeping in the mud. Apparently the underfeeding was due to the careless and hard-hearted French officer in control of them. The American soldiers and the French guards were all indignant at the treatment . . . Several Friends had strong scruples against making use of "war-slave" labor, since we have taken so firm a stand against militarism: they wanted to send food and aid into the camp without taking the work of the Germans. Others were willing to use their work because it so evidently was a pleasure for the poor fellows to get with people who would treat them as brothers. "*Heute is gleich wie Himmel gervesen"* ["Today is the same as heaven"] the eldest of the group said to Edmund Harvey after their first day's work. As one of them earnestly said, *"Es nacht ein kolossale Unterschied"* ["It's not a big deal"] to be asked not to run away, for the sake of the other prisoners and for the sake of the furtherance of our work, and then to be working with Friends and have no guard. They wanted to know who we were and what we believed, and we told them.

The matter was satisfied by the news that the day before Committee meeting, their living conditions were substantially ameliorated. And about paying them for their work: it was decided impossible to keep a minute record of the number of hours each prisoner helped us, but we will collect the addresses of as many as possible, form an estimate of the proper remuneration, taking into consideration the food and chocolate[25] we give them, and send the money to them after the peace is signed and they are returned. We can't do it now without embroiling ourselves with the French Gov't.

The Committee decided to put out a Mission Book—with a history of the beginnings of the FWVRC, the work of the English, the coming of the Americans, the work on the Somme, the concentration of the effort in the Meuse. A story of the work of each *équipe*. A list of the workers and their pictures, and individual histories—stories of COs in camp and prison (perhaps). Bright stories and anecdotes in the back. In all about 250–300 pages—to be printed in America, and got out when the Mission has concluded its stay in France. I'm delegated to organize the collection of material. Some job! I think I'll get somebody else to work right away on the details of gathering the more mechanical data . . . .

Tat Brown took me over into the Argonne forest, where there are still lots of munitions lying around in huts, although soldiers are occupied every day blowing up huge quantities of explosives. Thee'd think the war was still on by the rumbling roars which shake the windows from time to time. There was one hut in the woods with propaganda shells in it—the only kind of weapon which interests me enough to want it as a souvenir—little 37mm shells with tightly-rolled papers inside, printed in German. They are intended to be shot up into the air like a star-shell from a canon-fusil, burst, and scatter the leaves in the German trenches. Oswald Villard said that Germans told him on this trip through their country, that that shell did more to end the war than any other. They are quite a curiosity, I understand. Even Captain Marrauld of the French Artillery had never seen one.

On Saturday morning I got a ride in a side-car up to the village of Brabaut-en-Argonne. There I wandered about among the ruined houses seeing the skillful repairs that our men had made in those that were reparable, and hearing the sound of hammer and saw cheerily at work. I also saw the cooperative store in action—everything a body could want at remarkably low prices ... Village women coming in happy to be able to buy and not be robbed. The life of the village was taking on again, though slowly, tentatively.

Fred Chambers, my old chum, who now drives the Agricultural Dept.'s Ford, had to make a trip up to Varennes that afternoon, so he took me along. We passed through Aubreville and Neuville, where *équipes* are building and repairing, up to Varennes, which is shattered. One can still imagine its one-time beauty, lying on a hill-side beside the river. The old hostel at which Louis Seize and Marie Antoinette were apprehended on their attempted escape has been razed to the ground by shell-fire, but the little square heavy *donjon* [dungeon] tower where they were imprisoned is still standing. We drove around to the *équipe*, which is in a German dug-out on the lee side of the hill. The whole side of the hill is dotted with dug-outs—very attractive places, some of them, done in cement, and well-appointed inside. We

Entrance to one of the abandoned dug-outs in Verdun

delivered our goods, visited a little with the members of the *équipe*, and then set out on foot to the famous hill of Vanquois, some four kilometres distant. Over the shell-pitted country, across trenches and barbed wire, we went to where this huge murdered hill lay. We climbed up its steep side, all overturned with explosions and, on reaching the top found that it had none—the French sappers, during the war to dislodge the Germans, had tunneled deep in eight places along the top of the hill and had planted tons of high explosive—and then blew the whole backbone out of the ridge! One of the craters was at least sixty feet deep. Freddy and I let ourselves down into it by means of telephone wire. It was too steep to get out without help. Then, after viewing the shattered Bois de Cheppy from this desolate look-out, we thought we'd have a peep into the famous miles of saps which the Germans burrowed into the bowels of this hill. Before leaving the *équipe* at Varennes, Appleton (an English Friend) told us that many of the entrances had been smashed down by hand-grenades to keep folks out, because of dangerous weaknesses of ceiling, etc.

We found a good-looking entrance after seeing many plugged-up ones and decided to have a look inside. Each of us had a candle, and I had four matches. We lit them and went in; the tunnel was so small and narrow that we had to stoop, and it would have been difficult for two to pass. I felt rather adventurous. We stopped, listened—all we could hear in the deadly silence was the far-off drip-drip of water deep down the blackness of the tunnel. Slowly, for the way was steep and slippery with mud, and our candles dazzled, we descended, feeling our way. We found telephone wires over our heads, and I noticed that the flame of my candle was blown ahead by an incoming draft. Coming to cross-ways, we took the most promising-looking ones with increasing telephone wires and neglected to mark our turnings. Rooms appeared—some filled with munitions, others with sleeping quarters, and some even with forges and little work-benches. We found German wine-bottles on the floors, and I picked up a little German novelette which some fellow had been reading to keep his mind off the danger. Well, we had walked some fifty minutes before we decided to right-about-face and get out of that terrible burrow. I happened to be ahead; we went back over the way we had come quite quickly, but suddenly, we looked at each other and suspected that we had missed our path. However, the way went up and up, and we followed, until we were stopped short; the tunnel had been made impassable by a cave-in. We went back to our last turning and tried another tunnel. Freddy went first and nearly fell into a deep part of it that was full of water. Then we tried another tunnel, and I blew out my candle, to save it. By that tunnel we got back to a place deeper down where we had just come from. It certainly looked as though we were lost. I started to think about Tom Sawyer and Becky Thatcher, but didn't mention it to Fred. Then we started out again, slowly this time, watching the footprints and verifying where we had been before. All at once we came to a place where a casual glance would see no exit, but where we really had come in. We started up that, found our original footprints, found the draft coming in, and a three-minute walk brought us to the first gray shafts of daylight. My land, but they looked good! I thanked God in my heart for bringing us out safely. We had walked for an hour and a quarter trying to get out—and had spent altogether more than two hours in that *maudit trou* [cursed hole]. Fred and I were a little shaken up about it. It appears that Tom Sawyer was on his mind, too—he read the book for the first time just this winter. As he said, "that was an experience I never want again, but one I wouldn't swap for a whole lot." It was dark— after eight o'clock when we got back to Varennes, but luckily the fellows hadn't begun to worry about us. We ate something, and started back to Grange. I sang (or tried to) to cheer myself and annoy Freddy so he'd forget how nearly his Sylvia (familiarly known as Peggy) came to never seeing his 212 lbs. of Ohio manhood again.

Sunday morning was bright and warm: excellent weather for the trip to Verdun which many of us were contemplating. We took the morning train at Clermont and got into Verdun at noon. Joe Marvel and I left our packs and coats at the Y.M.C.A. there and started out to see "the greatest battleground of history" on foot. When we got out to the first fortified hill—Côte-St.-Michel, we were pretty tuckered by the heat and dust. There we fell in with some American soldiers who had come up from Toul to Verdun for the day in a Ford. They took us in, and we rode through those hills and vales of horror where the surface of the earth is pulverized and not a bit of earth can be seen—the most appalling thing I ever saw. One can't imagine it—

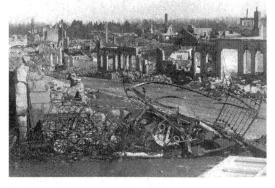

Land and homes in Verdun that were completely destroyed

it would take a Dante to invent such a scene. The terror of it is that it overwhelms you—ordinary battlefields are those whose grass is growing round the old gun-carriage wheel and sheep are grazing between the former trenches; the moon (the ground is so white)—or in Hell. One can't say anything that doesn't sound ghastly trivial.

The American soldiers, whom I got to like very much after hearing them talk—they were of America's best, I think—asked us why we didn't come with them down to Toul. Why indeed? We went! Through St.-Michel, Commercy, to Toul, following the Meuse, which was the front for a considerable period. The day was lovely and the Meuse Canal charmed our eyes. It was a handsome voyage—the sun went down in glory behind us, and we plodded along in the dusk, arriving at Toul about half past eight . . . Thence we took the Paris express, which brought us into the Gare de l'Est in the morning!

And yet I'd trade it all for one walk with thee up the Charles . . . .

Yes! Let's form a company of young radicals to spread the gospel of the new era in plays over the countryside! What if there be hardships and discouragements? We need them for our character! I don't believe Molière would have exchanged his experiences for a bed of roses!

A wonder and deep thankfulness come over me when I consider our magnificent friendship. *Courage et cœur, mon camarade! Si nous fixons nos regards vers la vie éternelle on sera heureux dans n'importe quelle épreuve! Dieu te garde toujours. C'est la prière de ton,* [Courage and heart, my comrade! If we set our sights towards eternal life, we will be happy whatever the tests. God protect you always. That's the prayer of thy,]

Leslie

April 3, 1919, Mary in Cambridge to Leslie in Paris

Dear Les,

I am sitting up in the old crooked tree in the Botanic Gardens. Spring is really here and thrills my soul. I hope thee has not been worrying since getting my last letter—I was so blue when I wrote it that I was selfishly thoughtless of thee, I am afraid—now I am a different girl—cares about lessons being all gone and spring coming fast, I shall be myself again soon. It takes a long time—and sometimes I get discouraged, but the blue spells are rare now, and I am going to live all the joy of every opening leaf and flower. Thy last letter described so strangely well the very way I felt before I was sick—

wanting oh so badly to do everything, and yet somehow not being able to spur myself to do it. Now *mon ami*—<u>do</u>, <u>do</u> be careful—thee must not be sick. Overworking puts one so far behind that it doesn't pay. I am so glad thee has the fencing for exercise—we must have healthy recreation mixed with our work to be able to serve the best—

The sun is getting lower in the sky and everything is so peaceful; the little pond makes me think of what thee said about feeling like a plant groping up thru' the water to the light. As I sit here writing to thee of the thoughts and ideals we shared and the breeze blows gently through the budding branches I feel the quiet of the Great Peace, and I am calm. Thee asks me if I do not keep needing inspiration—oh, *oui mon ami*, I could not live without moments like this. Nature is a great symbol of God as thee has so often told me and therefore is the great sympathizer and inspiration. How small (little) we feel ourselves in its presence, and yet how great is the soul of man. I wish thee had a chance to get out in the country some this spring—thee must, *il le faut!* [it's necessary!] Spring is the most beautiful season of the year, *elle est divine, n'est-ce pas!* [it's divine, isn't it!] (It is funny, thy letters are a mélange of English and French, so I catch the habit when I write to thee.)

Even if thee has a hard time thinking what thee wants to do later on, I am glad thee is what thee is, and not Bob Dunn—why should everyone need brains just like his? I feel it more and more that people have to serve in the way they are fitted. I felt for a while that I ought to force myself to work in a factory, but after talking with different people (Mrs. Davis for one does not want me to do it) I think that I would not be of most service there because I would be deadened by the monotony. Of course I believe we should keep in the movement of progress but I also believe that there are many ways. I remember vaguely having written thee something about a radical theatre—and how thee should write the plays and act, too. Of course that is just a flight of my imagination for the present, but I firmly believe that thee should feel around to find what thee likes and can do best and then link it up with thy constructive ideas. Thee has plenty of time yet to decide *ça viendra!* [what will come!] And thee has so many talents that it will be easy. Now I am a jack of all trades and master of none—here I am graduating from college in June and I am at sea. Margaret Garrison and I have been much interested lately in a Fellowship School on the Hudson about sixty miles from N.Y. They want some young radical teachers. I did not want to teach, but this looks as though it might lead to other things so we are looking in to it. How we should have loved to get into the Trade Union College, if it were only to scrub the floors—but they have such wonderful people and more than they need for everything that there is no hope there. I send thee the little prospective, I can imagine it will thrill thee to read it as it does me! [Leaflet enclosed—"Preliminary Announcement of the Trade Union College Under the Auspices of the Boston Central Labor Union"]

Next Saturday evening, Rufus Jones is to give a lecture in the Old South Church on the Friends reconstruction work in France. Francis G. Peabody[26] is to preside, and Horace is going to show his lantern slides. I am crazy to go—I think they expect a good audience; they sent out very impressive cards about it.

College, of course, seems entirely different to me now. I can enter into the life of it again and not feel wicked about wasting time. I have reconciled myself to graduating with a humble "cum" and am in for all that college life has to give until June. We are making our plans for class night, Bachelauriat (spelling!) and Commencement already—

the time just flies—before we know it, it will be all over. How I wish thee were going to be here for all the festivities. I shall miss thee, my comrade—though I know thee will be here in spirit.

> *Bonne nuit et adieu mon camarade et au revoir,*
> Mary

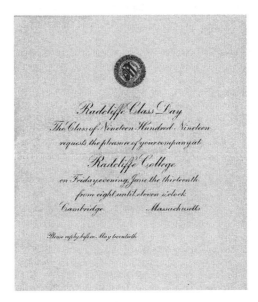

April 14, 1919, Leslie in Paris to Mary in Cambridge

Dearest Mary,

How my heart yearns to comfort thee, to cheer thee and strengthen thee in thy dark hour, Mary—and what a groping pain it is not to be near thee—where we can speak and say what is on our souls to say! Miles are long and hours are heavy for us to speak by letter—but thee must sometimes feel the love that I express to thee in spirit. Yet, so often I am heartened and encouraged to a new hold on life by the mere recollection of one or two of the many high moments in the past—how I wish I might be to thee the power and tenderness thee is to me! If I had more of the spirit, how much greater would be my sympathy—how much nearer I might come to being a friend worthy of thy friendship!

I never dreamt thy nerves would let down so terribly—which proves that I had no conception of the tremendous effort of the will thee was exerting in study. Thee does not do well to be either disappointed or angry with thyself! What, disappointed at not being able to study and work superhumanly? *Allons donc!* [Nonsense!] If I could ever study hard enough to threaten my health, I'd be proud of my powers of concentration. Angry? Why be angry at learning something that will be of inestimable value later and which no one on earth can teach—how far one can work efficiently? Oh dear, how heartless this all sounds—I'm sorry, Mary. But thee has had two unforgettable experiences—the greatest in life, I feel—of first contemplating the nearness of death (last fall) and now the vast terror of losing, more terrible than life, one's mind. And the Christian faith was potent to sustain thee where all else failed . . . Yes, Mary, thy religion is the true one—of the life. I've never feared for thee . . . one cannot feel that calm security for many of one's friends . . . Thee is out of reach of accident or death in any form. Life is only life when the source and water of it is thy pure love of God. Insofar as it is perverted by self, it becomes death, which is sin. As thee says, life is precious: nothing is more, for it flows from God. But we waste our effort in clinging to it— for inasmuch as we love and serve, we will have life now and forever.

God gives it, and no one can take it away but our self, and we sometimes tend to lose it by hugging it too close . . . This is my spirit speaking to thee, Mary, and my spirit's heart is high with love for the eternal loves and truths. Yet my natural self wants to fear for thee—made my breath come quick and sharp and then stop as I read thy letter. Oh, Mary, in me there are two men striving for control . . . and our friendship is helping the spiritual man—the man of God.

Thee will be well and happy when this reaches thee; already far from doubt produced by illness. Thee will have sung the songs we love, walked in nature's heavenly beauties, and picked flowers . . . .

Que Dieu te garde, mon camarade, soeur, et amie! [May God protect you, my comrade, sister, and friend!]

Ton,
Leslie

The time isn't long before my homecoming—

April 18, 1919, Mary in Cambridge to Leslie in Paris

Dear Les,

I have, lying before me on the desk, two splendid letters from thee, and I have so much to answer and tell that I don't know where to begin. It was strange thee should have guessed I was working too hard, and said that probably I had seen the futility of it already— thee has second sight . . . but I am not going to say anything about myself in this letter because I have come to the conclusion that the mind has a most powerful influence over the body, and the sooner we forget ourselves the better.

Today I had lunch at Mrs. Davis's—a cousin of hers who is in the new Fellowship School was there. Harry Dana read a thrilling letter from Lewis Gannett about the unrest in France and the attitude of French workingmen toward intervention in Russia. Let us just hope against hope that this great world struggle may somehow be settled by peaceful means. I certainly am anxious to meet Mr. Villard—he may perhaps feel freer to talk when he gets here, though I doubt it, as our state legislatures are trying to pass the most horrible Prussian-like bills about radicalism. Anyone who has in his possession (whether he believes it or not) any revolutionary literature, is subject to imprisonment for three to five years! This country is simply terrified at the word Bolshevism.

Day after tomorrow is Easter. Thee will probably go to the Russian Church to hear the beautiful choir music—what wouldn't I give to be there! Last Sunday I went to Appleton. The boys sang "In Pauperus Refugium" (if that makes sense) by des Pris (and did it mighty well—there certainly is nothing like voice training). I shut my eyes and pretended thee was in the choir—the rising and falling voices were so full of manly vigor, and the harmony carried me away as it does thee. I should like to go to an Easter service where only the Resurrection story was read and all the rest was music—it is the most beautiful means of expression, and as thee says, it adds to our power of giving again to others.

Easter Morning—out on the porch at 13 Hilliard St.

It is the most heavenly of heavenly days—warm and bright. I have been over to Appleton just for the singing (coming home before the sermon). They sang "O Filii et Filiae" by Leising who lived in the 17th century (I didn't like it very well) and then that wonderful "Credo" by Gretchaninoff! I don't know the fellow who sang the solo part—but it was great. The whole choir is going out to Wellesley this p.m. to sing in the Easter Service with the girls.

Last night at Elizabeth Peabody House they had two CO plays to which everybody we know who is interested in such things went. They were really remarkably well done, but unfortunately, the prison CO play, making the boy to look like Christ, was overdone—an awful shame. The acting was mighty good—a Jewish fellow with a lovely face took the part—but it dragged on and on with no real development or climax, keeping you tense and unsatisfied all the time. The authoress, a N. Y. girl, was there, and I couldn't help wishing she might be put through some good hard 47 drilling before she tried to write any more. She has got the right idea and is perfectly fearless— had a little socialist play she is trying to get acted in N. Y. She was interested in my interest in dramatic propaganda work—and took my name and address, saying she would write to me about it.

We sold YD papers and other lit. between plays and afterwards I saw Oliver Larkin's[27] name on the petitions that we passed out and had signed. I made Victor hunt him out and introduce him to me. I have heard so much about him lately. He designed and made the scenery for the plays—a very clever chap, I guess—he is studying for his MA at Harvard now and doing all the designing on the side. Thee knows him pretty well, doesn't thee? I liked him very much.

I don't know whether in my last letter I told thee about Rufus Jones's lecture in the Old South Meeting House. It was wonderful! He is one of those men that is simply overflowing with the spirit of love, isn't he! He told all about the work in France in such a vivid, sympathetic way—and afterwards Horace showed and explained some of his slides. Now I want to hear Mr. Harvey some time.

My cousin Frederick Eliot has come home—he is the chaplain I told thee about who helped with the wounded in the station at the same time thee did. His trip has made him hopelessly conservative, I'm afraid—he saw nothing but the inside of a hospital most of the time he was there, and has no idea of the real French people and what they are thinking about. What wouldn't I give to really know what is happening over there across the water—our papers are so biased and distorted that we feel like blind people groping around in search of something we know not what—we only trust the people and wait. We will be the slowest to change here because we are so far behind—

The Lawrence strike is holding out still—but the children are starving—it is terrible, terrible. The telephone strike that is on now here is exciting—we haven't been able to call up or be called up for days, but it looks as though in spite of strike breakers, the telephone girls will get the best of it. Burleson[28] will have to give in (public opinion, even the Transcript, is against him!) and they will probably get collective bargaining and a raise in wages.

I walked along the river yesterday, and the whole place was alive with springtime. I felt like singing again as I haven't for a long time—"*Comme la vie est belle*" ["How beautiful life is"] over and over. Thy answering that part of my letter that I asked thee not to, made me unhappy and yet happy—*Je ne puis pas m'expliquer, probablement parce que je ne me comprends pas. Comme tu dis c'est l'exhortation—*

l'idéal que nous donnons l'un à l'autre qui le fait si précieux—Tes lettres
m'ont aidé, tu ne sais pas comment, pendant mes "blues." C'est drôle, mais
en pensant comment finir ma lettre, les mots suivants venaient dans ma
tête et me voulant pas partir—alors je te les dit—[I can't explain myself,
probably because I don't understand myself. As you said in your exhortation—the ideal we share makes it so precious—Your letters
have helped me, you have no idea how, during my "blues." It's funny,
but in thinking about how to finish my letter, the following words
have come to my head and don't want to leave me—therefore, I say
them to you—]

"May the peace of God which passeth all understanding, which
the world can neither give nor take away, be and abide in thy heart
from this time forth and even forever more."

Thy comrade,
Mary

April 26, 1919, Leslie in Paris to Mary in Cambridge

Dearest Mary,

Like the difference between a vivid, many-colored life of work
and service and the sudden vast strangeness and loneliness of a mind
under strain—such was the change between thy last letter and the
one from Gloucester. What a wonderful nature thee has to have
strength to throw off disappointment and discouragement! Thee
grows in my eyes every time it happens. Deep within there is growing humility, yet the fire of love and purpose flames stronger than
ever, unessentials being burned clear in those most terrible times.

The Louvre is open now; I went in and wandered about amid its treasures, but so far have had but the fleetingest glance at things which I ought to take time really to see.

How about Russia, Mary? Many Friends have a strong concern to go and be friendly by helping them, and also realizing the wonderfully different system of spiritual life that they have there. Their Christianity (I mean the faith of the peasants, by which they live) is as different from ours as the Gospel of John is from the Epistles of Paul. And look at their literature! And the absolute marvelous revolution they are carrying through to a new order! I think a few years in Russia would be a tremendous inspiration, and make for a firm, bright background for service at home. These Friends Missions offer unique opportunities to serve, and to serve personally. I feel that I ought to try to prepare myself a little by taking Russian language at Harvard for the rest of my time there; I don't think they'd refuse me for service if I knew some of the tongue . . . Doesn't thee remember that talk of Scott Nearing's at Garry's when we wanted to go to Russia? It seemed so impossible and different! But the Friends' Service Committee are sending more people to Russia; and preparing the way for young people just out of college to give a couple of years to work there . . . My desire to go there may evaporate—I can't tell: certainly it hasn't come upon me all of a sudden, but rather slowly formed. What does thee think of it?

This school of the Fellowship's on the Hudson sounds very interesting: young teachers! The fire and inspiration of a young teacher is one of the greatest lacks in modern education. Has thee and Garry heard any more about it? Ah, but if thee's way over there near New York, and I am in Cambridge, it looks as though our companionship might be from afar off as it is now! Are circumstances to be against our being near each other—to keep us from communing, exchanging experiences, hopes, sorrows, and strengths? Is our year and three months of separation to be drawn out? It would be hard for thee to leave thy family, and thee knows what thy going means to me.

Eh bien! I'll not think of it. Faith and love should carry us over any obstacle, and difficulties are often set that we may be deepened and strengthened. One thing I love to look back upon—and that is that my love for thee has always been an inspiration and stimulus to me, even though it so fills my being that one might think I wasn't good for anything else. Last spring I did better in my studies after I knew thee; religion and God have been dearer to me ever since we first met. Truth is clearer; without the possibility of doubt I have come to know where the eternal verities lie—and eternal life is bright and near . . . But we are still young, and what a priceless privilege it would be to be able to be near each other, in work yet a little while! Yet, I must not ask selfishly for a comradeship which must mean infinitely more to me than to thee, and I can wait . . . .

Two of the fellows and I went to the Russian Church for the midnight service before Easter morning. It was an intensely interesting and solemn occasion. Most of the Russians there were of the wealthy classes; finely gowned women and brave officers throwing out chests that glittered with medals and decorations of the Tsarist regime. The only really poor I saw were two very old women, with wonderful faces. The place was crowded, but we were standing near the front. At a certain point in the service, I think just before the procession went out to bring in the resuscitated Christ, everybody lit a candle and held it . . . making a charming group of faces aglow. But the *grande dame* next to me had her mind off her candle, because she calmly set fire to the feather on her hat.

There were a couple of startled exclamations from the rear before, bravely tapping her on the head, with a cool courage unsurpassed in perilous moments, I extinguished the spreading conflagration . . . We stayed until after two a.m. and then walked home across Paris. Would that thee had been along to lead us a dance along the Seine as thee did the others along the Charles! Of course Horace can unbend! So can I!

I'm so glad that thee is going to enjoy thy last spring at school . . . I'm much happier that thee should be graduated with honor and a bright laugh and moments, countless ones, of joy to others, then with great honor and a pair of glasses and a headache! *Voila!*

Good night, Mary, and God keep thee!

Les

April 29, 1919, Mary in Cambridge to Leslie in Paris

Dear Les,

What a letter from thee yesterday! When I saw how fat it was, I went and curled up on my couch, surrounded by cushions, and was transported to France. Thee certainly knows how to make things seem real, and I could just see thy tramp in the rain with the Burnand girls and all the boys; the work at Grange-le-Comte, the war prisoners, and thy horrible adventure underground—what a narrow escape (didn't thee wonder what a Mary would think at the time, as well as a Peggy?!) I was so thrilled with the German socialistic propaganda that was shot from French guns to help bring about the revolution. That certainly is the only kind of gun to have.

And the book—just another little thing added to thy duties! I thought Ronald was going to help with that. I would worry about all thee has to do, if thy last letter didn't sound so bright—as long as thee is so enthusiastic, I know thee is in good health.

I am sitting at my desk here in my cozy room at Barnard writing by the light of two tall candles, and a beautiful bunch of crimson roses nods down at me and fills the room with fragrance. This afternoon was our Cercle play and it went off beautifully—the blessed girls pretended that I had something to do with the success and sent me these wonderful roses. *Ça m'a bien touché, tu sais.* [This greatly touched me, you know.] Oh we have had such a happy year together. We are going to wind up with a little supper at our house before the elections for next year.

These roses make me think of the ones thee gave me at this time last year when I was coaching an Idler, does thee remember? I have one still in my Oxford Book.

I am glad this Cercle play came to give me confidence in myself again, for the other day I was called up by the dean and lectured for an hour about being too unconventional. She could not understand why I should like to walk at night and such things. She had heard of one thing I did, and I know now that perhaps I shouldn't have done it—that is dance on a great big table out in the hall at one of our dances. Miss Boody was shocked to death when I did it only with a spirit of fun. She cannot see the young person's point of view at all and would always have me sit conventionally in the parlor— never doing anything out of the ordinary—oh I couldn't talk with her—she made the world seem all black and wicked and I won't look at it so—if one does it will get so. Thee mustn't worry, I haven't been doing anything thee wouldn't think was absolutely all right. I just at times am seized with an impulse to run wild through nature—but always with my face toward the stars. Miss Boody could see only mud, poor woman; what wonders of life must pass her life.

As I left her office she held my hand for a minute and looking me earnestly in the face she begged me "to not be revolutionary," just for one week! She little knew how I felt (for I couldn't seem to express myself, Les, tho' I tried oh so hard)—that moral struggles and idealism will always, always conquer in the end. The only reason that I felt discouraged was because I felt myself such a poor person to prove it to her—But I will, I will someday.

I was so interested in what thee said about Horace because it was so much what I had been thinking—he is a rare fellow, but mighty hard to get at. I realized how fortunate I was to be able to talk on serious things with him because we both know thee so well that it is a bond between us.

Ah well, good night—I wish thee were here for a good old talk—I have been thinking hard this spring and what thee said that the Burnand girls said about marriage and social reform, together with thy account of Jim Norton and his wife and their work, make me feel that it is in the end a matter of great enough love. If by marriage two people are stimulated to greater love for mankind they ought to marry, but the love must be very great if they are serious reformers—*Je ne sais pas—je ne sais pas*—[I don't know—I don't know—]

Thy true comrade,
Mary

May 2, 1919, Leslie in Paris to Mary in Cambridge

Dearest Mary,

I want to tell thee what Ronald and I saw in Paris yesterday, the International Labor Day. The Syndicated workers shut down every activity of the city, including street-railways, subways, shops, theatres—everything. It seemed like a different world . . . and in spite of the drizzly weather, the streets were thronged and outside of a rare motorcycle or auto, the rustling tap of feet and the murmur of voices filled one's ears. But it was not the hushed voices so much as the tense, quiet, earnest manner of the people which struck the keynote of the day. They were as one; they were remembering past strikes, and they weren't celebrating, but thinking for the future. The lily-of-the-valley, sold in the streets to bring good-luck on May Day, found its way to few button-holes; the others were decked with the bright red Socialist rosette, looking like a bright drop of the blood of the international workers.

The syndicates had arranged for parades and manifestations, but Clemenceau, the detested, ordered prohibiting demonstrations and brought troops into the city in great numbers and got cannon placed all around the fortification, pointed on Paris. He is mortally afraid of a revolution. On the morning of May first, a girl who lives across the street from him saw his car draw up to the mansion quadruply guarded and the Tiger come out of his door, look quickly up and down, hurry into his Limousine, and crouch 'way down in the seat while the car whirled away at top speed.

In the afternoon, I walked up towards the Gare de l'Est looking for trouble. When I got to the Boulevard Magenta I heard the roar of a crowd, and looking up, I saw the wide street black with people and red banners sinking and rising in the mass. When I got closer I saw that the passage was being blocked by mounted *gardes republicaines* [Republican guards], brass-helmeted and plumed. Apparently they were reinforcing a large body of *agents de police* [police officers].

Every window was full of faces—all looking toward the struggle. One man I saw gazing up the street. The eye that was towards me was blind but it had a look of wild eagerness and hope, and with the high-flung attitude of his head, he was a page out of the future. The eye that was blinded by the system under which he suffered was fixed in wild hope on the red flag of his fellows, and not seeing, it saw far and high.

Pushing on into and mixing with the crowd (I had civilian clothes on) I heard that half the paraders had got through the cordon of "*flics.*" The men were hotly indignant at being stopped in a peaceful parade. "*Oh, la, la, la, la!*" "*Ah, les flics! Quelle race de chiens!*" "*Quelles sales bêtes!*" ["Ah, the cops! What a breed of dogs!" "What dirty beasts!"] At this moment, the crowd in which I was, reformed to try to break through. The cavalry dug their heels into their horses, drew their sabres, and clattered down on us, striking right and left, and drove the crowd before them, as there were no doorways nor alleys for it to get into. But it wasn't driven far, and it came right back with a deep-chested roar when the *gardes* retreated to their first post. The sabres were too much for many of the men; up and down the street they began tearing up the cast-iron grills at the base of trees, and breaking them into chunks handy to throw. Then an army wagon, with French soldiers in it, came through the cordon toward the people. The soldiers waved at the people, flourished their caps, and leaned out of the wagon to shake hands with the people. Cheers of "*Vivent les poilus!*" welled. ["Long live the poilus!" (Poilus is an informal term of endearment for infantrymen, literally "hairy ones.")] The police charged again. The ambulance arrived to carry off the wounded. I saw one man, with his head bound with a bloody bandage, come back to the attack. Young boys and women showed not the slightest fear of the *flics* and rallied each other to go forward. A crowd of *cheminots* [railway workers] got together to make a manifestation in another street. I thought the trouble was all over and started down-town again. But it seemed that the crowd's ire was up; they picked up a lot of those cast-iron *plaques de fonte* I spoke about, broke up a shed, tore down a tree—and made a barricade against the cavalry. Revolver shots were fired and the whole thing looked critical. The crowd howled at the inmates of houses that wouldn't open the grills and the doors below to give the workers a means of retreat from the infuriated sabre-strokes.

The people sang the song that commemorates the action of the troops of the 17th who, when ordered, refused to fire on the people. Sang it with emphasis. Shifting north the crowd invaded the Gare de l'Est and there was a free fight between *flics* and workers with sabre-charges by the mounted guards.

Ronald and Frederick Kuh[29] went up to the Place de la République, whither many processions of workers were bound. With several thousands of others, they got in before the cordons of police and guards were formed to plug all the entrances to the Place. Even regular French cavalry were there to support the police. They did it half-heartedly and would rein in their horses to keep them from trampling the crowd, and the crowd cheered them and talked with them, whereas the *gardes* urged their animals onto the people. Ronald saw many cases of heroism on the part of the boys and girls, and instances of cold-blooded, unspeakable brutality directed against the defenseless and the weak. Women were beaten . . . Ronald and Kuh both were struck heavily in the face because the crowd they were in wouldn't give way quickly before the blows of the police. Kuh, who is with the IWW and not a pacifist, was nearly won over to our stand by the sight of the degradation which the force brings to those who use it.

May 3

I read today in the papers about the demonstrations on May Day in America. It seems that there were demonstrations and red-flag parades in Boston as well as the larger cities. But I doubt that the unions closed everything up as completely as the Syndicates did in Paris. America is just about the most reactionary country in the world. More work is to be done there before the great day than anywhere else.

May 5

Tomorrow I'm leaving for Grange-le-Comte to carry out thy injunction to seek Nature in the youth of the year. How I wish I were out today in the Meuse under the blessed sunshine and not gazing out over the chimney-pots of Paris!

Que Dieu te garde!
Les

FRU members relaxing on the porch of a house that they built

12

Leaving France

IN THE SUMMER OF 1919, Mary was finishing her exams and joining in graduation events. Leslie meanwhile continued his job of documenting the work of the Mission. He came upon a trove of printing equipment and movable type, which had been sent to the Unit in 1917, but had not been used since. He cleaned up the press, probably with the help of his brother Ronald, who had worked in the printing industry before his incarceration as a CO. In June, Leslie started another newsletter, *L'Équipe*, telling about the Friends' work in his breezy, somewhat humorous style. The first issue announced his intentions:

> "*L'Équipe* was born in a stable, in that part used as an atelier by the veterinary. There, in the humble calm cradled by the fragrance of the hay, the equine aromas, and acrid horse-liniment, the first number came into being . . . Struck off by The Augean Press, *L'Équipe* has Herculean aspirations. It would clean up things with rushing rivulets of truth, and is not above pilfering a golden apple or two from the unsuspecting Hesperides. *L'Équipe*, published by

a *Sociètè Anonyme* (you must imagine the acute accents over the e's) welcomes brief contributions in prose, verse, or pen-and-ink, which amuse (humorous), tickle the aesthetic palate (artistic), startle or irritate (true). The *Sociètè Anonyme* cannot be expected to feed *L'Équipe* with the mental pablum he requires. The S.A. is too busy setting type, mixing inks, and cleaning out hay thrown in by absent-minded Aggies."[1]

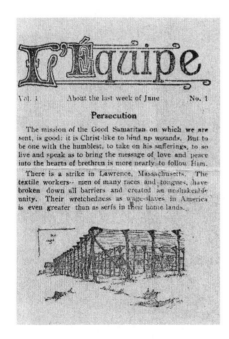

This first issue included a brief article on the textile strike in Lawrence, Massachusetts, probably using some of the reports from Mary's letters. The second issue included a humorous essay on tending the "wicked, unscrupulous, and totally unprincipled" goats at the Farm, written by C. M. and illustrated with silhouettes of workers. On a more serious note, Leslie reprinted a statement from the group "*Clarte*"[2] protesting the peace treaty;

signers of this protest included, among others, the French authors Anatole France and Georges Duhamel.

The paper had a small audience, and Leslie's friends rallied to support it financially. Their backing could not sustain the work, however. The second issue carried this notice: "The paper has great possibilities: one can imagine stencil printing and two or three color work; and the fact of an intimate, mobile medium for expression should interest every member of the Mission. If properly nurtured, its future is bright. But the *Sociètè Anonyme* is going home! If you are at all interested in continuance of *L'Équipe* make your interest known at once in writing to *L'Équipe*, Grange. Is it to be thumbs down?" Sadly, no one offered to continue publishing the paper and Leslie's two issues were the only ones published.

Leslie's work in France was coming to an end. The work of the Friends Unit had begun tapering off. Refugees were back in their villages. Some semblance of community life had been reestablished. Friends had provided relief to 1,666 French villages and more than 46,000 citizens. The Mission planted 25,000 trees, mostly fruit trees in the Verdun area, giving each family five trees and many more for the community.[3]

The workers began heading home to America and Great Britain. Several Friends moved on to new service projects in other countries: Belgium, Russia, Germany, Serbia, Poland, and Austria.[4] In summarizing the spirit that undergirded their work, Rufus Jones spoke in Paris to a gathering of Unit workers about the work of the Mission:

"Ever since I was a little child, the building of cathedrals has made me marvel—the way those men translated their faith in these glorious structures . . . A great thing has come to us. Though I cannot be in a cathedral without having every fiber in me respond to the glory of the place, yet I would rather have part in this work we are doing than share in the building of a great cathedral. This translation of Christianity is greater than any cathedral-builders ever made. It has come to you to put your lives into this. Two hundred years from now they will not remember your names; they will not have a roll on which every name is listed. But this thing which you are doing will never cease, for when you translate Love into Life, when you become organs of God for a piece of service, nothing can obliterate it. To-night I feel, as I did this morning in Notre Dame, an emotion that throbs through my whole being. Thank God we can have our little share in this age in translating the love of God into terms of human service and that we can fight, not with guns, not with bombs, but with the sword of the Spirit which is the word of God."[5]

At the FRU General Meeting in May, Leslie spoke in favor of going to Russia to continue working with the peasants, feeling that the Russians had much to teach the Americans, "both in attitude towards people, new institutions, and good lives." He considered studying blacksmithing and agricultural machine repairs during the summer in order to leave for Russia "with no Mission supporting me, to wander from village to village helping mend their tools."[6]

Eventually, however, Leslie made plans to return home. He had been in France for more than eleven months. He hoped to be back in Cambridge by the start of the fall term to resume his undergraduate studies. On his twenty-second birthday in August, he started his vacation exploring Strassburg. While there, he found a quiet place in the mountains to write and ponder his future. He sailed for New York on August 30, 1919.[7]

Ronald decided to continue his work with the Friends. He met with each German prisoner who worked for the Friends and offered him an opportunity to write a letter to his family and have his photograph taken. Ronald, along with Constance Gostick, Mary Kelsey, and Solomon Yoder, traveled to Germany in December 1919, remaining until the following March. The travel was arduous, but they were met with kindness and warmth. They visited three hundred families of the prisoners who had worked with the Unit, providing letters and photographs showing that their sons or husbands were in good health (unlike the German families themselves who were often undernourished and suffering). They also brought wages estimated to cover the value of the labor given by the men while they worked with the Friends. Although the prisoners did not return to Germany for many more months, the visit of the Friends offered encouragement to their suffering families and the funds to help alleviate some of their hardships.[8]

By the time Leslie left France, most of Unit members were headed home or to new postings. A few remained and, in the spring of 1920, one after another of the centers were closed down, with all available equipment and supplies packed and dispatched to the new fields of Poland and Vienna.[9]

May 9, 1919, Leslie in Clermont-en-Argonne to Mary in Cambridge

Dearest Mary,

Up on the flank of a hill bright with fruit trees in blossom, thee has been with me, close at my side for hours . . . On the other side of the valley, the sun has been shining blessedly on the village of Brabant-in-Argonne. The light and warmth soften the terrible aspect of those houses of the hamlet which are ruined. Clouds—as tumbled and yet as stately as a prince's dreams of empire—have floated away over the valley. The cuckoo has been singing off in the woods; a crake grated his strange cry as he flew close to the swift brook which flows down the green bottom; bees hummed among the blossoms over my head; the gentle wind blows white petals down upon me. The slope is yellow with dainty flowers and the sweet, thin, rushing twitter of the little birds is in the air.

Mary, my heart is full. What an ingrate I have been to let myself forget God's blessings! How they have been heaped upon me! He gives me to drink in the beauty of nature, He makes me capable of holding high spiritual beliefs and hopes, He gives me faith in life eternal, and He gives me a comradeship and rare understanding with my ideal among women. Why have I not praised and loved Him at all times with my whole heart?

It is a blessing to be up here in the area where work is going on. One can't picture the life and spirit of it until one is in it. My job up here has been to collect material for Reconstruction and to take photographs of the work. This morning I climbed a long, rickety ladder and accosted Pere Guichard, who was mending his roof which had been badly damaged by shell-fire. He was very affable and is a most interesting old man—a Jack-of-all-trades and a master carpenter. I took his picture on the roof and hope to write his story.

Yesterday the Mission doctor took me on his rounds: we went to Parois,[10] Aubreville, and Neuvilly, and came back by way of Clermont, a splendid ride, and productive of several good pictures . . . .

It's hard for me <u>not to see thee</u> at thy Class Day and Commencement; thee will imagine I'm there, won't thee? Just look over in one corner of the room and smile; I'll smile back . . . .

God keep thee, Mary . . . .

Thy,

Leslie

May 18, 1919, Mary in Cambridge to Leslie in Paris

Dear Les,

Again it is lilac season and the trees are their most gorgeous lush green. I have been sitting down by the river watching the sun and shadows drift across the hills and water. Oh it is beautiful, beautiful! I haven't had a letter from thee for nearly three weeks, but I have thy picture, and I was so glad to get it. Yes, thee looks much older (I won't tell thee how much), and yet, thee is just the same. I like the moustache very much. When I first opened the picture it seemed a bit strange, but it didn't take me long to see thy old self through the changes— now I feel as though I had always known thee this way. *Je ne vais pas te dire comme tu es beau parce que cela pouvait te gâter, même si tu n'es plus jeune!* [I'm not going to tell you how handsome you are because that could spoil you, even though you're not so young anymore.] Just think that thee has been gone nearly a year—doesn't it seem more than that to thee, though? When does thee plan to return?

I invited Horace to the House Dance that we have every spring at the dormitories (we had it last week), and he told me that thee and he are going to room together in thy old room in Matthews (I had seen his name in the "Crime" [The Harvard Crimson] for it) next year. Isn't that perfectly <u>great</u> for both of you. What fun you will have, and each will be an inspiration to the other for work. Horace was great fun at the dance—I got to know him much better. Ec. A is making him rather conservative, he needs thy enthusiasm to keep him radical!

A month from today is Commencement. I can't believe it, and yet I just live for the time when exams will be all over and summer here. We are probably going to take a little cottage down by the

ocean then—where Helen can have painting lessons with an artist
and Mother and I just loaf and invite our souls. I intend to be good
and strong before starting any job in the fall—what it may be I
haven't decided yet. The Fellowship School in New York is what I
should love to get in on, but I am afraid there is no chance for me as
there are to be only two women teachers and they prefer older ones.
I might get in to wash dishes though—I would take anything to be
able to help along the experiment.

Trade unionism is the thing that attracts me next—I should like
to be an organizer, and for that, I should go into a factory for a while
anyway this fall. But I really try not to think of the future yet—I have
all I can do to finish the year just now. The girls wanted me to do the
lead in the spring play "Milestones," and I was perfectly crazy to—
but the doctor said I would be a fool, and if I wanted to get my degree
this year, I had better not do much else besides my studying except
be out of doors or sleep. It is wonderful to <u>have</u> to go down by the
river and sit in the sun or stroll around the Botanic Gardens reading
the <u>Oxford Book</u> and absorbing the spring life. I have written a lot of
verses not good enough to show anybody else but which have helped
me mightily to find myself . . . .

The little verses "Thee and Me" that I sent thee at Christmas are
especially true of this spring when I am such a creature of moods.
It is in thinking of the high and beautiful things that we both love
that I can forget myself and really live.

Thy true comrade,
Mary

May 19, 1919, Leslie in Grange-le-Comte to Mary in Cambridge

Dearest Mary,

A letter from thee is a God-send! That is not to say that my morale is low and that I need God-send, but a little one-sided talk with thee makes me rich in joy and puts new happiness in the songs of birds, new grace in nature, and new human kindness into the faces of all whom I meet.

I am glad thee went to Appleton for the singing on Easter and gladder that thee told me about it. These little spoken links with dear things at home are more precious than thee can imagine.

And the CO plays! It does my heart good to hear of anything along the right road being put on. Of course, the overdoing is a real pity; still, the fact of plays about COs is like a trumpet sound through a chaos of noises . . . .

When we consider our own COs, we might spare a moment for those of Germany, doesn't thee think so? Our talks with German prisoners up here have opened our eyes. They estimate the number of Germans shot for refusing to serve at a quarter of a million. We didn't hear about that, did we? And there are many other things that aren't spoken of. A French officer, an eye-witness, told one of our workers that every tenth man was taken out of certain regiments from Marseilles and shot, because the people from the south were refusing to fight for what they considered the north's battles, and they had to be intimidated.

Up at Aubreville, behind the *équipe* hut, there is a crucifix at the cross-roads. Beyond the crucifix are piles of abandoned, unread pamphlets entitled, "Faith in God in War Time," got out by the American Y.M.C.A., and beyond these piles are the triple-barbed wire corrals for prisoners whose country laid down its arms five months ago. They are inside—underfed, hard-worked, and longing for home—and outside guards walk up and down, bayonets fixed—up and down. *Et c'est une guerre sainte. Comprends-tu?* [And this is a holy war. Do you understand?]

Ah, well! I don't mean to be morose. I can't be, after the laugh I had over Miss Boody's earnest request to thee. It's without question the funniest thing I've heard for a long while! "Don't be revolutionary, just for one week!" "Mary, please don't be yourself, just for eight days! Don't do your hair as you want to, but the way the other girls do it, and as I am accustomed to seeing it done!" Isn't it pathetic? Why doesn't somebody suggest that she use the valuable time she spends in looking through mud-colored goggles at progressive young ladies in writing a book called "Looking Backward" (starting with the present)?

Dance on a table? Why, of course! Isn't it the most interesting and dramatic event I could imagine for one of those same old stiff, shuffle-round-the-ring, I-almost-believe-in-Harvard and Radcliffe? Isn't it graceful? Isn't it gay? Hasn't it the free, pure, happy abandon of youth? Isn't it <u>dance</u> more than the shuffle on the floor? . . . No, she can't see it with her eyes full of dirt—how could anyone?

Does thee know, Mary, I wish thee would do something for me . . . don't take a lecture like that seriously, <u>even while it's being read to thee!</u> It does the young life more harm than good to attach importance to such a homily—And I'll tell thee how I've imagined thee's to do it! Just act! Pretend thee's a little girl of four and a half who's listening to the list of her peccadilloes—very penitently. Keep acting! Don't let Miss Boody get near Mary Peabody for one second with her old mud-tinted specs! And the funny part, if thee acts well, will be that Miss Boody will think that she's talking to thee, whereas she will be really pointing out mud-pies to a fairy child!

I have been learning some more sweet old French songs—we may sing them when I get home.

Que Dieu garde nos coeurs. [May God keep our hearts.]
Les

May 29, 1919, Mary in Cambridge to Leslie in Grange-le-Comte

Dear Leslie,

Exams are upon us. I have two at the very beginning and so much to do that I haven't courage to begin, so I have decided to gain some by writing to thee. I always feel refreshed and invigorated when I write to thee. Thy article in the last Reconstruction is beautiful, shining with thy splendid spirit. How I long to be out of college, rested and ready for work. I have almost decided to start in a factory somewhere around here this fall, and from there, get into Trade Union organizing. I am crazy to get started and to try to get some ideas across to our slow-as-cold-molasses labor. Thy thrilling description of May Day at Paris must be printed. If I can seize a minute in these hectic exam times I am going to make a copy of it and send it to "Young Democracy" in New York. Such a description from an eye-witness must be published—I should think labor was stirred up over there. How will it all end? Are there no Mr. Mustes and Rotzels over there to keep the peace and work by education and organization? Of course, as thee says, they are wonderfully organized already—I should think they could take things over peacefully before long.

Thee is thinking of going to Russia. It is a wonderful idea, but I am sure that when thee comes back here thee will see how badly this country needs thy help and will not be able to get away. I read thy description of May Day to Garry, and she was highly interested; she says that thee ought to go to Oxford for a year instead of coming home to Harvard—because they have such a wonderful economics department there. There is another idea for thee!

Just think that thee will be at home in three months—what talks we will have about ways of service, thy experiences, and the problems of the world.

Good night, Les—may God watch between thee and me while we are parted one from the other.

Thy comrade,
Mary

June 1, 1919, Leslie in Paris to Mary in Cambridge

Dearest Mary,

Finishing college must seem like a strange dream—a gentleness must lie in those last days, enveloping and infusing the excitement and gayety. As Commencement approaches, I feel ever more sharply the regret at not being there to see thee and rejoice with thee. But don't forget that the best part of me will be there anyway, happy in thy pleasure.

I came down from Grange to Paris about a week ago, getting a lift as far as Bar-le-Duc in a Mission car. The day was bright, and the spring countryside was soft, warm, and mysterious. The time I spent in the war-zone made me doubly anxious to stay up there as long as possible—and I'm going to get back as soon as I can after a visit to the manufacturing *équipe* at Dole in the Jura. I have never seen it, and since it is to close so soon, I feel that I must.

Yesterday evening we had a rare treat at the Hostel. Jeannette Rankin, Jane Addams, and Dr. Alice Hamilton, back from the Women's Congress at Zurich,[11] spoke to a gathering of Friends about what they had seen and done. Jane Addams said that she felt that pacifists in America during the war hadn't managed to get their message across. Something was lacking: a conciseness of thought, a completeness of speech, a *je ne sais quoi*. And now, in the coming social changes, the pacifist will have a hard time getting his message to the rising working classes, who will probably say that in not fighting for the social revolution, the pacifist is on the bourgeois side. This will be our task, and a tremendous one. She almost envied us our youth and the years before us. And that's just what Lewis Gannett said: that the pacifist is in reality the rejected of men—neither the militarists nor the social revolutionaries have any use for him.

But today I saw hope. I went to a great meeting held to demand general amnesty this afternoon at the Syndicalists' Meeting Hall, Rue de la Grange aux Belles. Anatole France was listed as president, but he was too sick to come. One of the three prominent men (in Socialist circles) who sat in the Tribunal was one who had been wounded by the *"flics"* on May First. His head was still bound with a big bandage, which nevertheless did not hide his face, and as the light from above struck his features, the resemblance to the pictures of Edgar Poe was startling. The same black long hair, pale face, broad forehead, thin, almost Semitic nose, and mouth a little on one side. The hope came to me in the speech of Georges Pioch,[12] who seemed to have great weight with the people. He said that theirs was the power, if they felt as one, that their irresistible authority lay in the general strike. And the beauty of it was its calmness, its great serenity, its peacefulness—this quiet, irresistible folding of arms. That whatever happened, the words of Scripture were deeply true—"They who take the sword shall perish by the sword"—that the working classes of the world wanted peace, and that they would have it even in their revolutions! Tremendous, frantic applause! I was almost carried off my feet—a shiver of joy ran through me; I hadn't realized that deep difference in the attitude towards violence of the bourgeois and the worker. At heart the worker is more of a peace-maker. It is with him that our lot is cast, and I rejoice in it . . . Another speaker, pleading for action to bring about amnesty, said that the bourgeois government had not learned anything from the war—that the gentleness, tolerance, and generous feeling that had grown in almost every soldier during his months and years of suffering and comradeship through martyrdom were unknown to the governors. And then he said that, stupid and cruel as the bourgeois may be, the working-class will know how to pardon them, to give them amnesty, in the new day. Mary, I never heard anything like it said and cheered for in a revolutionary meeting. It was noble. What heights the lowly are capable of reaching—miles above the Scribes and Pharisees[13] of today.

I have told thee, haven't I, that I hope to study Russian in my last years at Harvard and get into Russia to work with the peasants, on a Friends Mission? All that I hear convinces me that there is a spirit abroad in Russia not to be found in other countries, and I long to go there and work in Relief. Maybe that'll give me just the broad background to live a life of service on. But we must talk together.

Thee probably has a purpose and plan of much better service ... Be happy, Mary! Let's never forget that our lives are eternal—that this world is a step away from the forking of the roads—a beginning and not an end. Somehow the thought of God's love and eternal life make it impossible for us to worry: "to take thought for the morrow."

Mary, God keep thee—
Thy,
Les

June 4, 1919, Mary in Cambridge to Leslie in Paris

Dear Les,

Two exams are over, and the heat is perfectly tremendous—I just couldn't do Ec. tonight as I am stealing time to write to thee once more before Class Day. The time is just flying, and before we know it all the excitement will be over, and we will all fall into the summer vacation with a thump and be still for a while until we recover ourselves. I am afraid it will take me quite a while because I have had to take "doyse" [unknown word] to make me sleep in order to get through. Oh this is a funny world. I always thought I was an ox of strength until I suddenly found out I wasn't!

To come down to more practical things! I enclose a letter which Arthur Fisher wrote in today's Crimson. I think it is awfully good, doesn't thee think so. I wonder why the "Crime" [The Harvard Crimson] printed it—perhaps they felt they had to because A. F.

was one of the Editors-in-Chief once. The past "Harvard Magazine" had a great attack on the Crimson in it—it said that its editorial column is positively pathetic in its wobbling policy—that the paper does not represent the college and never will until all letters that are sent to it are printed and a better system for selecting the editors established. As it is now, most of the editorials are written by men running for the job and who are afraid to express any strong opinions for fear of "getting it wrong." The magazine suggested that a new daily paper be started, though it feared for its success because of the money behind the Crimson in the shape of graduated editors.

When I write next I shall be Mary Peabody, A.B., I hope.

Ton camarade,
Mary

June 18, 1919, from Mary in Cambridge to Leslie in Paris

Dear Les,

This morning was Commencement and now the college things are all over, and there is a great lull in the storm of excitement. The last time I wrote to thee we were still in the midst of exams—I will begin where they leave off and tell thee all about the wonderful events. The first thing was Class Day and what a perfect day it was! I was chairman of "our group" and so spent most of the day decorating the Ghirlandajo Room[14] where we were to receive in the evening. Flowers came in shoals, so really all I had to do was find vases for them. We received our friends from eight to nine, and then there was the class singing on the steps of Agassiz, the giving of our banner to the Freshmen, and the Glee Club songs. I shall never forget the sight, as I stood on the white steps there in the dark with a sea of faces below and the colored lanterns dancing in the trees—as we sang, the moon came up and flooded us with silver light; it was a happy omen. They asked me to sing with the Glee Club, which had meant quite a lot of practicing at the last minute, but I loved to do it—we sang that beautiful suite of German Dances by Shubert and some college songs.

After the singing, with all our guests we sat around under the lanterns and ate strawberries and ice cream while the orchestra tuned up—and then we danced. Victor, Horace, Hal, Harry and others were there—I had a great time looking after the eight men that I had invited, seeing that they had a good time and changed partners once in a while. It is great fun to be the lady of the day but a responsibility too! When the clock struck midnight, the gaiety ended, and laden with flowers, the seniors went their happy ways home.

With fear and trembling the morning after Class Day, I went to the office to see if I had passed all my exams. One of them (Ec. A) I was terribly scared of because I was feeling miserably when I took it, and it was a terribly hot day—but I got through it thank goodness. When I heard I had three As (one of them was not in Ec.) I certainly wished I had been able to keep on trying for honors—Ah well, it's all over now, and I am as happy as though I had had a "Summa."

On Saturday, the Alumnae had various festivities for the Seniors and 47 Workshop repeated Doris Halman's charming little play "The Playroom." It is one of the best things they have put on this year. On Sunday came Baccalaureate—the service was in the church there on the corner by the Washington Elm. Dean Brown of Yale[15] was the speaker. All the Seniors marched in caps and gowns while Dr. Davison played the organ; we all wore exactly the same white shirtwaists and skirts. I had such high ambitions for this service that it was a disappointment to me when Dean Brown was not what I needed him to be. He was good and said some splendid things about Industrial Democracy, but his whole sermon was trite and did not uplift me.

Next day

Some of the girls came in to my room then—and we sat up very late talking—we couldn't seem to bear the idea of going to bed when the next morning early we were all to scatter to the four winds. Now it is the next morning and they have all gone—how lonely the world is when one's friends go away. There are seven of us that have been fast friends all through college, and we have sworn that no matter how much distance divides us, we will think and care about each other just the same.

I am the last one to leave my room because I live so near. Everything is packed and I am waiting for lunch and the expressman before going home. It really hurt me to take down the pictures and curtains from my pretty little room. It seems like desecrating the happy memories that lurk in every corner. Oh, I have been so happy at college—in future years I shall probably look back and think that these were the happiest years of my life.

Well, to go on with the story of events. Class Exercises on the day after Class Day were great fun. Ethel Kidder's class poem was very lovely indeed—Ellen Collier's[16] history and the class will were awfully funny, at least to us of the class in the audience who knew the local points. Thee may see that the Giver of Gifts—(Kath[17] is one of my best friends so I had to forgive her) gave me a table upon which I might dance to my heart's content. It was a sweet little doll's table that came from the 10¢ store. I treasure it greatly! Kath whispered in my ear afterward that the censored line was "then the Dean got sore"—isn't that naughty!! The girls who knew of my affair with Miss Boody simply howled when I was presented with the table— and the others crowded around me afterwards to hear what it all could mean. I had to explain to so many different people, that I almost decided to call a class meeting and tell them all about it once for all!! Thee'll be amused perhaps at the gifts which other girls in the class that thee knows got.

The next event on the list is Harvard Class Day. Arthur gave us tickets to the stadium and it was such fun—a regular pre-war celebration—it was cloudy during the oration—but when everyone rose to sing "Fair Harvard," the sun suddenly came out and illuminated the paper ribbons and confetti that were being thrown everywhere. It was a lovely sight. In the evening, Victor took me to the yard to hear the Glee Club and then to "Mem" to dance afterwards. Howard Henners has proved a mighty good leader, and the Glee Club sang well (save for one fellow who was drunk and put them off a bit!). They sang a lot of new things that suited their voices beautifully. My, but I did miss thee, Les, as I sat there under the lanterns and the strong voices carried afar over the yard. We had such a happy time last year, didn't we? Harvard Class Day is thy day for me.

The next day was Commencement and that was the end. Now the summer lies before me, full of rest and sunshine. I am not going to think of a job until September and then scurry around after one.

I probably told thee that we are going to Ogunquit, Maine (almost to Nova Scotia), where Helen will have painting lessons. But before then we seniors have decided to have a farewell house party down at Garry's summer place on the Cape. We leave at nine o'clock tomorrow morning, to be gone a week. We are all crazy to get together and really see each other before parting for good. Write to me always at 13 Hilliard St. because I don't know the exact Ogunquit address—letters are sure to be forwarded. What a long letter I have written—it will make up for not having written for quite a while. Thy last letter telling about Jane Addams and wishing thee could be at all the fun here, came the other day—thee really thinks seriously of going to Russia, doesn't thee. I am glad that thee has no uncertainty about finishing Harvard tho'—for all our socialistic ideals, we love our college and realize its value, *n'est-ce pas!*

I have so much to say—so many thoughts and plans have been going through my head lately—but I can't write any more . . . I will save it for some other time. I can't believe that in three short months thee will be here—in fact I won't be able to write many more letters, will I? *Comme le temps passe vite! Que Dieu te bénit toujours* [How quickly time passes! May God bless you always].

Ton camarade,
Mary

July 3, 1919, Leslie in Grange-le-Comte, forwarded to Dunheed Cottage, Cape Neddick, Maine

Dearest Mary,

I have just read again thy letter of May 29 and renewed the strength and cheer it gave me; my heart has been with thee all through the exam period. Thee will excuse me for not having answered the delightfully promising invitation more materially, but the spirit is the real thing, and I shall be there.

Garry's suggestion is good; so is mine: to stay in Paris another year and go to the Sorbonne, but it's *toujours le sou, qui manqué* [always the money that I lack], and as far as I know now, I shall be back in Cambridge next fall ... How glad I am that thee is not going away! It is dear to look forward to the talks we shall have with one another. I am almost content to wait for thy picture, having good powers of anticipation and unfailing delight in the picture I already have!

Just now I am at Grange; and I am doing harder work (combined mental and physical) than ever before. The reason of it is a printing establishment which I am opening here to print a new Mission paper, called *L'Équipe*. Reconstruction has tried to cover two needs: the need for a touch between the various *équipes*, and the need for a report of the work to the outside World ... in trying to do both, I feel that it has not been a howling success in either. But Reconstruction, like the brook, will go on trying to straddle. We couldn't stop it now! A third need, as I see it, is a strong expression among our members of pacifist radicalism: that's the line along which Quakers ought to be made to think. Rotzels and Mustes are the men who will make a new and splendid era in the history of the Friends.

I'm so disgusted with the restraint of the censor that our new paper is going to be private—not sold, and distributed only among our members and friends . . . and it's going to be radical, amusing, and artistic. Very tiny to begin with, but with capacity for growth. This thing I send thee is the first job off the press.

The origin of the materials is interesting: the press came over from America when Horace did, in Sept. 1917, with an outfit of type. It could not be found in Paris. There it has lain, rusty, partly broken, for twenty months; then some of our transport men found it and shipped it up here. Here it would have stayed in its box if I hadn't taken it out and got it repaired and cleaned.

Breck Thomas, one of the secretaries, backed the idea strongly, and buzzed me over to the dump of material we've bought at Dombasle, and we picked out about thirty pounds of vari-colored printer's inks. From the same dump about 1,500 large sheets of beautiful yellow cartridge drawing paper was obtained, and we had most of the essentials. I got the carpenter to make me a case and distributed some type into it. We got the Mission artists interested, and they drew pictures for cuts and headings.

I've found some difficulty in getting proper help and have been almost working my little empty head off to get the scheme under way, but I think it'll go! Yet if I don't come back in the Fall, don't thee worry; I shall be safe in jail, put there by our beloved *Anastasie*—the censor.

Horace would be interested in the plan if he were here—I wish he were.

Thy,
Leslie

July 5, 1919, Mary in Cape Neddick, Maine, to Leslie in Paris

Dear Les,

A year ago today thee sailed from New York, didn't thee? I can't believe that a whole year has gone by, and yet it certainly seems that long since I have seen thee. Thy last letter tells about thy new venture *L'Équipe*—I think it is perfectly <u>great</u>—*bonne chance!*—thee is just the one to make it a success with thy enthusiasm and convictions—but what a tremendous amount of work for one man, I don't see how thee does it. It is no use telling thee not to do too much, but thee said thee would take care of thyself if I would take care of myself—and I wish thee could see me now. I have just been in for a glorious swim in the dear old Atlantic— the water here is cold, which makes it wonderfully invigorating. Helen and I are alone just now in this cozy rustic little cottage. Ogunquit (of which Cape Neddick is a part) is a sort of artist's colony—we came here so Helen could take painting lessons and I—well, I am just living real living—as happy and as carefree as a bird. I do what little housekeeping there is to be done and then explore the country on bicycle or on foot the rest of the time. The doctor said I must have a real vacation if I am going to take a job next fall—so I am following his orders! Next week I am going to begin practicing on the typewriter, for—a word in thy ear—Mrs. Davis has suggested that I go down to Lawrence in the fall to help Mr. Rotzel with his Trade Union organizing there. She says my languages would be a great help with the foreigners. I would live at the Fellowship House down there and probably come home for weekends if I could get off. Nothing is settled about this yet—I only thought I would make use of some of my extra time learning to typewrite—in case—

Now, Les, if *Anastasie*, or anything else, prevents thy returning in September I shall not forgive that person or thing—thee just must come home. It would be wonderful, wouldn't it, to go to Oxford or the Sorbonne—but I really don't think Harvard can get on any longer without thee! Mother wants me to go to England next winter with my cousin to study economics and see what the Labor Party is doing—but Lawrence attracts me more. If I decide to go to Lawrence—that is if Mr. Rotzel wants me, I shall probably go down from here some time near the end of August or beginning of September.

Does being a friend of the Editor give me any claim to a copy of *L'Équipe?* I am just crazy to see it as it comes out—thee will send it to me if thee can, won't thee? I am going to send this little "word in your ear" along to Horace—he is out west now canvassing for the Non-Partisan League—he has probably written thee telling about how he goes around in his little flivver and talks with the farmers. He is going to be out there most of his vacation, I guess.

Now, Les, I am sending thee this glossy copy (the one I had to have for the yearbook and the only one I have so far) of Mary Peabody, A.B.—If thee knows that young lady at all well, thee will be sure that she is not as hard-hearted and stony as the photograph makes her out. They seem to have taken out all or any expression that I may have—but I promised thee a picture and here it is. *Au revoir—à bientôt,* [Good bye—see you soon]

Mary

July 9, 1919, Leslie in Grange-le-Comte to Mary in Cambridge

Dearest Mary,

It has been centuries since last I wrote to thee and decades since the last letter came from Cambridge. This is the first time such a long interval between my messages has fallen; for days and days I have wished to write, but my time has been full, and at night I am so done that the morale of any letter I might write would be far below what it ought to be.

To begin at the beginning, I might say that now, as well as editor and photographer, I am publisher and printer (boss and devil rolled into one), and I do jobs for the Mission and *L'Équipe*, my darling, to please my friends and myself.

I have been working harder than ever before, but it hasn't really worn on me much, because we're out in the country here, and one can swim in the River Aire and bicycle through the lovely defiles of the Argonne forest. Yet, for a time, I lost all sense of nature, and when I stepped out the other day and saw the magnificence and delicacy of the Meuse sunset, I was surprised and could not take it all in, as if I were a man who had almost forgotten what appetite was and then had the door of a prince's supper-chamber thrown open to him.

An FRU member, Howard Elkinton, with the bicycle he used to travel among the various équipes

The morale of the Mission is high. Great work is being done and will continue long after I leave—perhaps into next summer and autumn, but the building work will close late this fall. I am sorry to be leaving so soon. That is why I am putting in so much effort now, so that with the feeling of work well done, the parting won't seem so hard.

I am writing to thee in the tremendous old fireplace in my room—which is also the home of the Augean Press—by the light of a good old fire. The shivering embers and the darting flames bring back the thought of those we watched together in Cambridge in the night in early spring. There was happiness and comradeship enough in our lives then for me to live on ever since. Does thee ever think of our walks along the Charles?

Next Day

It's tomorrow morning. Just then the fire died down on my beautiful thoughts and instead of binding them to cold paper, I sat and sent them to thee—messengers on the wings of night without a word and without a sound. And this morning, thy letter came—it's been delayed somehow, but it is all the more precious. How glad I am that things were so perfect for thy last days at school!

After hearing how thee and Horace both put it, I feel a sort of responsibility for H.'s happiness next year. I'm not used to responsibility of that sort, Mary! I was the youngest in my family (except Evelyn, whom I rarely had a chance to look after with Mother and Mildred forming sort of a clique to minister to our every whim), and the charge of *le bien-être d'autrui m'est u peu étrange* [the well-being of others is a little strange to me].

But still, I'm getting there. You people wouldn't believe it, but folks are so often taking Ronald for my younger brother, that I'm acquiring the sort of paternal air with him! Ah—don't whisper it to him, or he'll slay me . . . I'll certainly do my utmost for Horace, but he will do great things for me, too—keep me from the prodigal wasting of time that I was guilty of with good old Pack!

How lovely a summer thee will spend down in Maine! But thee mustn't try to swim to Ireland, because thee can't be sure of being as lucky as Harry Hawker[18]—there mayn't be an aeroplane passing to pick thee up if something goes wrong!

I shan't be in Paris for the Fourteenth, which promises to be one of the wildest of wild French celebrations. Almost everybody at Grange is going; they'll have to fight to get on the train, *je pense* [I think]. Somehow these Victory doings have no attraction for me . . . If it were another May Day, I'd go and leave everything. But as it is, no, *je reste* [I stay].

I think I'll start for home the first week in September . . . and I'm torn between my desire to take the vacation that's due me and write the play I have in mind, or abbreviate the vacation and do more publication for the Mission.

Ronald is staying on and doing splendid work in Paris—picking up French phenomenally quickly as well.

It is not long before I start for home—a little over a month and a half!

En attendant, soigné-toi, ma mie-tu auras besoin de toutes vos forces à l'automne. Que Dieu te donne sa paix. [As you wait, take care of yourself, my dear—you will need all your strength in the fall. May God give you peace.]

Les

July 21, 1919, Mary in Cape Neddick, Maine, to Leslie in Grange-le-Comte

Dear Les,

I am sitting on this wonderful beach with the sand dunes behind me and the gulls swooping along over the waves. If thee gets home in time, thee must come up here, and we will walk the length of the beach (three miles) at sunset and see the moon rise over the ocean—it is a wonderful sight. I don't know when I am going down for a job—perhaps about the first of September (though Mother wants me to stay until she and Helen have to go down for college).

When does thee sail? Thee will let me know as soon as thee decides, *n'est-ce pas?* I haven't had a letter from thee for quite a long while. I know thee must be very busy with *L'Équipe* and Reconstruction, too—Oh, I do hope the authorities won't interfere—how could there be anything sillier than this gagging process; it is everywhere here. Bob Dunn and Evans Thomas,[19] who have been organizing the textile workers in Paterson N. J., have had all their literature taken away and are now in jail awaiting trial. Bob is perfectly great—he says of course he knew it would only be a matter of time and only regrets that he couldn't have accomplished more before being locked up. What a world we live in! But really thee must not choose a French prison for thy permanent residence—come home to help out our radicals—I am sure American jails are much more sociable, and thee really ought to finish college to be able to appreciate the great advances of prison reform! But enough cynicism—I hope thee is having wonderful success with *L'Équipe*, as I know thee is, but I also hope that *Anastasie* will not make thee late for registration!

We do so little here, and yet if I started to write in detail, I could go on and on. The swimming is so glorious and the blueberry patch so thick that I divide my time between the water and the meadow— with a bit of Dante or the "Great Society" thrown in at intervals. The "Coop"[20] is sending me an Underwood typewriter—I am crazy to begin on the touch system and only hope I will get some kind of start on it before Fall.

Boston has just emerged, as thee probably has heard, from a street car strike.[21] Mother went down the other day to a meeting held by this Mr. Hickson[22] (the Episcopal layman who is curing so many people), and she said that the city was a sight! The traffic police were nearly driven insane by droves of flivvers and trucks jammed with people. Mother came in to Boston to get her train from Harvard Square in a huge truck with settees on it—it was pouring rain and everybody's umbrella dripped down everybody else's neck. The Car- men's Union certainly tied things up, and they got what they de- manded, too, an eight-hour day and a raise in wages. When labor is organized it can certainly get anything it wants, can't it.

It certainly is great having a mother who is such a good sport. Helen is away all day long painting, so Mother and I do all kinds of things together—at least we swim and berry and walk together. The other evening we walked ten miles back into the country on the pret- tiest, most rustic old roads. As soon as one leaves the summer set- tlement of artist folk, this region is most quiet and antiquated. I never saw so many weather-beaten old farmhouses, which seemed to have a ghost looking out of every cobbwebly [sic] window and only one dim spooky light off in the kitchen somewhere. I don't see how, if the farms out west are anything like these (but of course they are not) that Horace ever dares drive up to the door in his little flivver and begin by discussing crops and end with Non-Partisan League. It must take a lot of pluck—I admire him for it. Arthur Fisher is out there too, doing the same thing—he writes that it is desperately tiring work. There must be a lot of adventures, though, to keep things interesting.

Thee will be interested to hear that Mr. Rotzel was unable to find a house to live in in Lawrence this summer (the one that he finally found was refused him after he had rented it, when they found out who he was) so he and his wife and little girl are living in tents on some land they managed to hire. One tent is used as a sort of library or meeting room where people come for literature, meetings, etc. They are hoping to get some kind of a house in the fall for a "Fellowship House." If I go to work with Mr. Rotzel I shall probably live there. Anyway, tents won't do for the winter.

> À bientôt—ton camarade,
> Mary

July 23, 1919, Leslie in Grange-le-Comte to Mary in Cape Neddick, Maine

Dearest Mary,

The fire is before me, and the shadows are dancing silently and madly on the wall behind me. I have been gazing into the fire, and seeing in it a picture of life—flames of love and passion girdling the body of the wood—leaping out upwards, gesticulating as though to leave the wood, still clinging and consuming, and sending out warmth and light. Think of an eternal body and an eternal fire!

I do hope that thy plan of working with Harold Rotzel comes through—it's such a splendid one! My few fortunate days with him were an inspiration, and of course thy languages will be a tremendous help! Why didn't I ever think of that? Italian, French, German! Good gracious, when you think of the people at Lawrence, nothing could be more opportune or valuable for thee than to be able to speak to them in their own tongue, and if I know Harold Rotzel, I'm sure he'd be anxious to have such an able and devoted aide. But does thee know, I still have a feeling deep down that the best thing thee could possibly do to start in up there would be to get a job as a factory hand. I know thee would bless the experience after thee had gained it, and that touch and knowledge of the lives and struggle of those whom you will try to reach will be an open-sesame in thy talks with them. I feel this is true, Mary—doesn't thee? . . . The other night, we had here Constance Gostick,[23] a member of the Mission who is leaving for England. She is a fine woman: a welfare worker in a big factory in Hull; she is straight and sympathetic—pacifist, Socialist, and everything else; she says that the most valuable experience she had, that helped her to see straight into the lives of the girls, was working as they did, living on the same money and sleeping under the shadow of the big chimney. She learned what it was to have no thought from morning till noon but dinner and food . . . she lived on the seven shillings a week for three months and couldn't stand it. Her brain was going to a standstill and perpetual hunger was too much for her. Now she <u>knows</u>. It gives her clear sight, firm speech, utter fearlessness in dealing with employers, and the most complete sympathy with the toilers—and admiration for their stamina which keeps them up under the strain.

But I must tell thee about the Conference. It was held last Saturday and Sunday in the store-room of the Grange, cleared for the purpose. About three hundred and fifty members of the Mission were present, and Henry Hodgkin, a very prominent English Friend, and Roderic Clark, just out from two years in prison (before which he was one of the founders of the [British] Mission).

The Friends are alive, Mary. If they aren't all Socialists, at least the best of them are pacifists and COs, and they're all fully aware that there are many things rotten in the state of Capitalism as well as of Denmark. Notable words were said by Hodgkin. He gave us the clear call back from the deadly old-man attitude to life, to the courageous, adventurous child-spirit—that life must be lived for personality and not possession.

Fred Libby (the pacifist Andover instructor who sailed with me from America) made a stirring appeal for thought and Christ-like activity on our part. He said, "The work of those three ministers in the Lawrence strike marks an epoch in American history—an epoch!" He made a tremendous impression. Thee doesn't know what an electric thing the act of these three men has proved to be. It will galvanize men to action for the ideal all over the world.

Wright Baker is a young English Friend who has been in the Mission from the beginning. He is the head of the Transport Department. As such, he looked so young that he had to grow a beard and moustache to get business men to listen to him. The striking thing is that he looks so marvelously like the average artist's conception of Christ that one is almost fascinated to look at him. He is accustomed to wear a white smock about, which heightens the impression. His beard and hair are a golden brown. In the General Meeting (or Conference), he got up and told why he got into the Mission, why he stuck, and why he is leaving it. The Mission, with its sustained friendship and idealism, it seems, has made a new man of him: not sure of truths, wanting to get on in the world, and mortally shy—shy to painfulness—that's what he was. Now he's going back to work for those who spent so many years bringing him up, and his ambition is gone—he is rich with a wealth of friendship and faith which he never could even have glimpsed without this experience. Last night, in the Forum Meeting, his eyes, which are blue, seemed to have shimmering deep flame in them—they burnt right through me. You feel capable of the greatest things in your heart when you see a man like that. And when a Friend suggested slow revision of the social order—point by point—Wright Baker got up, and, in a manner so humble and yet so fearless that it took all possible sting out of a directly opposite thought, said that Christ's way was a complete overthrow of the old man and the full life of the new, that it was by his faith in man that so many men came to him—not because he cautiously advised them to prudently change their plan of life point by point.

Mary—what does thee think—I'm learning to speak! That is, I don't stutter, burble, and forget as I used to. I spoke a couple of times in the course of the meetings—only when I felt I had to and couldn't keep still any longer. But in these Forums we're having, I'm going to take every opportunity to improve. Heaven knows I need it!

The Mission is harder and harder to leave, the longer one stays. What friends the Friends are! People whom one would never suspect of warm, kindly, tolerant feelings suddenly show them—and you wonder where you can have been looking all this time not to have seen! I'm afraid I really must join the Friends—<u>must</u>!

For recreation, we had games on Saturday afternoon before tea. They put me on the entertainment committee, and we certainly did our best to get everybody into the games, which, although we do say it, were fairly well chosen. But before lunch, H. Hodgkin (who is the Secretary of the new Council for International Service, formed by the London Friends) asked all those who had at heart future service in Quaker Embassies or otherwise to meet him after lunch. There was a big crowd, and from time to time, people got up and voiced the desires and plans they had been thinking over. Ronald was up from Paris for the Conference; he told the meeting he wanted to go to Austria and gave his reasons. He wants to work in Vienna as one of the people, if possible, to spread the pacifist and CO ideal, and help the men of the new world who are trying to communize Austria. And I think he'll go sometime before very long; Charles Rhoads seems to think it quite possible that way to Austria will open very soon. Thee sees, Mary, that one of the Friends' ideas is not to have all "miniature Missions" working in these countries, but Friends here and there taking up residence and the sort of work they wish to do in foreign countries where the pacifist ideal is needed. I certainly envy Ronald his opportunity and wish him God-speed in his undertaking.

One very strong point worked out by the Committee on Future Work which met here at Grange, was the principle that the directing, planning, and spreading of effort of whatever nature was to be done entirely by the workers in the field, without referring back for instructions from home committees. This strong element of initiative and responsibility is one of the greatest incentives I know.

I spoke for Russia, because I believe that we can learn things from Russia, in attitude towards people, new institutions, and good lives. It is striking that Augusta Townsend,[24] who keeps house for the Mission *équipe* at Solesmes where we have four Russians (wrongfully kept prisoner by the French) to help us (we pay them), expressed a vital interest in Russia. Just the way they act—the things they silently do for her and the expressions of their faces have made her anxious to go to Russia to learn from them and to carry the Western message of goodness and pacifism to them.

But enough! Thee must be seriously sick of this terribly drawn-out story about the Meeting.

Horace's work is extremely interesting—I wonder what his reaction to it will be. Fred Libby, who is not yet a Radical, wants to get in touch with Townley, the organizer of the League. He thinks that in organizations like that lies the hope of the future.

Against the big, cold Atlantic I can only present a little, cool stream—the Aire River. But in this stream I have been swimming, day after day—and I'm getting to love it. It flows down through a green meadow between Rarecourt and Augeville, with fresh, supple trees on each bank. Our only beach is the soft greensward from which we run and dive into the water—I have been trying so hard, that at length I began to feel at home and confident in the water. And that, as thee said last summer, is a feeling without a like in the world.

Good-night, Mary, good-night. God keep thee,
Les

August 2, 1919, Mary in Cape Neddick, Maine, to Leslie in Grange-le-Comte

Dear Leslie,

When I let myself, I worry about thee—for it is a whole month since I have heard from thee. I try and think that thee is all right—that thee has written and something has happened to the letter, but then I fear that perhaps thee is sick or that thy fearless speaking of the truth has gotten thee into trouble. How I wish I could see across the ocean and know what thee is doing.

Now I will pretend that I have just had a letter from thee saying that thee is well and happy—and I answer that I am the same and wish thee the very happiest of birthdays—for this is a birthday letter, though it didn't start much that way. I hope thee will get it on time. It is funny that thee should manage to get in two birthdays in France when thee is staying only a little more than a year.

This bit of goldenrod I enclose is thy birthday flower and mine, too. I wanted to press some lacy sea-weed on my letter, but the tide was high when I went down to get it, and I don't want to wait until tomorrow.

Twenty-two is a fine age to be, isn't it—with every sunny day that goes by up here I feel myself growing in strength and purpose for the work ahead. As thee said in one of thy letters once, "I feel as though I were on the threshold of the world about to enter life." How marvelous it is to be alive—there are so many beautiful things to love and such eternal truths to give solidity and reality to all the symbols. When we are blue or discouraged, it is only for a while, and usually because we are physically tired—for soon the old spontaneous joy comes back, and we feel that we can do and share anything.

By the way, glorious news—Roger Baldwin and Brent Allinson are out [of jail]! Isn't that wonderful—also Bob Dunn and Evans Thomas, whose case was tried last week, and the fight for free speech at Paterson seems to have been won—for the police have backed down entirely; now they can go on with their organization in peace!

I heard from Horace yesterday; he seems to be working very hard and succeeding, too—for he got thirty members for the Non-Partisan League last week. I wrote him about *L'Équipe* and he was much interested—wants to hear more.

Helen is really painting some lovely things of the rocks and ocean here; she works indefatigably and just loves it. Next week is her twenty-first birthday, and I am trying to get a couple of her best friends to come down and spend the weekend as a great surprise. I do hope they can, it will be such fun.

I don't seem to write much about current events and really important things in my letters to thee—but we are all so disgusted with the Treaty that there is no use talking about that, and, well thee knows what I think on other things—we will have great comparings of ideas when thee comes home.

The postman will be here in a minute. Here's hoping he brings a letter from thee! *Heureux anniversaire, mon ami—Cette lettre t'apporte les meilleures souhaits* [Happy birthday, my friend—This letter brings best wishes].

De ton fidèle camarade,
Mary

August 13, 1919, Mary in Ogunquit Beach, Maine, to Leslie in Grane-le-Comte

Dear Les,

At last the silence is broken and two letters have come from thee—one enclosing *L'Équipe* and the other telling about the Conference. Perhaps I wasn't glad to get them! I don't know whether thee will get this letter before thee leaves—the mails are so slow—but I thought I would risk it and write one last letter. Thee must be sure to let me know the name of the boat thee sails on, so that I can watch for its arrival in the paper. My! Won't thy family be glad to see thee, and some other people too!

I was so interested in what thee said about my going into a factory, for that is just what I have decided to do. Mr. Muste and Mrs. Davis both think that I could help better with the organizing later if I went into a mill at Lawrence for a few months. So about the middle or last part of September I am going down to apply for a job, no matter what, in the textile mill. I would go before then, but Mother insists on my staying here as long as possible, and I must say I don't want to leave this glorious beach.

I must tell thee about how we celebrated Helen's twenty-first birthday the other day. With several of the girls in her painting class, we went in swimming here in the surf and then collected a great pile of driftwood. For supper we roasted corn over the fire to eat with the rest of our feast. And after supper we danced around and played games on the smooth hard sand. Then followed stories and experiences told around the fire and then—we curled up in blankets and went to sleep around the fire. We were way along the beach by the sand dunes where never a soul passes, and it was glorious. How I wish I could describe the marvelous light effects that we saw. First there had been a glorious sunset, and then the moon rose over the ocean, making it seem alive with silver snakes. Then about midnight the sky flashed purple and gold and green with northern lights—I never saw such a sight. It rayed out from one point and made one think of the star the shepherds saw the night Christ was born—for it filled the heavens with brilliant light. I was awake most of the night tending the fire, so I got every bit of the loneliness and wonder of the ocean and sand stretches at night. Then in the morning came the delicate pink dawn and the vivid sunrise. It was all an experience we shall never forget, and Helen said it seemed as though nature had prepared it especially for her, it was so absolutely perfect.

I was so interested in thy description of the Conference—to think that Ronald wants to go to Austria and thee to Russia! Thy family will be scattered to the four winds if Clarence should depart too. Evelyn will just have to stay in the U.S. so that we can have the fourth wind to refresh us here!

Thee says that thee feels thee must join the Friends. It is funny—or rather interesting that I have been thinking seriously of it myself for quite a while. I have grown so tired of church forms and creeds that mean nothing, that my heart is drawn to this simple belief in living the Gospel of Love. Of course everything such as family ties bind me to the Unitarian, the liberal faith—so many of my relations have been Unitarian ministers; I must say, a faith that makes us all ministers appeals to me more.

I am glad thee has gotten to love the water as thy foster-element. If thee gets home before the end of Sept., thee must come up here and have a swim on this glorious beach, and then we can walk way along the sand where the white birds scream. I have written some verses about the ocean and the birds, which I will show thee if thee has some metrical thoughts to show me in return! I hope thee took the vacation and has written the play thee spoke of in thy letter. I tell thee, I will read thee my poems if thee will read me thy play— that is fair, *n'est-ce pas?*

As the last bit of land disappears out of sight when thee sails home, say good-bye to beautiful France for me, too. Although I did not have time to get to know her as thee does, yet I love her as the home of Lamartine, Vigny, Daudet, and all the others, and one needs only a glimpse to prove the truth of "*La Belle France.*" I know how thee must hate to leave the Mission—it has meant so very much to thee—the spirit of the Friends and the opportunity of service—it is a great chapter in thy life, isn't it. And I know what wonderful work thee has done over there too—Horace was right when he said thee had inextinguishable enthusiasm, and I add—unlimited ability as only one of many things. *L'Équipe* certainly proves that. I don't see how thee ever did all the things thee did do.

Eh bien, au revoir! I can't believe that this is my last letter—I must stop for want of light as the sun has long since set.

Adieu mon camarade et au revoir,
Mary

August 17, 1919, Leslie in Strasbourg to Mary in Cape Neddick, Maine

Dearest Mary,

Voilà que je t'écris de Strasbourg [Here is what I write to you from Strasbourg]: or rather, *Siehe, ich schreibe au dich von Strassborg. Es jammert mich, dass ich gar schlectes deutsch schreiben un sprechen kann, aber du kennst wieviel ich mich von deutsch gebraucht habe.* [See, I am writing you from Strasbourg. I pity myself that I cannot write and speak German, but you know how much I needed German.] (Oh what dog German!)

It is a beautiful town—and what a relief of cleanliness after the slovenly towns of France! And they don't rob, either. Things cost a little more than half as much as they do almost anywhere in France.

I've been swimming in the Rhine this afternoon, a current of about nine miles an hour, I guess. It's great fun. You dive off the float some distance from the bank, and then try to get back to shore. You do it, about one hundred and fifty yards downstream . . . and the general spoken language on the beach is German; it gives me a queer feeling.

In the morning, I dropped into a Protestant church. The sermon was in German, and I thought it excellent—the bits that I understood. He was urging fearlessness and courage—which were alone possible in love. He spoke with great fervor—paid no reference to the change of masters in Alsace . . . a far better sermon than even the better ones of those we hear at Appleton.

In my chamber I found a Luther New Testament which I have been reading with benefit. Probably they have them in each spotless room in the old house. At the table at dinner was a Sunday-school paper in German, and I'm listening to some very beautiful hymn singing by two girls across the court. Just imagine what a pleasant surprise and feeling of peace—after not seeing or hearing anything like that in France!

Just yesterday—my birthday—I started on my vacation, which will only last a few days, for I am to sail on the 30th, according to latest reports. I have a bicycle, which I got from the Mission, and am going to start off tomorrow morning, if it is fine, and cycle down to Schlettstadt and Ribeauville and on to Colmar . . . near which I hope to find a quiet spot where I can be for a few days. Sh! I want to write a play. And I want to have it legible by the time I see thee.

My feeling of sureness in an undying and superb friendship between us is nothing compared to the eagerness with which I look forward to the unknown and Christ-like things thee is going to do. Let us hope that thy duty and mine may go hand in hand . . . maybe the coming year will point our futures more clearly than today does.

I have an idea which is growing on me. The more I see of the best Christians I know: T. Edmund Harvey and others among the Friends, and Harold Rotzel, Muste, and others, makes me feel that the really healthy Christian way to act, if we haven't done it earlier, is to work in a humble job as one of the people—<u>try to be</u> one of the people. But there is the consideration that certain kinds of work give us no opportunity for soul-life at all. These are the frightful, mechanical, automaton operations in certain factories. And another thing—a nervous character should have more or less peaceful surroundings. Hurry and worry will burn us out, Mary—I'm giving up caring for the rush of college good times—although I shall enter it again, probably, when I go back.

I think now that the best thing in the world I could do is to study blacksmithing and agricultural machine repairs during my summer and after I graduate and go to Russia—with no Mission supporting me, to wander from village to village helping mend their tools; by service like that, one can talk to a man; I could never feel here that I had a right to talk to a man who had worked and suffered—I wasn't in his class . . . I've had enough of the deadening influence of the comfortable; it never made a man yet.

Ronald is going to Austria for a couple of weeks (if he can manage the papers) to look around and see what he can do. His purpose, as thee knows, is to get away from the Mission as soon as possible and be a real apostle.

Forgive this garbled talk; thee'll be able to read into it what I mean. It isn't long now before I'll see thee—a few short days!

God watch over thee,

Les

August 23, 1919, Leslie in the Alsace French region to Mary in Ogunquit, Maine

Dearest Mary,

I'm having a new experience! Imagine thy Leslie up on one of the highest of the Vosges Mountains, Le Ballon de Guebwiller, above a mountain lake. He came up here four days ago and has been far from human habitation ever since—alone with the forest and the west wind. Ah, thee should hear the west wind strike the trees a mile away and surge by with a gathering roar, whelming the bowed heads of the beech and the fir!

I came up here to fast and invite my soul and to write. This is the fourth day of my fast, and I feel much better than I did at the end of the first. My head is very clear. I feel almost disembodied, my desires are sprightly, and I want to sing all the time—to experience and express the deepest of human emotions. A feeling of life underneath, of original freedom from every burden!

It's curious, the condition one gets into fasting. One has no inclination to crave food at every moment, nor does hunger obsess one's mind. As a rule one is free to think clearly at will. But when thoughts of food do come, and one doesn't forcibly drive them away, the imaginings are sublimated—of the most esthetic nature. The stomach has been translated into the spirit. One thinks of a good meal with the same sense of enjoyment of the beautiful that a musician remembers a beautiful harmony—As different as possible from the appetite of the senses with which one ordinarily approaches a meal . . . I wish I might always have, as spirit looks toward the flesh-pots of Egypt as I have now! [sic]

But I must call a halt today, as I have to go down from the mountain, along through Colmar, Schlettstadt, and Strasbourg to Ban-le-Duc and Grange. For I'm getting ready to go home! I must just pick up my little knapsack—I have no blanket, and I've slept these four nights in a pile of leaves—and go down to the little inn, get my bicycle and fly down the long, winding mountain road . . . My mind is filled already with the wistful joy of meeting thee again and hearing thy voice *"Mon cœur s'ouvre a ta voix, comme s'ouvrent les fleurs au baiser de l'aurore"* ["My heart opens to your voice as the flowers open to the kisses of the dawn." [Lyrics from an aria in the opera "Samson and Delilah" by Camille Saint-Saëns.]

I have been very near to thy spirit, Mary, in these days on the mountain. The other day I climbed to the wind-swept top and gazed down the valley to the sunrise, to see the Alps standing through the haze, powerful yet delicate to see . . . and I thought of thee and thy strength and swift beauty.

I've written a play here; I can't tell whether or not it is worth keeping; but at least it isn't a trick of ideas or a sport with words in the mouths of puppets. I've tried to put real things into it—and I hope I've not utterly failed.

Is thee still studying the typewriter? Hard at first, *nest-ce pas*, but when one has mastered the keyboard and been accurate (!), speed will come.

I'm finding it hard to leave the Mission—the group of friends unique in my life—where I've grown and spent precious days. But T. Edmund Harvey and his wife have gone; Charles Rhoads is going—the Mission is rapidly diminishing . . . and I'm the last one in France of our group which came over in July.

But Ronald has a great opportunity! He is going to Austria to spy out the land and see where he can do good—and in about two months he will probably be there! He has won the hearts of the Friends over here. Everybody, I think, likes him deeply. I hate to go away and leave him—we haven't been together much in the last years, and we mean so much to one another. But he will be inspired and inspiring wherever he goes!

Arrivederci, Maria mia,

Thy,

Les

Epilogue: Their Story Continues

FOR A BRIEF AND INTENSE TIME, Leslie and Mary lived up to the best of their ideals. They worked to improve the lives of workers and to repair the ravages of a war they both opposed. They dreamed of a new world order and hoped that America was ready and able to step up to the challenge.

Leslie and Mary continued their courtship when he returned home from France. On Christmas Day in 1919, they were married in a Quaker-style ceremony at Mary's home at 13 Hilliard Street in Cambridge. Her uncle, a Unitarian minister, officiated.

Leslie returned to Harvard and finished his bachelor's degree and a Ph.D. in English in 1923. He followed it with a year of research as a Sheldon Fellow in England. There he discovered, in the legal archives kept in the Public Record Office, unknown details of the killing of Christopher Marlowe, later embodied in his first book *The Death of Christopher Marlowe*. This and his second book were among the first books published by Nonesuch Press, a firm established by David Garnett, who had been a member of the British Friends War Victims Association working at the manufacturing facility at Dole. David was a close friend of Leslie's co-editor on *Reconstruction*, Francis Birrell.

After two years of teaching, one at Harvard and one at Yale, he spent another year at Yale as Sterling Senior Research Fellow until the completion of his second book, *The Commonwealth and Restoration Stage*. In 1927, he went to New York University as associate professor of English and then moved to the Quaker-founded Haverford College in Haverford, Pennsylvania, where he taught until 1941, living on campus next door to Rufus Jones.

Leslie became a well-respected Elizabethan scholar, focusing in particular on Shakespeare and the Elizabethan theatre. He found enjoyment in digging through piles of musty papers and became especially known as a literary sleuth. While on a Guggenheim Traveling Fellowship, searching through records at the British Museum, Leslie found unknown letters by the poet Percy Bysshe Shelley, written to his wife in 1814; these were the basis of his book, *Shelley's Lost Letters to Harriet*. (This author would like to think that Leslie would be pleased that his own letters have also been "found.") In 1930, Leslie was elected a Fellow of the Royal Society of Literature.

Mary taught for a while at the Shady Hill School in Cambridge and then spent the rest of her life traveling with her husband and assisting him in his research. She developed a special interest in Elizabethan music and presented programs of song and poetry.

Their love lasted more than seventy-five years. On their seventieth wedding anniversary, in 1989, Mary and Leslie Hotson reflected on how they sustained the joy and wonder of their Christmas wedding day throughout their married lives. "You need a love and you need a dream," Mary said with conviction. "Something to sacrifice for . . . something really important to live for . . . Life is so wonderful, so joyful . . . we've always looked for and found the beauty and truth in love."[1]

The ideals that sustained them through their marriage found fertile ground in the realities of the Great War. They were then highly educated, deeply spiritual, adventurous young people rising to the challenge of extraordinary times, pacifists during a time of patriotic militarism who were daring to transform their idealism and principles into action. They were also just an ordinary young couple trying to maintain a budding romance under the difficult conditions of wartime.

Author's Note

WE ANSWERED WITH LOVE has been a labor of love for more than fifteen years. In 2001, my husband, David, and I acquired a large collection of letters from Richard Murphy, an antiquarian bookseller from Connecticut. He had purchased all of the papers from Leslie Hotson's estate for their autograph value—Leslie had corresponded with many of the top literary figures of the 1930s and '40s and with many Shakespearean actors. At the time, David and I operated an antiquarian bookstore specializing in books and pamphlets by or about Quakers. In fact, we were the largest dealer in out-of-print Quaker materials in the world. We were offered the letters because they had "Quaker content."

David carefully sorted the letters and put them in chronological order, and I transcribed them. As we worked, we constantly interrupted each other with, "Listen to this . . . " and shared passages that caught our attention. We soon realized that Leslie and Mary had a story to tell, and they told it in a new and exciting way. Their letters captivated us both. We fell in love with this young couple.

We are grateful to Leslie's relatives for permission to publish these letters. The couple did not have children and did not designate a literary heir in their wills. Their niece, Janet Hotson Baker, Ronald's daughter, met with me and shared stories about her family. Peter Diaconoff, Evelyn Hotson's grandson, contacted other members of the family and obtained their permission for the project. Mary's sister Helen did not have children.

Over the next ten years, as time permitted, I spent hours in research. I knew very little about the Great War and felt that the letters needed to be put into context. I read books about World War I, conscientious objection, the great influenza epidemic, the Espionage Act, the rise of Bolshevism, trade unions and labor strikes, and the roles of women during the war and its aftermath.

Jack Shetter and Don Davis at the American Friends Service Committee Archives provided invaluable help while I pored over administrative letters, monthly reports, newsletter articles, diaries and letters from other Unit members, photographs, and other documents and materials. I am especially grateful for permission from the Archives to reprint materials, including photographs.

The staff at the Swarthmore College Peace Collection provided documents about the pacifist and social activism organizations in the Boston area. I had an "aha!" moment when I discovered that Mary Peabody's mother, Anna Peabody, and Anna Davis served together on the same committee dealing with COs—the missing link connecting Leslie, a Swedenborgian from Brooklyn, with Mrs. Davis, the Quaker coordinating the work of the AFSC in Cambridge.

At the Harvard and the Radcliffe archives, I was able to read Leslie's and Mary's personal files, including their college applications. Yearbooks, reunion letters, college newspapers, and written histories of the two institutions provided a wealth of background material and helped me identify some of the classmates mentioned in their letters.

And I had fun getting sidetracked. Leslie and Mary were acquainted with many fascinating people: Roger Baldwin, A. J. Muste, Jeannette Rankin, Jane Addams, Eva Le Gallienne, Harry Dana, and of course Rufus Jones, all of whom had whole books written about them but who could only serve as little more than footnotes to the Hotsons' story. Other equally fascinating people were not as well documented, but I enjoyed discovering what I could, including details about Anna Davis, Horace Davis, Helen Peabody, Frederick Peabody, Mary Stone McDowell, and Francis Sayre. I wish I could have included more of their stories.

Leslie's co-editor, Francis Birrell, was a member of the Bloomsbury Group in England, so I spent hours reading about the antics of Virginia Woolf, Vanessa Bell, John Maynard Keynes, and Lytton Strachey (none of whom had anything to do with the reconstruction work in France, but what fun!). I also read parts of the writings of Emmanuel Swedenborg and the *Oxford Book of Poetry* and dipped into novels and plays Mary and Leslie recommended in their correspondence.

Eventually, I knew it was time to start writing. In 2008, I joined a writer's group in Durham, North Carolina. They patiently put up with my efforts as a beginning author while I worked on the first drafts of Leslie and Mary's story. I had been an engineer, and I needed many drafts of my first chapters to rid my writing of the passive voice I was accustomed to using in my former profession.

Because of other obligations, this project sat on a back burner for several years, but I continued to be drawn back into the Hotsons' story. I set a deadline for the project when I learned that, in 2017, the AFSC would celebrate the one hundredth anniversary of its founding. I joined

the First Time Book Writers Meetup Group in Shrewsbury, Massachusetts, and more recently, The Writers' Loft in Sherborn. Some wonderful
writers in these groups provided me with support, critiques, and encouragement in completing the writing and in publishing the book. I am
grateful to all of them.

The first reader of the complete book, Martha Schwope, made many
useful suggestions. She surprised me by offering to translate and transcribe
the French passages that are such an integral part of Leslie and Mary's correspondence. Any mistakes in editing these passages or interpreting the id-
ioms as they were used a hundred years ago are mine.

Gwendolyn Towers offered thoughtful comments and suggestions.
The book is certainly better for her help. Marjorie Turner Holman, an
experienced personal historian and published author, helped me clarify
the arc of the story and eliminate some of the extraneous material in the
early drafts. Paula Stahel and Francie King stepped up to edit the book
under a tight deadline; they did a wonderful job—I hope I did not re-
introduce any egregious errors. And finally, I am so grateful to Robin
Brooks, an excellent book designer, who brought the book to life; not
only did she design a beautiful book, she offered encouragement and
support throughout the scary process of letting go of the project.

Bibliography

Archives

Harvard University Archives. John Leslie Hotson personal student folder.

Radcliffe University Achives, Schlesinger Library. Mary May Peabody personal folder.

American Friends Service Committee Archives, Friends Reconstruction Unit 1917-1920.

Swarthmore College Peace Collection.

Books

Barry, John M. *The Great Influenza: The Epic Story of the Deadliest Plague in History.* New York: Viking, 2004.

Blair, Karen J. *The Torchbearers: Women and Their Amateur Arts Associations in America, 1890-1930.* Bloomington, Indiana: University Press, 1994.

Bright, James W. *An Anglo-Saxon Reader, Edited with Notes and a Glossary.* New York: Henry Holt and Company, 1891.

Brown, Carrie. *Rosie's Mom: Forgotten Women Workers of the First World War.* Boston: Northeastern University Press, 2002.

Early, Frances H. *A World Without War: How U.S. Feminists and Pacifists Resisted World War I.* Syracuse, New York: Syracuse University Press, 1997.

Farr, Gail E., Brett F. Bostwick, Merville Willis. *Shipbuilding at Cramp's Shipyard.* Philadelphia Maritime Museum, 1991.

Foner, Philip S. *Women and the American Labor Movement From Colonial Times to the Eve of World War I.* New York: The Free Press, 1979.

Forbes, John. *The Quaker Star Under Seven Flags 1917-1927.* Philadelphia: University of Pennsylvania Press, 1962.

Frost-Knappman, Elizabeth and Kathryn Cullen-DuPont, editors. *Women's Suffrage in America: An Eyewitness History.* New York: Facts on File, 1992.

Fry, A. Ruth. *A Quaker Adventure: The Story of Nine Years' Relief and Reconstruction.* New York: Frank-Maurice, Inc., [1926].

Gale, Oliver Marble, compiler. *Americanism: Woodrow Wilson's Speeches on the War—Why He Made Them—and—What They Have Done.* Chicago: The Baldwin Syndicate, 1918.

Gill, Gillian. *Mary Baker Eddy.* Reading, Massachusetts: Perseus Books, 1998.

Hagedorn, Ann. *Savage Peace: Hope and Fear in America, 1919.* New York: Simon and Schuster, 2007.

Harvard University Class of 1920 Anniversary Class Reports, 1925-1965 (published every five years).

Hentoff, Nat. *Peace Agitator: The Story of A. J. Muste,* New York: Macmillan, 1963.

Jones, Mary Hoxie. *Swords into Plowshares.* New York: The Macmillan Company, 1937.

Jones, Rufus M. *A Service of Love in War Time: American Friends Relief Work in Europe, 1917-1919.* New York: The Macmillan Company, 1920.

Morison, Samuel Eliot. *Three Centuries of Harvard, 1636-1936.* Cambridge, Massachusetts: Harvard University Press, 1937.

Perry, Bliss. *The Amateur Spirit.* New York: Houghton, Mifflin, 1904.

Pringle, Cyrus, edited by Rufus Jones. *The Record of a Quaker Conscience: Cyrus Pringle's Diary.* New York: Macmillan, 1918.

Quiller-Couch, Sir Arthur. *The Oxford Book of English Verse 1250-1900.* Oxford: Oxford University Press, [1917] (originally published in 1900).

Radcliffe College Class of 1919 Fiftieth Reunion Report, 1969.

Radcliffe College Class of 1919 Year Book.

Selincourt, Hugh De. *A Soldier of Life.* New York: Macmillan, 1917.

Selleck, George A. *Quakers in Boston 1656-1964: Three Centuries of Friends in Boston and Cambridge.* Cambridge, Massachusetts: Published by Friends Meeting at Cambridge, 1976.

Stephens, D. Owen. *With Quakers in France.* London: C. W. Daniel, 1921.

Swedenborg, Emmanuel. *The True Christian Religion: Containing the Universal Theology of the New Church.* New York: Swedenborg Foundation, 1946.

Swedenborg, Emmanuel. *The Delights of Wisdom Pertaining to Conjugial Love.* New York: Swedenborg Foundation, 1891.

Preliminary Announcement of the Trade Union College Under the Auspices of the Boston Central Labor Union, Spring Term, April 7 to June 14, 1919.

Articles

"What is Radcliffe Doing to Win the War?" *Radcliffe News*, May 17, 1918.

"Violating Traditions." *Harvard Crimson*, March 1, 1919.

Committee of 100 Friends of COs. "Who Are the Conscientious Objectors?" Brooklyn, New York: May 1, 1919.

Frost, J. William. "Our Deeds Carry Our Message: The Early History of the American Friends Service Committee." *Quaker History* 81: 1-51.

Howlett, Charles F. "Quaker Conscience in the Classroom: The Mary S. McDowell Case." *Quaker History* 83: 99-115.

Kauffman, Susan. "Hidden New Jersey: Gloucester City: Philadelphia's Historic Immigrant Port of Entry." Web Blog Post, July 28, 2013 (accessed July 30, 2016).

Powell, Kathy. *New Haven Register*, "Christmas couple still coos after 70 years," December 25, 1989.

Periodicals

L'Équipe, 1919.

Reconstruction, 1918-1919.

Relevance: The Quarterly Journal of the Great War Society, Volume 13, No. 2, Spring, 2004.

Photography Credits

The background image on the cover and the AFSC star on page 2 are used with the permission of the AFSC Archives. The illustrations on the following pages are also used with permission: xii, 5, 6, 24, 90, 120, 148, 150, 151, 153, 162, 170, 179, 181, 188, 192, 193, 195, 196, 206, 210, 290, 293, 296, 316, 318, 341.

Snapshots on pages 69, 71, and 72 were taken by Mary Peabody and enclosed in her letters, 1918.

The following images are from the Library of Congress website [https://www.loc.gov] with no known restrictions on publication, accessed August 17, 2016:

Page 30. Davis Photo Co., Copyright Claimant. *Panoramic view of Camp Dix, New Jersey, United States Army Cantonment.* Circa, 1918. [item/2007664144]. No renewal found in Copyright Office.

Page 134. *St. Louis Red Cross Motor Corps on duty Oct. 1918 Influenza epidemic.* 1918 [item/2011661525]

Page 137. *Hospital, Camp Devens, Massachusetts* (between 1909 and 1920) [item/93509754]

Page 153. *T.O.M. Sopwith—Airplane.* (about 1915) [item/2001704152]

Page 64. Bain News Service, Publisher. *W.D. Haywood leads Lowell strike parade.* (date created or published later by Bain, 1912), [item/ggb2004010357]

Page 258. *Strike in Lawrence, Massachusetts, with many children on sidewalk,* 1912 [item/89714967]

The cover portrait of Mary Peabody and the illustrations on pages 130, 203, 220, 222, and 300 are from the Schlesinger Library, Radcliffe Institute, Harvard University.

The cover portrait of Leslie Hotson and the illustrations on page 8, 178, and 233, are used courtesy of the Harvard University Archives.

The images on pages 20 and 142 are used with the permission of the Cambridge Historical Commission.

The image on page 164 is from the National Archives Catalog website [https://catalog.archives.gov] with unrestricted use, accessed August 17, 2016, *Scene in Boston Mass. on Armistice Day.* Id/23921423, record 165-WW-75C-41.

Page 66. Printed postcard *50 Le Havre: — Le "Rochambeau", de la Cie Generale Transatlantique.* Paris: Levy et Neurdein Reusis, no date.

Notes

Introduction

[1] Jones, Rufus M. *A Service of Love in War Time: American Friends Relief Work in Europe, 1917-1919*. New York: The Macmillan Company, 1920, p. 9.

[2] ibid., pp. 7-8.

[3] London Yearly Meeting, "To Men and Women of Good-Will in the British Empire" in Jones, Rufus M., p. 4

[4] ibid, p. 4-5.

[5] Frost, J. William. "Our Deeds Carry Our Message: The Early History of the American Friends Service Committee." *Quaker History* 81: 3-4.

[6] The William Penn Charter School was the first Quaker school in America, established by William Penn as a day school. At the time Grayson Murphy attended, it was a boys' preparatory school.

[7] Jones, Rufus M., pp. 10-12.

[8] Lewis Gannett was a Harvard student who went to France with the first Friends Unit. He served as co-editor of the FRU newsletter, *Reconstruction*, and conducted the correspondence for the Mission. After the war, he became a journalist, writing the daily book review column for the *New York Herald Tribune*.

[9] *Reconstruction*, Volume 1, No. 7, p. 101.

[10] Morris Leeds was a Haverford graduate and co-founder of Leeds and Northrup, a respected manufacturer of electrical measuring and control devices. He used his position as a business leader to urge Philadelphia Quakers to become more involved in social reform. Joseph Henry Scattergood was serving as treasurer of Haverford College when he was asked by Quakers to investigate the possibility of sending young men and women to do relief work in France. He became the first Chief of the Friends' Reconstruction Unit and was a member of the original Red Cross Commission to France.

[11] Jones, Rufus M., pp. 42-45.

[12] Frost, J. William, p. 12.

[13] *Reconstruction*, Volume 1, No. 7, p. 103.

[14] Jones, Rufus M., pp. 17-18.

[15] Sermaize-les-Bains is in the Marne Valley in northeastern France. After the Armistice, the town became the headquarters of the Verdun Project. Rufus Jones called it "a dreadfully devastated town."

[16] Jones, Rufus M., p. 30.

[17] ibid., pp. 65-66.

[18] ibid., p. 64.

[19] Forbes, John. *The Quaker Star Under Seven Flags 1917-1927*. Philadelphia: University of Pennsylvania Press, 1962, p. 45.

Chapter 1. Answering the Call

[1] Leslie's personal student file, Harvard University.

[2] Mary's personal student file, Radcliffe College.

[3] Leslie Hotson personal folder, AFSC Archives.

[4] Swedenborg, Emmanuel. *The True Christian Religion: Containing the Universal Theology of the New Church*. New York: Swedenborg Foundation, 1946, p. 298.

[5] The League for Democratic Control (LDC) was formed in April 1917 and worked to preserve the nation's democratic liberties. The League divided its activities among four committees: The Committee on International Relations advocated a negotiated peace as the only lasting and effective settlement; the Committee on National Service demanded full exemption from service under military authorities for all COs (Anna Davis and Anna Peabody served on this subcommittee); the Free Speech Committee watched for attempts to restrict democratic standards of free speech, free assembly, and free press; and the War Finance Committee urged that revenues be raised by laying financial burden on those best able to bear them. Robert Dunn of Harvard served as Executive Secretary. [Printed flyer, League for Democratic Control, 120 Boylston St. Boston, Massachusetts, July 1, 1917, Swarthmore College Peace Collection.]

[6] Early, Frances H. *A World Without War: How U.S. Feminists and Pacifists Resisted World War I*. Syracuse, New York: Syracuse University Press, 1997, p. 101.

[7] These poems and others referred to in letters from Leslie and Mary were not saved with the letters and have not been found.

[8] Swedenborg, Emmanuel. *The Delights of Wisdom Pertaining to Conjugial Love*. New York: Swedenborg Foundation, 1768. According to Swedenborg, when perfect love is found in an ideal marriage, it leads towards real spirituality and the joy of mutual sharing.

[9] Leslie saved this sprig of lilac, and it is still with his letters.

[10] Henry Wadsworth Longfellow (Harry) Dana, a graduate of Harvard, was dismissed from his professorship at Columbia in 1917 because of his association with an anti-war organization, the People's Council of America for Democracy and Peace. He moved in with his aunt, Alice Longfellow, in Cambridge and became active with Harvard and Radcliffe students in the anti-war, socialist, and trade union movements.

[11] Leslie's high school Latin teacher, Mary Stone MacDowell, had been dismissed from her teaching position and was on trial because of her pacifist stance. Her brother, Carlton MacDowell, was part of the first Haverford Unit of the FRU working in France, so her case had special significance for Leslie. Academic freedom in public schools became a controversial issue during the war. Anyone even suspected of not supporting the war was required to give proof of his or her loyalty. Mary McDowell challenged this law in court, seeking justice on the issue of pacifism and academic freedom.

[12] The Quakers originally used "thee" rather than the more formal "you" as a form of address for everyone regardless of social status, emphasizing their belief in the equality of all people. By the early twentieth century, "thee" was mostly used only within families or among close friends.

[13] Quiller-Couch, Sir Arthur. *The Oxford Book of English Verse 1250–1900*. Oxford: Oxford University Press, 1917.

[14] *Radcliffe News*, May 17, 1918, "What is Radcliffe Doing to Win the War?" reported on a patriotic mass meeting, held on May 15, to encourage students to enter fully into war work, supporting the actions of the government and the activities of the Red Cross. One of the speakers, Hilda Stewart, Radcliffe Class of 1919, spoke about the perceived indifference among Radcliffe students, saying, there are "those who think and talk and those who feel and don't talk. The former represents the comedy in life, the latter the tragedy."

[15] Camp Devens in Massachusetts was established on September 5, 1917, as a temporary cantonment for training soldiers and served as a reception center for recruits.

[16] Young Democracy was a movement of college students and young adults. Its purpose was "to awaken the youth of America to the consciousness of their power and their responsibility to humanity; to fuse the energies and ideals of the young into a co-operative unity, to the end that they may have a voice in the construction of their own future and the determination of their own destiny; to invite the co-operation of all existing young people's societies, in order that the youth of America may present a united front on problems vital to us all; and to establish bonds of international good will and fellowship between young people of all nations." [Flyer on Young Democracy letterhead, Swarthmore Peace Collection.]

[17] The Henry Jewett Players, America's first resident professional theater company, was based in Boston. The Idler was Radcliffe's drama club, which presented performances of plays written, directed, and acted by the students.

Chapter 2. Ronald's Story

[1] The Selective Service Act, Article I, Section 8, gave Congress the authority to declare war and raise and support armies.

[2] Peace churches, particularly Brethren, Quakers, Mennonites, and Amish, advocate Christian pacifism or Biblical nonresistance. Active membership in one of the peace churches was at one time sufficient for obtaining CO status in the United States. But during World War I, even members of the historic peace churches had to defend their beliefs before exemption boards.

[3] Fort Slocum/Davids Island, New Rochelle, New York, is an eighty-acre island in Long Island Sound. During World War I, the island was one of the busiest Army recruiting stations in the country. More than 100,000 soldiers per year were processed through this facility.

[4] Committee of 100 Friends of COs. "Who Are the Conscientious Objectors?" May 1, 1919, Brooklyn, New York, p. 15.

[5] William Cramp and Sons Shipyard in the Kensington District was one of the largest manufacturing establishments in Philadelphia, employing 10,500 people. (Farr, Gail E., Brett F. Bostwick, Merville Willis. *Shipbuilding at Cramp's Shipyard*, Philadelphia Maritime Museum, 1991, p. 14.) The Gloucester City Alien Internment Center was opened in 1912 to relieve the overcrowding at Ellis Island. The facility had a small infirmary for immigrants and was also used to treat the soldiers stationed at the nearby shipyards. (Kauffman, Susan. "Hidden New Jersey: Gloucester City: Philadelphia's Historic Immigrant Port of Entry." Web Blog Post, July 28, 2013.)

[6] Samuel Bunting was a prominent banker from Philadelphia; he served as Personnel Secretary of the AFSC.

[7] Leslie to Mary, May 27, 1918.

[8] Ronald Hotson to Lillie Hotson, May 29, 1918. Letter in AFSC Archives.

[9] Ronald Hotson to Lillie Hotson, May 29, 1918. Letter in AFSC Archives.

[10] Statement of Ronald Hotson to the Exemption Board. Letter in AFSC Archives.

[11] Camp Upton, the closest induction base to the Hotsons' home in Brooklyn, was located in Yaphank, New York, on Long Island.

[12] Pringle, Cyrus, edited by Rufus Jones. *The Record of a Quaker Conscience: Cyrus Pringle's Diary*. New York: Macmillan, 1918. During the Civil War, Pringle was conscripted into the Army. A CO, he would not allow his uncle to pay for his release, and he refused to do any military duties. He was severely tortured during his time in prison. He was finally released through the personal intervention of President Abraham Lincoln.

[13] Frederick P. Keppel was Assistant Secretary of War under Newton Baker. He was responsible for civilian relations and non-military aspects of Army life, including relations with the Red Cross, YMCA, and Army chaplains.

[14] Bliss Perry was a professor of English literature at Harvard between 1907 and 1930. Prior to that, he was editor of *The Atlantic Monthly* for ten years.

[15] The Cercle Française gave Radcliffe students the opportunity to hear and speak French. The Cercle cooperated with the French Department and the Library to institute the Salle Française. Mary was secretary of the club during the 1917-18 school year and president of the club during her senior year.

[16] At the request of Ronald's daughter, the texts of his letters are not included.

[17] Selincourt, Hugh De. *A Soldier of Life*. New York: Macmillan, 1917. The author, an Englishman, writes about national affairs in a nation at war and reveals the spiritual realities of the Great War.

[18] Sarah Haydock Hallowell was a member of the Friends meeting in Cambridge and the sister-in-law of Anna Hallowell Davis.

[19] Boris Stern, Harvard Class of 1918, enlisted as a private on May 27; he was promoted to corporal in November and fought in the Saint-Mihiel and Meuse-Argonne offensives.

[20] Beatrice (Trixie) Julia Jones was a member of the Radcliff Class of 1918. She served as secretary of the Socialist Club her junior year and then as president in 1917-18. She was also with Mary in the Choral Society, Music Club, and Idler Drama Club.

[21] The Philadelphia Monthly Meeting of Friends meeting house on the corner of Fourth and Arch Streets was built in 1804 on land granted by William Penn and still serves as the center for the Philadelphia Monthly Meeting and Philadelphia Yearly Meeting.

[22] Moloch was a deity from the Hebrew Bible whose worship was marked by the sacrifice of children by their own parents. The term is used to refer to anything which requires an appalling sacrifice.

[23] The first paragraphs were originally in French. Only the English translation is included.

[24] The Church of the New Jerusalem is a historic Swedenborgian church in Cambridge. The building is a Gothic Revival stone chapel built in 1901, located near Harvard Square.

[25] Evelyn Rose Hotson was Leslie's younger sister by five years. She attended high school in Waltham, Massachusetts, and then was a member of the Radcliffe Class of 1925. After college, she married Rev. Andre Diaconoff.

[26] The first paragraphs were originally in French. Only the English translation is included in the text.

[27] Perry, Bliss. *The Amateur Spirit*. New York: Houghton, Mifflin, 1904.

[28] The Craigie House was Henry Wadsworth Longfellow's home in Cambridge; Alice Longfellow, his oldest daughter, was living there with her nephew, Henry Wadsworth Longfellow (Harry) Dana.

[29] Dr. William Worcester was one of a long family line of Swedenborgian ministers. He was a Harvard graduate and served as the second pastor of the Cambridge Society of the New Jerusalem from 1911 to 1936.

[30] Henry and William James are buried with the rest of their family in Cambridge Cemetery. The plot has six family headstones in front of a brick wall with the surname "James" inscribed on a stone centerpiece.

[31] Leslie probably meant the Charles River between Boston and Cambridge.

[32] Clarence Paul Hotson was the eldest of the four Hotson children. He applied for conscientious objector status but was denied an exemption. He entered the military as a non-combatant and was discharged in June, 1919, as a corporal in the Medical Department.

[33] Mary was visiting her father and stepmother and her two half-brothers in central Massachusetts.

[34] Harold Rotzel was a young pacifist minister who had been forced to resign from his church near Worcester, Massachusetts. He was a co-founder of Comradeship, which tried to explore ways in which members could most effectively organize

their lives in the way of truth, non-violence, and love. [Hentoff, Nat. *Peace Agitator: The Story of A. J. Muste.* New York: Macmillan, 1963, p. 47.]

[35] Lloyd H. Donnell of Framingham, Massachusetts, was an absolutist CO. He was furloughed to the FRU from Fort Riley, on September 1, 1918.

[36] Frederick J. Libby was a Quaker from Exeter, New Hampshire. He first served in the canteen at Amiens; on October 29, 1918, he went to Normandy to supervise the closing of the Red Cross activity in that region.

Chapter 3. Aboard the Rochambeau

[1] The S.S. *Rochambeau* was built for the Compagnie Generale Transatlantique (CGT) fleet in 1911, by Chantiers and Ateliers de St. Nazaire. The ship weighed 12,678 gross tons, was 598 feet long and 63 feet wide, and had a service speed of fifteen knots. The ship carried 2,078 passengers (428 in first class, 200 in second, and 1,450 in third. [from printed postcard *50 Le Havre: — Le "Rochambeau", de la Cie Generale Transatlantique.* Paris: Levy et Neurdein Reusis, no date.]

[2] *Relevance: The Quarterly Journal of the Great War Society*, Volume 13, No. 2, Spring, 2004.

[3] *Relevance*, Volume 13, No. 2, Spring, 2004. The German campaign was effective, sinking 1.4 million tons of shipping between October 1916 and January 1917. On March 17, 1917, German submarines sank three American merchant vessels. The United States declared war in April 1917, in part as a response to German resumption of unrestricted submarine warfare. In the end, of the 360 German submarines that had been built, 178 were lost, but more than 11 million tons of shipping had been sunk.

[4] Stephens, D. Owen. *With Quakers in France.* London: C. W. Daniel, 1921, pp. 14-15.

[5] Forbes Robertson was a great Shakespearean actor who performed several times at Harvard's Sanders Theater. He published several volumes of Shakespeare arranged for the stage.

[6] Joel 2:28, King James Bible.

[7] Francis Bowes Sayre was a professor at Harvard Law School. In 1913 at the White House, he married Jessie Wilson, the daughter of President Woodrow Wilson. He was traveling to France to take charge of the camp activities of the American Army YMCA and to assist in the establishment of YMCA centers at American military bases to provide recreation and canteen facilities.

[8] *Chasseurs Alpins* [literally, Alpine Hunters] were the elite mountain infantry of the French Army. When the United States entered the war, units of the French Blue Devils, so nicknamed because of their blue uniform with flowing cape and jaunty beret, toured the country helping raise money for the war effort. Irving Berlin captured their spirit in song describing them as "strong and active, most attractive . . . those Devils, the Blue Devils of France." ["The Blue Devils of France," 1918.]

[9] Gustave Doré was a French artist, illustrator, and engraver. He illustrated and self-published an edition of Dante's *Inferno* in 1861, which has been widely reprinted.

[10] A fireless cooker is a box with soapstone or other insulating materials around the sides and tops. Food is heated to the boiling point in a pot on the stove; the pot is then placed in the cooker. The retained heat continues to cook the food. Although it takes longer to cook using a fireless cooker, the system is efficient, cost-effective, and reliable.

[11] A pastille was a pill-shaped lump of compressed herbs or incense, which was burned to release its medicinal properties.

Chapter 4. Summer Sojourn

[1] Forbes, John. *The Quaker Star Under Seven Flags 1917-1927*. Philadelphia: University of Pennsylvania Press, 1962, p. 53.

[2] ibid., p. 41.

[3] *Reconstruction*, Volume I, No. 7, p. 111. The Foyer International or Students' Hostel was the first student residence in the Latin Quarter and has been open to students of all nationalities since World War I. The building was demolished and rebuilt in 1928.

[4] The Gironde is a navigable estuary in southwest France, at the meeting of the Dordogne and Garonne rivers near Bordeaux. The lighthouse, Phare de la Gironde, is located at the mouth of the Gironde.

[5] *Horace* is a play by Pierre Corneille and *Scapin's Deceits*, a play by Molière.

[6] The letters of the Unit members were subject to military censorship, and they were not permitted to write of anything that could compromise the war effort.

[7] By 1828, Quakers in America had split into two branches: Hicksite and Orthodox. The conflict between the two groups concerned beliefs about the importance of the Bible, the role of the Inner Light, and the nature of salvation. Hicksites, following the teachings of Elias Hicks, believed that the Inner Light must be the primary source of truth and that the Bible was only a secondary source, while Orthodox Quakers believed that the Bible must be the primary authority on the truth. The final split came in 1827, when Orthodox Quakers tried to impose a formal doctrine of faith, or creed, on the Philadelphia Yearly Meeting. Because the Hicksite Quakers believed that adhering to a creed would interfere with freedom to follow the Inner Light, the separation eventually spread throughout the Society in the United States and continued in many regions until the mid-twentieth century.

[8] Industrial Workers of the World (IWW) is an international radical labor union founded in 1905.

[9] Peter Arrell Brown Widener II, who attended Harvard from 1915 to 1917, was a first lieutenant in the Sanitary Corps. In France he was on the staff of Brigadier General J. F. T. Finney, chief of chemical surgery, A.E.F.

[10] Quentin Roosevelt, the son of President Theodore Roosevelt, was a fighter pilot in the U.S. Army Air Corps. He was killed in aerial combat over France on July 14, 1918, and buried by the Germans with full military honors.

[11] William Southworth, Harvard Class of 1918, organized The Union for American Neutrality at Harvard and served as secretary. While in the FRU he built houses until he was lent to the Red Cross and put in charge of a center for distributing supplies to the French refugees. After the war, he went into the State Department and was assigned to embassies in Peru, Mexico City, and Paraguay. He died in 1925 of complications from an appendicitis operation.

[12] The Hotel Britannique, an old apartment house on the Avenue Victoria, was the residence for many of the FRU workers living in Paris.

[13] Mary's cousin, Frederick May Eliot, attended Harvard Divinity School and was ordained in 1915. During the next two years he served as associate minister at First Parish in Cambridge. In 1917, he transferred to Unity Church, St. Paul, Minnesota, where he served for twenty years, except during a leave of absence in 1918-19 spent at a military hospital in Tours, France. From 1937 to 1958, he served as president of the American Unitarian Association.

[14] Saint-Germain-en-Laye is one of the wealthiest suburbs of Paris and includes the National Forest of Saint-Germain-en-Laye and the Chateau de Saint-Germain, built in 1539 on the site of earlier castles.

[15] Maurice H. Gifford of Lindsay, California, was a Quaker who worked for the FRU in Violaine, Marne; he was a graduate of Whittier College.

[16] Porphyry is a deep brownish purple igneous rock with large crystals prized for monuments.

[17] The rest of the letter is in French. The English translation only is included in the text.

[18] Hilda Holme, a Quaker from Baltimore, was an elementary school teacher. In 1918, she was assigned to the Friends Unit at Pompadour, and then in 1919 she was tranferred to Bar-le-Duc (Meuse). After leaving France, she worked with the AFSC soliciting funds for an expansion of the work in the devastated areas of eastern Poland.

[19] Henry B. Strater was a Mennonite of Louisville, Kentucky. After the war he became a noted painter, illustrator, and printmaker and worked at the Academie Julien and the Art Students League, as well as the Ogunquit Summer Art School.

[20] Jesse Packer was a physician. He and Mary Pancoast Packer, a social worker, were from Newtown, Pennsylvania. They were assigned for most of their time with the FRU at the Hospital du Château.

[21] Edwin C. Zavitz was a member of the Haverford Unit from Coldstream, Ontario, Canada.

[22] George Hervey Hallett, Jr., Harvard Class of 1916, entered the service on August 26, 1918, and on September 3 was transferred to the Casual Detachment, Conscientious Objectors, Camp Lee, Virginia. He was discharged on December 17, 1918. Bob Dunn was a Harvard student who did not join the FRU; he was a radical but not a conscientious objector. Brent Allinson, as a Harvard senior, served as president of the International Polity Club and helped found the Harvard Union for Neutrality. He was appointed to the Diplomatic Service in Switzerland, but lost the position when the *New York Tribune* exposed him as a "pacifist." He was then drafted and refused to serve in the military. He was eventually released from the penitentiary at Leavenworth after two years' incarceration, when his sentence was "remitted by direction of the president."

[23] Naked Translations, February 6, 2004, accessed March 17, 2016 (www.nakedtranslations.com).

[24] In 1917, the Cadet School for the First Naval District was established on the Harvard campus, and Harvard offered a special course leading to an ensign's commission. The Naval Radio School was started in the spring of 1917. It expanded so fast that within six months almost all of the buildings north of Harvard Yard,

including Memorial Hall, had become "ships." By the end of the war, the Naval School covered Cambridge Commons with temporary barracks. At one time, the enrollment at the Radio School reached five thousand men. Radcliffe students often socialized with the "Radio boys" at dances and other activities. (Morison, Samuel Eliot. *Three Centuries of Harvard, 1636-1936.* Cambridge, Massachusetts: Harvard University Press, 1937, pp. 458-459.)

Chapter 5. *The Great Influenza*

[1] Barry, John M. *The Great Influenza: The Epic Story of the Deadliest Plague in History.* New York: Viking, 2004.

[2] ibid., p. 382.

[3] Jones, Rufus M. *A Service of Love in War Time: American Friends Relief Work in Europe, 1917–1919.* New York: The Macmillan Company, 1920, p. 120.

[4] Margaret Garrison, Radcliffe Class of 1919, later served as a social worker in public relief work, then as a psychiatric social worker in a family agency.

[5] In modern times, Scott Nearing is best known as an advocate of simple living, but in 1918 he was an outspoken, radical anti-war activist and socialist. In 1915, he was fired from his teaching position at the Wharton School because of his social activism. He then joined the American Union Against Militarism and became a founding member of the People's Council of America for Democracy and Peace. He published a series of pamphlets for the Rand School, including *The Great Madness: A Victory for the American Plutocracy*, which resulted in his indictment, in April 1918, under the Espionage Act for alleged "obstruction to the recruiting and enlistment service of the United States." The trial against Nearing, the Rand School, and the American Socialist Party did not take place until February 1919, after the war ended. Nearing was found not guilty. (https://en.wikipedia.org/wiki/Scott_Nearing, accessed July 3, 2016.)

⁶ Le Baron Russell Briggs was the second president of Radcliffe College, serving from 1903 until 1923. At the same time, he was dean of Harvard's Faculty of Arts and Sciences. During his tenure, the college increased its geographic and ethnic diversity. Before Briggs left office, he asked that Radcliffe become a college for women within Harvard and was refused. In his final presidential report, Briggs wrote, "I believe that ultimately Radcliffe will become a women's college in Harvard, but that neither institution is as yet prepared for such a union." (http://www.radcliffe.harvard.edu/le-baron-russell-briggs, accessed July 3, 2016.)

⁷ Arthur D. Fulton was a member of the Friends Unit from Baltimore, Maryland.

Chapter 6. Reconstruction Work

¹ Jones, Rufus M. *A Service of Love in War Time: American Friends Relief Work in Europe, 1917-1919.* New York: The Macmillan Company, 1920, p. 128

² ibid., pp. 36-37.

³ Forbes, John. *The Quaker Star Under Seven Flags 1917-1927.* Philadelphia: University of Pennsylvania Press, 1962, p. 57.

⁴ Adrian buildings were prefabricated, one-story frame buildings with tarpaper roofs, built to provide double-decked bunks for ninety-six soldiers. *Blocus* is the French word for blockade and, I assume, the buildings took their name from the small military forts used for defense.

⁵ *Reconstruction*, p. 145.

⁶ Leslie to Mary, November 10, 1918.

⁷ Jones, Rufus M., p. 139.

⁸ Leslie to Mary, October 6, 1918.

⁹ Jones, Rufus M., p. 69.

[10] *Jocelyn* is a four-act opera by Benjamin Godard, best known for the lullaby for tenor, "*Oh! ne t'éveille pas encore*" commonly known in English as "Angels Guard Thee."

[11] Frederick Clifton Packard, Harvard Class of 1920, was Leslie's roommate at Harvard. He enlisted in the Harvard SATC in October 1918, leaving for officer training in Kentucky in November. After completing his degree in 1920, he taught at Harvard as an associate professor of public speaking.

[12] Pierre Monteux was a French conductor, noted particularly for his interpretations of Russian and French music. He was conductor at the Boston Symphony Orchestra (1919-1924), where he introduced a number of new works by French composers.

[13] Karl Muck was the chief conductor of the Boston Symphony Orchestra from 1912 to 1918.

[14] Miss Bertha May Boody became dean of Radcliffe College in 1914. She graduated from Radcliffe in 1899, and received an A.M. degree from Columbia in 1912. She taught for nine years in the Cambridge School for Girls, before Mary attended high school there. In 1926, she wrote *A Psychological Study of Immigrant Children at Ellis Island*. Although her middle name is May, she was not related to the May family.

[15] In February 1918, the Drama League of America held a one-act patriotic play competition for amateur playwrights. One hundred and forty plays were entered, mostly by women. (Blair, Karen J., *The Torchbearers: Women and Their Amateur Arts Associations in America, 1890-1930*. Bloomington: Indiana University Press, 1994, p. 156.) Doris Friend Halman (Radcliffe Class of 1916) and Rachel Lyman Field (a Radcliffe Special Student) won prizes in the contest. (Reports of the President and the Treasurer of Harvard College, 1917-1918, p. 263.) Rachel Field became a novelist, poet, and author of children's fiction. She is best known for her Newbery Medal-winning novel for young adults, *Hitty, Her First Hundred Years*, published in 1929.

Chapter 7. Armistice

[1] Gale, Oliver Marble, compiler. *Americanism: Woodrow Wilson's Speeches on the War—Why He Made Them—and—What They Have Done.* Chicago: The Baldwin Syndicate, 1918, p. 73.

[2] Stephens, D. Owen. *With Quakers in France.* London: C. W. Daniel, 1921, p. 254.

[3] The Armistice agreement was for thirty days, but it was renewed until the formal peace treaty was signed at Versailles in 1919. The conditions of the Armistice were developed based on President Wilson's Fourteen Points, which took many of the principles of progressivism and translated them into foreign policy, including free trade, democracy, and self-determination.

[4] The Junkers were members of the Prussian and East German landed aristocracy. They dominated all the higher civil offices and officer corps of the army and navy.

[5] Garfield Cox of Crawfordsville, Indiana, was a Quaker and professor of public speaking at Wabash College. He was a delegate to the World Conference of Friends in 1920 and then taught political economy at the University of Chicago.

[6] R. F. Alfred Hoernle was a professor in Harvard's Department of Philosophy from 1914 to 1920.

[7] The Women's Trade Union League (WTUL) was an organization of both working class and well-off women formed in 1903 to support the efforts of women to organize labor unions and to eliminate sweatshop conditions. The Consumers League was formed in 1899 to promote a fair marketplace for workers and consumers and to ensure safe working conditions.

[8] The Red Flag Riots were a series of violent demonstrations in Brisbane, Australia, in 1918-1919 against socialists and others that returning soldiers considered to be disloyal. The demonstrators carried red flags, which were associated with trade unions and banned under the War Precautions Act. The Bolsheviks, founded by Vladimir Lenin and Alexander Bogdanov, were a major organization consisting primarily of workers who considered themselves the leaders of the revolutionary working class of Russia. Their beliefs and practices were often referred to as

Bolshevism. During the Russian Civil War of 1917-1922, they executed representatives of the autocracy and threatened people who spoke against their regime.

Chapter 8. Still More Work to Do

[1] *Reconstruction*, Volume 1, No. 8, p. 130.

[2] ibid.

[3] Fry, A. Ruth. *A Quaker Adventure: The Story of Nine Years' Relief and Reconstruction*. New York: Frank-Maurice, Inc., [1926], pp. 90-91.

[4] ibid., p. 91.

[5] *Reconstruction*, Volume 2, No. 3, p. 50.

[6] Jones, Rufus M. *A Service of Love in War Time: American Friends Relief Work in Europe, 1917-1919*. New York: The Macmillan Company, 1920, pp. 227-229.

[7] Fry, A. Ruth, p. 95.

[8] *Reconstruction*, Volume 1, No. 10, p. 155.

[9] Sophia Fry was a member of the prominent Fry family who ran a successful chocolate business in England, established in 1822. Her family was involved in many social and philanthropic causes.

[10] *Reconstruction*, Volume 1, No. 10, p. 156.

[11] *Reconstruction*, Volume 2, No. 3, p. 50.

[12] Jones, Rufus M., pp. 229-230.

[13] ibid.

[14] *Reconstruction*, Volume 2, No. 3, p. 49.

[15] Jones, Rufus M., p. 233.

[16] The "Liberty" Truck was a three- to five-ton standardized vehicle designed for the United States Army and produced by fifteen different manufacturers starting in 1917. The gasoline-powered truck had a four-speed transmission and a top speed of about fifteen miles per hour.

[17] *Reconstruction*, Volume 2, No. 5, p. 79.

[18] Jones, Rufus M., pp. 233-235.

[19] *Reconstruction*, Volume 2, No. 8, p. 129.

[20] The Hindenburg Line was a system of defenses in northeastern France, stretching from Lens to Verdun, constructed by the Germans during the winter of 1916-1917.

[21] Charles Walmsley and Geoffrey Franklin were British Friends and members of the War Victims Committee assigned to the Paris office at Rue de Chemin.

[22] Eva Le Gallienne made her stage debut in 1914 at the age of fifteen. After moving to New York, she became a Broadway star and, in 1926, founded the Civic Repertory Theater, for which she was director, producer, and lead actress.

Chapter 9. Documenting the Work

[1] Francis Birrell, *Reconstruction*, Volume 1, No 5, August 1918, p. 78.

[2] Lewis Gannett, *Reconstruction*, Volume 2, No. 2, April 1919, p. 12.

[3] *Reconstruction*, Volume 1, No. 4, July 1918, p. 60.

[4] Leslie to Mary, April 8, 1919.

[5] Leslie to Mary, May 9, 1919.

[6] Jones, Rufus M. *A Service of Love in War Time: American Friends Relief Work in Europe, 1917-1919.* New York: The Macmillan Company, 1920, pp. xi-xv.

[7] The French government often confiscated the property of landowners who were pro-German and used it to support the French war effort.

[8] Bright, James W. *An Anglo-Saxon Reader, Edited with Notes and a Glossary.* New York: Henry Holt and Company, 1891.

[9] *Samson et Dalila* is a grand opera in three acts by French composer Camille Saint-Saëns, with libretto by Ferdinand Lemaire, based on the biblical tale of Samson and Delilah.

[10] Henry Tatnall (Tat) Brown was a member of the Unit from Moorestown, New Jersey. In 1934, he served as chairman of the AFSC for one year. He later wrote several works on American journalist, poet, and author Christopher Morley.

Chapter 10. Mary's Senior Year

[1] Mary to Leslie, February 10, 1919.

[2] Gill, Gillian. *Mary Baker Eddy.* Reading, Massachusetts: Perseus Books, 1998, pp. 436-439, 675.

[3] Liberty caps were red, brimless, cone-shaped hats used during the American Revolution as a symbol of freedom.

[4] The Russian Cathedral in Paris is dedicated to St. Alexandre Nevski, Duke of Novgorod, a Russian hero who was canonized for saving Russia from the Swedes in 1240. This church was established in 1861. After the revolution of 1917, many Russians took refuge in Paris, and the cathedral became a place of regular meetings for this community. This church is still the largest Orthodox church in Paris.

[5] Thomas Edmund Harvey was a pacifist, social reformer, and politician. During the war, until 1920, he served as head of the British War Victims Relief Committee.

As a Member of Parliament, he helped draft the section of the Military Service Act of 1916 that required COs to perform service as a condition of their exemption from enlisting in the army.

[6] Abner Carroll Binder was a Quaker member of the Unit from Mechanicsburg, Pennsylvania, and a 1916 graduate of Harvard. In France, he met his future wife, Dorothy Walton of Minneapolis, who was also working for the AFSC. After the war, he became a journalist, starting at the *Minnesota Daily Star* covering labor issues.

[7] Eugène Brieux was a French dramatist who attacked the social issues of his day, including the education of peasant girls, corruption in politics, the unfairness of the dowry system to poor girls, gambling, venereal disease, and the injustices of law.

[8] Sir Ralph Norman Angell was a British journalist and one of the principal founders of the Union of Democratic Control. He was a member of the executive committee of the League of Nations Union and was awarded the Nobel Peace Prize in 1933.

[9] Leslie included a long passage in French. The English translation only is included in the text.

[10] The League of Free Nations Association was an organization working for the establishment of a new and transparent system of international relations, human rights, and world peace through disarmament.

[11] Georges Clemenceau was prime minister of France from 1917 to 1920. At the Paris Peace Conference in 1919, he advocated for harsh treatment of Germany and was instrumental in negotiating reparations from Germany and the return of Alsace-Lorraine to France. He considered Woodrow Wilson too idealistic in his promotion of the League of Nations.

[12] William Henry Dana helped begin the Trade Union College in Boston in 1919 and later taught at various workers colleges in Boston, New York, and Pennsylvania.

[13] The Rand School of Social Science was started in New York City in 1906 to educate workers. In 1919, during the "Red Scare," New York state officials tried unsuccessfully to close it down, alleging it was a front for the Communist Party.

[14] The class marshals at Harvard and Radcliffe wear red tassels at graduation.

[15] Ethel Kidder, Radcliffe Class of 1919, was the class poet; she was active in the drama club and Idler.

[16] Oswald Garrison Villard was an 1893 graduate of Harvard; he was a journalist, civil rights leader, and a founder of the American Anti-Imperialist League. Charles J. Rhoads of Philadelphia served as the chief of the Friends Reconstruction Unit in France from November 1918 until the end of the Mission.

[17] Jordans, a village in Buckinghamshire, is a Quaker center with one of the oldest Friends' meeting houses in England and the burial place of William Penn.

[18] Paul M. Cope of Atlantic City, New Jersey, was a Quaker lacking one year of graduation from Westtown. He was furloughed from Camp Dix to the FRU. Henry Stabler, a Quaker and CO from Sandy Spring, Maryland, was due to be sent to Leavenworth, but was in the hospital and missed his Board of Inquiry hearing; he was furloughed from Camp Meade to the FRU in August 1918.

[19] *The Suffragist* was a weekly newspaper first published in 1913 by Alice Paul for the Congressional Union for Woman Suffrage.

[20] While at Harvard, Hood Van den Arend, Harvard Class of 1922, served as president of the Socialist Club.

[21] Richard Bassett was a painter who received his degree from Harvard cum laude. As a child, he had studied art in Switzerland and Paris.

[22] General Tasker Howard Bliss was Army Chief of Staff in World War I and was appointed by President Wilson to the Supreme War Council. He was a supporter of the French Marshall Ferdinand Jean Marie Foch as Supreme Allied Commander. At the Armistice, Foch advocated for terms that would make Germany unable to pose a threat to France ever again, but was overruled by French Prime Minister Georges Clemenceau. After the war, General Bliss was a delegate to the Peace Conference.

Chapter 11. Political Activism

[1] *America is at War!* New York: Collegiate Anti-Militarism League, 1917.

[2] Roger Nash Baldwin earned his bachelor's and master's degrees at Harvard. He taught sociology at Washington University and later became a social worker. He was a member of the American Union Against Militarism (AUAM), which opposed American involvement in World War I, and headed the AUAM's Civil Liberties Bureau to protect the rights of COs. On October 9, 1918, Baldwin was arrested for violation of the Selective Service Act after refusing to appear before the draft board; he served a year in prison. He eventually became the first director of the American Civil Liberties Union. Emily Greene Balch was a professor at Wellesley College. She became an internationally known peace activist and helped found the Women's International League for Peace and Freedom, serving as the first secretary. She was awarded the Nobel Peace Prize in 1946.

[3] Mollie Steimer, in *Savage Peace: Hope and Fear in America, 1919* by Ann Hagedorn. New York: Simon and Schuster, 2007, p. 11

[4] Hagedorn, Ann. *Savage Peace: Hope and Fear in America, 1919.* New York: Simon and Schuster, 2007, pp. 150-152.

[5] ibid., pp. 53-57.

[6] *New York Tribune*, April 3, 1918.

[7] Flyer, "Suggestions for Securing New Members and Organizing Local Branches," Young Democracy [1919].

[8] Wilson, Woodrow, September 30, 1918, in *Women's Suffrage in America: An Eyewitness History* by Elizabeth Frost-Knappman and Kathryn Cullen-DuPont, Editors. New York: Facts on File, 1992, pp. 316-317.

[9] Foner, Philip S. *Women and the American Labor Movement: From Colonial Times to the Eve of World War I.* New York: The Free Press, 1979, p. 274.

[10] ibid., p. 276.

[11] Frost-Knappman and Cullen-DuPont, p. 317.

[12] Brown, Carrie. *Rosie's Mom: Forgotten Women Workers of the First World War.* Boston: Northeastern University Press, 2002, pp. 13-14.

[13] Foner, pp. 292-293.

[14] Brown, pp. 17-18.

[15] ibid., p. 20.

[16] ibid., p. 187.

[17] Abraham Johannes Muste was a pacifist, political activist, and Quaker minister. He became a member of the Fellowship of Reconciliation shortly after it began in 1916 and volunteered for the Boston chapter of the Civil Liberties Bureau. In 1919, he became involved in union organizing and continued working for labor and against war for the rest of his life.

[18] The Industrial Democracy movement was promoted by the Industrial Workers of the World (IWW) to involve workers in making decisions and sharing responsibility and authority in the workplace.

[19] The address by President Woodrow Wilson at Mechanics Hall was the unofficial beginning of his campaign to persuade the American people to accept the League of Nations. Republican Senator Henry Cabot Lodge of Massachusetts led the opposition to the League.

[20] The rest of the letter is in French. The translation is included in the text for clarity.

[21] *Harvard Crimson*, March 1, 1919, "Violating Traditions." The campus newspaper reported that "A week ago a student on the Yard was forced by about thirty-five of his classmates to burn papers which he owned dealing with the Lawrence strike." The unnamed author of the column condemned these actions, stating, "Freedom of conscience is one of the principles for which Harvard has always stood. The University was one of the first in the country to divorce itself from association with any particular church. All races of all religions and beliefs are admitted on an equal footing. This fact makes the University what it is—a small world within itself. These traditions of Harvard are too sacred to be violated."

[22] Rev. Cedric Long was a national organizer for the Amalgamated Textile Workers Union and a member of FOR.

[23] Frank Keddie, a Scottish Quaker, was one of the witnesses who testified before the Senate on the Bolshevik Revolution in February and March 1919.

[24] E. Carleton McDowell, a member of the first Haverford Unit, was from Cold Spring Harbor, New York. His sister was dismissed from her teaching position at Brooklyn Manual Training High School (Leslie's alma mater) because of her pacifist stance.

[25] The Friends Units were well supplied with cocoa and chocolate from the Quaker-owned Fry and Cadbury companies, British manufacturers of chocolate products.

[26] Francis Greenwood Peabody was a Unitarian minister and Harvard professor of theology. He is noted for introducing the study of social ethics to Harvard. He taught that Christians are called to social action, and he helped start a campus organization, which promoted public service in the community. He was not closely related to Mary's family.

[27] Oliver Waterman Larkin received his B.A. from Harvard in French and Latin in 1918 and M.A. in 1919. He served in the U.S. Army from 1918 to 1919 as a private in the Medical Corps of the 73rd Infantry Regiment. While at Harvard, he directed plays and designed scenery for Lincoln House in Boston. He taught at Smith College and Iowa State University. His series of six books on the development of American art won the Pulitzer Prize for History in 1950.

[28] In 1913, Woodrow Wilson appointed Albert Burleson to the position of Postmaster General. From June 1918 through July 1919, the Post Office Department operated the country's telephone services. After the war, improvements in working conditions and wages for women were reversed as returning servicemen filled jobs. Burleson refused to discuss new contracts with the telephone operators or to allow the phone companies to negotiate. On April 15, 1919, the members of the Boston local voted to strike and members began picketing outside the exchanges. Burleson

was also involved in enforcing the Espionage Act and had ordered postmasters to send to him any suspicious material that they found.

[29] Frederick R. Kuh was a member of the Unit from Chicago. After leaving the Unit, he worked as a journalist.

Chapter 12. Leaving France

[1] *L'Équipe*, Volume 1, p. 1.

[2] Clarté was an organization founded by Henri Barbusse to rally the world's intellectual elites in support of an internationalist ideology based on communist ideals.

[3] Jones, Rufus M. *A Service of Love in War Time: American Friends Relief Work in Europe, 1917-1919*. New York: The Macmillan Company, 1920, p. 240.

[4] ibid., p. 239.

[5] ibid., p. 242-243.

[6] Leslie to Mary, August 17, 1919.

[7] Leslie to Mary, August 17 and 23, 1919.

[8] Jones, Mary Hoxie. *Swords into Plowshares*. New York: Macmillan Company, 1937, p. 80; Fry, A. Ruth. *A Quaker Adventure: The Story of Nine Years' Relief and Reconstruction*. New York: Frank-Maurice, Inc.,[1926], pp. 320-322.

[9] Fry, p. 99.

[10] Parois, near Aubreville in northeastern France, was the site of a temporary World War I airfield built in 1918 for the U.S. Army. After the Armistice, the airfield was turned over to the French government and returned to agricultural use.

[11] Jeannette Rankin, Jane Addams, and Dr. Alice Hamilton were representatives to the Women's Peace Congress at Zurich in May 1919. The Women's Interna-

tional League for Peace and Freedom (WILPF) was founded in 1915, with Jane Addams as its first president.

[12] Georges Pioch was a French journalist, literary critic, and outspoken pacifist.

[13] "Scribes and Pharisees" is a reference to Matthew 32:13. The Pharisees were mostly middle-class businessmen who enforced obedience to Jewish law. The Scribes were a subset of the Pharisees who studied the law and wrote commentaries. Jesus charged these sects with hypocrisy because many of them outwardly observed the rituals of Judaism but were inwardly corrupt.

[14] A painting of the Madonna and Child attributed to Domenico Ghirlandaio is in this drawing room in the Agassiz House at Radcliffe College.

[15] Charles R. Brown was dean of the Yale School of Religion.

[16] Ellen Collier, Radcliffe Class of 1919, was active in drama while in college and eventually became an archaeologist.

[17] Kathleen Sandiford, Radcliffe Class of 1919, majored in chemistry and became a biochemist. As the class Giver of Gifts, she wrote:

> "Why there's Mary Peabody," said Alice.
> "Yes, said I," and giggled. "What's the matter?" asked the Caterpiller.
> "Oh we know a beautiful rhyme for Mary, but it's been censored."
> "Well, give Mary the table, and the lines that haven't been censored, and
>   she'll supply the rest."
> "Mary had a little dance,
> And then she had some more.
> This time on a little table,
> But _____ "
> "That's as far as the National Board of Censors got," said Alice.
> Can you supply the rest, Mary?

[18] Harry George Hawker was an Australian aviation pioneer. After the war, he attempted to become the first to achieve a non-stop flight across the Atlantic. On May 18, 1919, he and his navigator, Kenneth Grieve, set off in a Sopwith biplane.

They crashed into the ocean after fourteen hours of flight and were rescued by a passing freighter.

[19] Evans Thomas was a Presbyterian pastor in Scotland. He was a conscientious objector and went on a hunger strike while imprisoned at Fort Riley during the war.

[20] The "Coop" was, and still is, a cooperative store serving the Harvard community. It opened for business in 1882 in a student dorm room and moved to its current Harvard Square location in 1906.

[21] In July 1919, Boston's elevated train workers walked off the job.

[22] James Moore Hickson, an Australian Anglican, formed the Emmanuel League of Prayer to pray for the sick, wounded, and mourning people affected by the war. In March 1919, he arrived in Boston and carried his healing ministry to Episcopal churches throughout America.

[23] Constance Gostick, a member of the British Unit, was assigned to Charmont, Marne, Le Château.

[24] Augusta Townsend was a member of the Unit from Poughkeepsie, New York. She was a teacher with experience in nursing and social work. After the war, she worked for the AFSC in Poland and helped solicit funds for Russian relief.

Epilogue. Their Story Continues

[1] Powell, Kathy. "Christmas couple still coos after 70 years," *New Haven Register*, December 25, 1989.

Index

Page numbers in *italics* denote illustrations.
The letter "n" denotes the number of the note in the Notes section.

Made in the USA
Columbia, SC
12 June 2017